Introducti

This book is dedicated to the thousands of individuals who choose to leave school, college, university, paid employment (even their life partner) to pursue their dreams of self-employment.

Unlike other books on starting and running a business, this book does <u>not</u> deal with the logical, technical, legal or financial aspects of self-employment.

Far too many books, courses, institutions, advisers, celebrities and "gurus" tell you that running your own business will be easy. They tell you that it's simple, that your journey will be all plain sailing and that your success is guaranteed.

This is simply <u>not</u> true.

We know that self-employment can be a very lonely experience with feelings of isolation, frustration and even desperation on occasion for many. You have no-one to turn to for help or share the emotional roller coaster journey of starting and running your own business.

Very few can understand or appreciate (let alone empathize) what you're going through, what you're facing and the key daily decisions and consequences you're having to make and experience.

We do.

Thousands of self-employed people struggle to balance work and family life, maintain a lifestyle, win new clients, deliver work on time, and ensure they get paid what they're contractually owed.

Starting and running your own business is not all sunshine and rainbows.

1

Be mentally prepared because this is no ordinary book on self-employment. Be prepared to change your beliefs, your perceptions, and your attitude towards who you are, what you offer and who you can turn to for help, guidance and support – when you need it.

Whether it's working from your office in the back bedroom, at the end of the garden, serviced office space or a commercial unit on an industrial estate, running your own business can be a very difficult, challenging and even traumatic (as well as rewarding) time.

Don't be like the many who find the courage to start a business and who then wrestle with the emotional challenges of self-employment, un-aided, un-supported and without anyone to help, guide or support them. People give up on their dream, when all they needed was a little bit of encouragement, support and practical advice, to address a particular problem, from someone who's actually experienced and resolved the exact same issue.

Our book is ideal for anyone who is self-employed or is considering self-employment. We share powerful, practical and proven ways of dealing and coping with the many emotional issues, challenges and obstacles that being self-employed can present on a daily basis.

This book does <u>not</u> tell you how to prepare cash flows, Profit & Loss or Balance Sheets, register for VAT, write a business plan, build a website or generate sales.

No, it doesn't. It's more powerful than that.

It goes a lot deeper than that. It prepares you mentally and spiritually to live and experience your life purpose. It prepares you for success doing what you want to do - getting paid the real value you offer while excelling at what you love to do.

If you are considering self-employment or are currently running your own business, then learn to start trusting your instincts and your gut right now and choose to invest in yourself by buying this book and prepare yourself to learn how to <u>avoid</u> the pain, anguish, stress and cost that many self-employed business owners (including us) have had to endure.

This book logs the many mistakes an entrepreneur can make, the issues, challenges, obstacles we have to endure and the painful process we go through to learn from these mistakes, grow and become resilient. We've written this book to help you avoid making the same painful mistakes in the early days, so that you don't have to repeat them.

You need to change your thoughts, beliefs, and attitudes towards self-employment, becoming self-employed and your future success. Start adopting an open mind, open heart and a selfless approach of **giving** excellent service to those who need what you have to offer.

If you can adopt that mindset from the outset, you are in for an incredible transformation of who you are – personally, professionally and commercially.

When you see this symbol throughout the book, pause and reflect. Make notes. Answer the question or complete the exercise. This will greatly assist you.

One last thing and we think it's important…

We want you to get real value from the practical information we share in the following pages.

If you need additional help, guidance or support in working towards your personal, professional or commercial goals and objectives, then our contact details are at the end of the book. Please accept our invitation to get in touch and to share your thoughts, experiences and feedback from applying what we share in the book.

Ready? Now, let's make the next 12 months the best you've ever had...

Fraser J. Hay and Elsabe Smit
January, 2017

Resilience:
How to conquer the fear and challenges of self-employment

Copyright

Published By The Ps, Qs and As Limited.
2nd Edition, January 2017

Table of Contents

In the Beginning ...

ES: I had known for years that I was eventually going to be self-employed. The time for me to take that first brave step came in 2009. Early in the year I had a casual conversation with a man who said I should have a look at Fraser Hay's website.

I had no idea who Fraser Hay was, but at the time I had a vision of his name in neon lights. The moment stayed with me as an item on my to-do list. I did nothing about it until August, when I found an on-line ad Fraser had placed for a free marketing consultation. This ad was on one of the many on-line community websites, and we shall call this community The Water Cooler.

I contacted Fraser and we had a telephone conversation about what I do and the marketing for my business. During that conversation, I felt that something deep in me resonated with what he had to say. The conversation was all about marketing rather than my field of work, but I had over the years learned to recognize the feeling and act on it.

We discussed my requirements, Fraser's requirements and an agreement to exchange skills.
And the rest, as they say, is history.

FH: Ever since I lost my eye in a shooting accident at the age of 15, I have regularly questioned key events in my life, and regularly reflected upon key decisions and occurrences in both my commercial and personal life.

Over the last 20 years I have helped and assisted many different business owners from over 50 countries around the world, and have many hundreds of testimonials from those whom I have assisted.

At a time, when I was conducting live research and testing the idea of a franchise model of offering people the opportunity to become a marketing coach, little did I know what an impact a seemingly innocent click of a mouse on one online social network would have on my life, or on the richness and true value of the insights I was about to gain and the advice and assistance I was about to receive.

One day in August of 2009, I was drawn to follow up and connect with a woman who had clicked on my online profile on The Water Cooler. What happened in the weeks and months to follow is detailed in the following pages. Names and amounts have been changed to protect the guilty, but everything else you will read is a frank, honest and accurate representation of our journey and the challenges that ensued.

Make yourself a coffee, settle into your favorite chair, and be mentally prepared for a rollercoaster of a ride into self-employment that I believe may just have an impact on your life too. For the rest of it as they, is your future.

Let's make your next 12 months the best you've ever had.

 Remember, when you see this symbol throughout the book, pause and reflect. Make notes, answer the question or complete the exercise.

21 August: The First Steps

Italics indicate initial conversation.
Bold Italics indicate later response.

ES: You have done a massive amount of work getting everything in place. Now you are sitting back and waiting. You have thrown out the bait, and you are waiting for your catch to come to you. You are getting slightly impatient, because you have thought that by now things will start happening, and it is not even slow, there is nothing at all.

You are wondering where you can improve and what went wrong. I can assure you that you cannot improve on what you have created and that nothing has gone wrong. You are focusing on the details, when your attention should be on the bigger picture. Yes, you are always telling people to look at the bigger picture, and now it is time for you to follow your own advice.

What you have got in place now is not your life's work. It is in fact only the first building block.

FH: You mention I've spent a lot of time on the detail. It's true, but I don't think I'm a perfectionist. I just hope to implement what I've learned from the lessons already so others can benefit. Over the last 5 months, I've completely re-written my coaching programme and extended it to 12 sessions, which has been a challenge and a half, but it has also enabled me to create another product, to allow people to benefit from what I have to offer without committing to the full programme, and hopefully this will open me up to a whole new audience as well.

Are you in effect saying, enough getting ready to get ready, and now is the time for me to start pushing the boat out and reaching out and promoting to a wider (international) audience?

ES: It is also not about attending to the detail. Yes, you are good at getting the detail right, but that is a given and not a reason for concern. For example, someone may be a good fashion designer because they can visualize and create new looks, but they will only become brilliant if they also learn to sew and understand the intricacies of the processes that will be used to make their creations become real. You can see the bigger picture, and you have no problem with also doing a spell check and adding highlights where necessary. You do that intuitively.

It is also not just "enough of getting ready to get ready". It is about looking wider. You have perfected about 10% of your life's work, and you are now ready to start working on the next 20% and get a glimpse of the other 70%. Yes, you need to go international, but not quite yet. There is still some work to be done.

Over the past few years you have been working hard, but if you want to be honest, you will acknowledge that you have in fact been hibernating in a comfort zone. It is time for you to come out of that comfort zone and face your demons. That is what will open the sluice gates for you.

FH: I think I can relate to that. I've been busy testing lots of different approaches in trying to establish credibility in preparation for pushing the boat out and getting ready to take things to the next stage. I have done some talks and workshops to help build the credibility. Are you saying that once I stick my head above the parapets or get my message out to my true audience and not only that in The Water Cooler, I will begin to be true to my self/heart?

ES: Yes, it is time to get to your true audience. The Water Cooler has been your comfort zone and you are nearly ready to get out to your real audience. You have lots of credibility where you are now, and that is a very solid building block for your future. You are going to re-write your self-employment books. If you had done this a few years ago, you would have been locked up, but

the time is right for you to become your true self and you are a master.

ES: You are saying but those demons have nothing to do with your work? You are wrong. Imagine a river that is flowing really strong - so strong that nobody can cross it. Then the river reaches a point where it splits into a number of deltas. You can cross any of those deltas with ease. Where is the mighty river?

You have been focusing really hard on one or two deltas, and you have been telling yourself that this is your solution - just ignore the other deltas and the river will keep flowing.

What you have not realized is how much energy you use to ignore the other deltas. They are in the background, yes, but it is as if you build new structures with your right hand while you are pushing everything else back with your left hand. And you thought that the occasional pain in your wrist and shoulder was from typing too much. It is in fact your body saying to you that the strain of pushing back is too much.

FH: I think I understand. I have had my share of successes on The Water Cooler, but I have also had a difficult time of dealing with detractors and nay-sayers, only because some of the way they behave is not in my genetic makeup, and dare I say it, yes I do get hurt when all I try to do is help and assist people in the one area I think I can help. But it would appear, there are one or two "experts" who love to negate what I do or spread innuendo and untrue gossip, putting people off from working with me (and probably the people most in need of what I offer). I simply cannot fathom out why, as my intentions are always 100% noble and have no interest in making enemies – (Sorry I appear to be not good at boardroom politics).

I think I may have allowed myself to be affected too much by the nay-sayers, and this has made me question who I am. In private and in business I am two different people. In private I am a very spiritual person, but I think the wider commercial perception of me may be this aggressive commercial animal, which is not quite 100% true. I live to serve. I think there is a difference.

I'm also confused by your analogy of the deltas. Are you saying that being so focused this year on The Water Cooler, I have missed other deltas or opportunities, and thus I have lost momentum and flow?

ES: The Universe consists of balance. If you only get praise, you should be very concerned, because at some point the praise needs to be balanced by criticism. Where there is lots of praise and no criticism, you should expect some serious flak coming your way, and if you do not expect it, you could feel devastated when it comes. If you get equal amounts of praise and criticism at the same time, count your blessings and keep working. For every person you lose, you gain more. For every person that criticizes you, another is attracted to you.

You have not missed any opportunities. You have delayed an insight that is now due. Once you have the insight, there will be a floodgate of opportunities opening up to you. You will recognize them and grab them.

You are saying but surely there is a line to be drawn between your personal and professional life? You drew the line. It was not there before. You need to remove the line, so that you can again have one single flow of energy. That is what you are waiting for.

FH: Are you saying by this, that more and more of my personal beliefs are shining through in my work life, and moving more from head to heart in both private and professional life? My passion is for spiritual matters and marketing, but combining the two to an appropriate audience, can be difficult. Having been married for 21 years I know what Wendy (my wife) has been like in coming round to some of my ideas on life. (I was shot when I was 15 and lost an eye, and it can fairly change your perspective on life.)

ES: This is the delta. You have been dividing yourself into Fraser the business man and Fraser the spiritual being. And you have been thinking of Fraser the spiritual being as Fraser with an interesting hobby (spirituality) which can be attached or detached as required. You are one being who is spiritual, and you happen to live your spirituality by means of your business. Trying to not do it results in divided energy, being physically tired and having those aches in your arm and shoulder.

So you were shot when you were 15. Why did you lose an eye? You may have been thinking that you lost an eye and therefore it crippled you. It sounds to me like you turned one eye inside and this is where the division (your deltas) began?

How do you get to remove this line and consolidate your energy? You forgive the person who caused you to draw the line. And before you jump to conclusions about forgiveness, let me explain.

FH: I felt inspired to write a poem "Gratitude without Attitude" this morning after reflecting on our conversation, and I consciously thought of all the people who've had a pop at me, and allowed me to get my blood pressure up, and simply thought I don't care anymore - what they think has no effect on me now - if anything it's probably made me better, I just don't want any unnecessary grief which it appears they go out of their way to throw at me.

ES: People act in specific ways to help us discover ourselves. When you no longer get grief, check your pulse – you will have reached the end of this incarnation. When you do get grief, detach yourself and ask what they are teaching you about yourself.

There was a time when your energy was flowing in one single direction - you were a strong river. Then you chose to use some energy but ignore other energy. You saw the results and concluded that this was the right decision. Yes, it was the right decision at the time.

What you did was channel your energy into your professional life with great success. But you have reached the end of this cycle, and you are now entering a new cycle. For this new cycle you need to consolidate your energy again.

You say you do not want to cover old grounds again because it is too hurtful? Look at yourself. Remember the person you were before you chose to split your energy, and look at the person you are now. You have a lot to smile about and be grateful for.

FH: I am a little lost at the energy splitting concept. Am I trying to be something I'm not? Am I not allowing something to happen that should? (If so, what is it?) I wonder whether I should be focusing on the "self-employment" side of things or more of the spiritual side.

For me, I think that **the meaning of life is to discover your gift**, and that the **purpose of life is to share it**. That's why, over the last few months I've been focusing on helping people who want to work for themselves and not necessarily those who are already in a business. Many business people deem themselves experts, and their ego can react negatively towards a third party offering to help or guide them – they often resist the help being offered, whereas "newbies" are open to it.

Helping people to identify their life's purpose and realize it by starting a business, serving others and contributing to humanity, and allowing me to coach and guide them, fills me with great excitement, passion and dare I say it – "light".

As I write this I also get a feeling that some people on The Water Cooler are like a dribbling brook or softly running stream, but view me as a high powered jet hose, and there may be conflicting energy levels there.

Is that also what you mean in terms of energy - that I need to balance my passion and enthusiasm to be more acceptable with others so that they can cope with me rather than mistrust me?

ES: The energy split is where you try to be the business man with no spiritual side – like trying to be a nose with no face.

Imagine how your life would have been if there was no need to split your energy. You would have been happy but mediocre.
Because of what happened, you focused on your career and you tasted success. And now you want more. That is the reason why everything happened - to drag you out of your comfort zone. You have had massive successes, but they are small in comparison to what lies ahead of you.

FH: I think I am still a little unsure how you mean – "split your energy". Can you expand and simplify for me? Feel free to be as blunt as you need to be.

ES: Do you know of anyone who has written a sensible book about the spiritual aspects of self-employment? I can feel you stagger back. OK, you will not have written it by tomorrow afternoon, but it is bound to happen. You have already had enough experiences which you looked at from one dimension. You have successfully navigated your way around and through many different experiences so far.

It is time to get off the field, and go and sit on the pavilion, and re-live and observe those experiences you have had on the field. You will get a completely different view when you observe not just the person next to you on the field, but rather yourself, the person with you, the entire field and the area around the field. That is what you will be exploring and writing about. That will blow people's minds. This is why you need to "lift your head above the parapet" and look wider than the very small comfortable market you have explored so far.

There are a number of challenges waiting for you, where you will explore a much bigger market. You will be extremely successful, and at times you will be battered and bruised, but with every experience you will be both on the field, playing, and sitting on the pavilion observing Fraser and everyone and everything else, learning and then teaching others.

Forgiveness is about understanding that everything happened for a reason and you are so much better off because of it. Forgiveness is about saying "Thank you for teaching me a lesson in life that is precious and priceless".

Forgiveness is about recognizing and acknowledging a great teacher rather than rejecting a person who made you feel like a failure. You chose to feel like a failure, and you chose to take on challenges. That is what you need to understand so that you can consolidate your energy.

 This is really important. How does the above definition of forgiveness differ from how you understand it?

FH: Are you saying I've allowed myself to listen too much to others' opinions instead of just cracking on and allowing them to judge me by results instead? I think that's what came out as I wrote that poem this morning.

ES: Your poem indicated that you understand what forgiveness and gratitude are about. Now is the time to become more consciously aware of this. Have you forgiven the person who took your eye away – and at the same time gave you a new perspective in life? And I am not talking about "I forgive you because I am morally superior and judging you from on high". I am talking about "I forgive you because you have given me an awareness of myself as a spiritual being from a very early age, and without you I would have had a much different life which would have been small compared to what you opened up for me. I thank you from the bottom of my heart for forcing me to look inside when otherwise I would not have done it, because I am now reaping the benefits."

You have had great successes in the past few years. Now is the time to come out of your hibernation and consolidate your energy with gratitude. You have everything in place and it is excellent and according to the book. Well done.

FH: I'd love to know what "energy" or feeling you get about my new coaching programme and 90-day marketing plan.

ES: About the coaching program - (this is purely intuitive and not rational), go with it. You are already pushing the boundaries and you are a bit shaky about your reception, but trust and go with it. Listen to all the feedback you get, and feel in your body where the feedback sits. Do not try to interpret the feedback, just feel where it sits. You will learn from it.

About the 90-day marketing plan, it is not complete. There is an entire module missing. You drafted it and removed it because you doubted yourself. You need to finalize it and put it back. When you finalize it, trust your intuition.

Your time has come to re-write the book in your own terms. You are ready to be noticed internationally and to be incredibly happy. There are massive challenges ahead of you, and you need all your energy for them.

The difference this time will be that you will not approach the challenges with an attitude of "I will show you". You will approach them with the view of "This is exciting! What more can I do? What else is there that I cannot see yet? How much more is inside of me that I am only now becoming aware of?"

FH: Perhaps I have been hot headed in the past. Many have doubted me or mistrusted me, and I have had to prove myself. I suppose now I have nothing to prove. I now accept that what I offer can and will help those who need it. I'm just curious as to whether I neglect all the hard work that's been done, or whether I am to build on it, or if something else is to come along

ES: You will not neglect anything. You will build on a very solid foundation and see with astonishment and gratitude what you build.

Right now you are the biggest fish in the fish bowl. It is time for you to start growing into the biggest fish in the ocean. And the key is not the perfect product you have in place. The key is forgiveness, and understanding how people have helped you shape yourself, and feeling gratitude for that.

FH: I think I'm beginning to see that letting go may just help open the flow again. By the same token, I really want to develop my spiritual side, as dare I say it, I've had a year of bizarre happenings - perhaps there's more opening up now than I actually realize. I just wish I knew what the timetable for change is. I want to be mentally prepared for what's coming. Do you have any more insight on any of this?

ES: All I can say is prepare to "go out of your mind" – in a good way. Your brain is simply a control panel. If you focus entirely on what your brain can do or try to be "mentally prepared", you will miss many clues and build up an incredible resistance. You will put your brain aside more and more often, and listen to your unconscious. What you receive may not always be rational, but is a painting or a beautiful song or a sunset rational? What is the time table? How long is a piece of string? Forget about time. This is not another block that you need to tick off in a checklist. This is a journey. Enjoy the ride.

This book will take you into areas of your life that you have not explored before. If you insist on proof and rational explanations, you will be frustrated and now would be a good time to stop reading. Are you ready to push the boundaries? Are you ready to "go out of your mind"?

FH: Elsabe, you have triggered something in me, what I don't quite know, and happy to give you a testimonial to use on The Water Cooler or your website.

I would also like to extend my gratitude, by making you a proposition that I think could work well for both of us.

I would like to extend a FREE place on my full working for yourself coaching programme to help you get your business up and running in exchange for your help and ongoing assistance in developing my spiritual side and opening me up to the true possibilities that lie ahead.

I look forward very much to your comments, answers and insight.

Some things happen for a reason, and I have no doubt, we were meant to connect.

ES: Thank you. I accept your offer. I have been waiting for it, not knowing that it will come from you. It will be my honour and pleasure to work with you both spiritually and on your programme.

Gratitude Without Attitude

Thank you to my family, I see you each day
Don't say a word, you already have
In your own special way

Thank you to my peers, to each and every one of you
Thank you for your input and seeing it from a different point of
view
Thank you for the gift to question, to reflect and to ponder
Its only when we take time out
We really appreciate the wonder

Thank you for the daily lessons, the challenges and the fun
Thank you each and every single one of you
for my work is far from done.

Challenges and Obstacles, they help us in our plight
For opportunities are hidden everywhere,
Often visible with hindsight.

Critics come, and critics go
But we should stop and ask, why they think it so
In to our daily lives they do appear
We should spend more time listening but many choose not to hear

We are all a fish in a pond of size
Sometimes it grows before our eyes
But we can grow ourselves from the lessons learned
Why do some still choose to swim against the current?

But first catch your breath, to get in your flow
One deep breath and let it go
Energy doesn't start nor stop that is the norm
It merely changes in its form

Stop counting and measuring, comparing the contrast
Let your hair down, and have a blast
Be true to yourself and have the right attitude
For its starts with yourself and paying gratitude.

Forgive and forget, and wipe the slate clean
Unburden your heart, you know what I mean
Be thankful and grateful for all the lessons you've learned
Be supportive and helpful to all those concerned.

Stop and reflect on how you have grown
And be thankful for the errors that many have shown.
The next chapter in your life is about to arrive
It's time to embrace it with passion and drive

Thank and forgive and acknowledge the few
that have helped you in your growth and to become the new you.
Thank you.

 Are you at a crossroads? Do you feel directionless or surrounded by people who do not understand your ambitions? Do you feel there is something massive waiting for you that you are struggling to put into words? Make some notes on where you are in your life at the moment. These notes are only for your eyes, so you can be as honest as you want..

You are not a Human Doing. You're a...

..human being.

(article written by Fraser)

Whether it's working for yourself, relationships or whatever, the process of creating your optimum outcomes and achieving your objectives tends to follow a replicable process.

1. Being
2. Thought
3. Words
4. Action

We tend to create the experiences we desire in ourselves first of all (in our mind), then we communicate our thoughts in words, plans, documents, diagrams etc. and finally we (or others) implement our words and plans with real physical perspiration by implementing our plans of action.

In terms of our working for your self, it starts with -

a) **WHY** you want to work for yourself and what you want to offer – **MINDSET**
b) **WHAT** needs to be done, or what do we want to achieve – **STRATEGY**
c) **HOW** will we achieve it. – **TACTICS**

Now, many people seek immediate results. They want to know HOW to address the problems, without thinking or analysing the problem. They seek the knowledge on HOW to fix it. Some seek the knowledge and even implement it, only for the problem to rear their ugly head again purely because they didn't look for the root cause to discover WHY they weren't generating the results they want.

Many people manage to work for themselves but simply place themselves on an enduring quest for more results without wanting to know WHY the poor (or no results) keep occurring, or WHAT it

FRASER HAY & ELSABE SMIT

is they really want to achieve. They are often simply reacting to situations and the symptoms of bad, poor or ineffective habits without thinking or planning.

At a slightly deeper level, it could be argued that many people simply aren't aware of all the steps in the process. They continue to drift through life reacting and without achieving their objectives, primarily because they hadn't set any. They're simply not achieving what it is they want to be, do or have.

Some would argue that the action part of the process is the last part of the system to be put into place. After all, thinking allows you to formulate your ideas and initiates certain universal processes to begin, and your thoughts and ideas encourage others to buy into your plan, and want to assist you in achieving your own goals and objectives in working for yourself. Many people simply don't have the confidence (or mindset) to be what they want to be, so they stumble at the very first block.

Why do you think people need a business plan to persuade investors to buy into their idea? You come up with your thoughts; you document them and tell others your thinking, your ideas and your plans. The objects you see and touch, including the events you experience, are all effects of your thoughts.

Many people look for or try to create different "effects" without analyzing or considering the root causes. They simply fail in managing to work for themselves because they don't start at the beginning of the process.

Remember, the manifestation of the results and how we will achieve them are the last part of the process. We must go back and revisit our strategy (our words) and our mindset (our thoughts). **You are a human being, not a human doing. Some would argue that thought is the only cause.**

The results we generate working for ourselves are the outward manifestation of our thoughts. (Tactics=Strategy + Mindset.)

25

It starts with MINDSET.

The results and what we experience with our 5 senses in the physical world of business is an effect produced or created by a cause (thought).

Think for a second. The end results from your thoughts can't create - they've been created. They can only be experienced (and quite often, these experiences are not the ones you really want to be, do or have.) Are they?

Conversely, your thoughts cannot experience - they can only invent, imagine and interpret. We need a world of relativity to experience (through our senses) that which we create in our minds. Many want to experience results from working for themselves without first having created in their mind what it is they want to achieve, or expressing their dreams in written form allowing them to attract the resources they require.

Have you ever tried asking for directions from someone in a strange city without telling them where you want to go? Think about it. What's the plan? What's the destination? What do you want to be, do or have?

From a perspective of working for yourself, if your thoughts and mindset are negative, then its ultimately predictable that you will have a negative experience.

Self talk like "I have no leads", "I need more traffic", "I have no pipeline", "no appointments booked in for next month" simply reinforce your negative thinking and mindset that what you have been doing hasn't been working, and therefore it needs to change.

Stop dwelling on the past, or more specifically regrets of the past, which are manifesting the experiences that you don't want now. It's time to change your mindset. It's time to change your thoughts.

Choose to **be** positive, and become aware of your change of mindset, and start making positive plans for the future.

Stop waiting for the opportunity to arise or that elusive deal to come to you. Seize the moment and create the opportunities you want. If you want good results from working for yourself, by implementing good positive tactics (online or offline), then you want positive experiences as a result of implementing a positive plan of action.

But first, think about, and consider why you want to work for yourself, and then decide to create a plan for the next 90 days.

So in terms of your working for yourself, what do you want to be, do or have?

   Reflect and make notes on what you have just read.

21 August: Terra Incognita

ES: You told me about "Terra incognita" and the co-incidence of this term coming into your awareness twice in a short time, and then you consciously accepted the term and used it in your blog. But if you stand back and look at what happened over the past few days, you may find a different meaning there. Were the words like a road sign to you?

FH: Upon reflection, four significant things have occurred in three days –

- I discovered the term terra incognita in a book and it resonated with me
- I decided to write an article ("Your Unique Selling Point and Elevator Pitch") about it
- I picked a random book from my library ("Dianetics" by L Ron Hubbard) and the opening chapter was about it too.
- Our first conversation screamed demons, new pathways, journey and high time I ventured into terra incognita too

It's become very apparent that it's time for me to set sail, and "open up". OK, I understand that, I'm just a little unsure as to how it's all going to unfold, without me going cuckoo, taking my eye off the ball business-wise or undoing all the hard work I have put in over the last 3 years.

ES: You have entered terra incognita in your spiritual awareness. This takes a lot of courage. I am not just talking about any fears you may have from a religious point of view - we have been so brainwashed to mistrust anything we cannot see and touch, especially if those things touch our hearts.

Expanding your spiritual awareness can have unpredictable results, for example "seeing" people that might not be real,

28

hearing voices and wondering about schizophrenia (been there, done that, had some interesting experiences and questions with someone who became schizophrenic at around the same time I accepted my clairaudience) or even more inexplicable things. On the article "You Are not a Human Doing, You Are a Human . . . ": It is interesting how we climb from one set of stairs to the next in our lives and how we became aware of it.

FH: A lot of what I believe in, I haven't actually expressed in the written word, or spoken about, and this week (and being fortunate enough to be introduced into you), has acted as a catalyst or door opening for me.

ES: You are not one-dimensional at all, and I wanted to use the analogy to indicate where you are heading. The sequence of "mindset, thoughts, words, action" says you are on a stair. Time to climb to the next stair!

You talk about mindset, which implies that a person must have a mind to set. Can you expand a bit more on your understanding of "mind"? Why is it that a person can have less than half a brain and function normally? How do stroke victims regain some functionality when parts of their brains get permanently destroyed?

FH: Mind, in my opinion is NOT Brain. The brain is like the CPU, and processes data it pulls into RAM from the universal wide web (super-consciousness). Mind is the very essence within the whole of the body (almost like our own private virtual neural network), and is replicated down through to each cell in the body. Our mind is the unification of the energy (microcosms) collectively in the one human being, and the collective consciousness or universal mind is "everyone and everything."

Brain is the hardware, the physical the body. Mind is the intangible.

ES: Also, why is it so important to focus on what you want rather than on what you do not want? It is true, but I would like to hear how you explain it. Is it a platitude that makes sense to you or can you explain the mechanics behind it?

FH: We live in a probable reality. Our 3-dimensional reality is much denser than other parts of the universe and this can cause the time delays of manifesting what we think about into being. Personally, I feel it is better to concentrate on that what we DO want for it draws them to us. Concentrating on what we don't want maintains the status quo (in my opinion) for nothing new is created.

Our mission in life, (I think) is to recognize that we are consciousness in form and are here to enjoy abundance and experience the beauty of our existence in 3 dimensions.

The problem for many is, the ego gets bogged down with the physical and thus don't spend enough time experiencing the spiritual side. It's all about balance and being selfless. Many souls, when in physical form, love the short-lived pleasures and gains from one-upmanship, sex, greed etc. and deny themselves the long-term bliss of eternal happiness which comes from remembering/and experiencing the spiritual side and contributing to others.

After all, we derive happiness from giving. Isn't that what working for yourself is all about?

 How do you explain your current discomfort with where you are in your life? It is not a physical discomfort that you will lose by going to the gym. Eating or drinking does not help – don't kid yourself. Do you really think any financial discomfort will go away if you win the lottery? You know it is at a much deeper level than that. If you had to stretch your mind and your vocabulary, how would you describe your current state?

30

22 August

ES: Your understanding of the mind vs the brain is spot-on.
We will talk a lot more about the Law of Attraction and specifically about judgment.
Have a look at this article:

Want to Prove the Law of Attraction? Focus on What You Do Not Want

So, South Africa is getting a new president, and it is probably the man that half of the country wants, while the other half of the country does not want him.

The criticism of this man has been as loud as the support for him. And both the support and the criticism ensured that enough energy was generated for his party to win, and probably for him to become president.

There has been lots of publicity covering the wishes of the followers of Mr. Zuma, and also a group on the social website Facebook that wanted to get a million signatures against Mr. Zuma.
How did this happen?

The Law of Attraction states that we must focus clearly on what we require, and then be willing and ready to receive. Once we meet all of these requirements, our wishes materialize because all the energy is used to attract to us exactly what we wanted.

And if most people in a country focus on a single person, then that person receives all that energy and grows stronger all the time.

Should the group on Facebook have been the counterpart of the followers of Mr. Zuma to create balance? No.

The Universe does not judge. People judge. People spoke about and thought of Mr. Zuma for months. Some people did this in a positive sense and added their positive judgment. Other people spoke of and thought of Mr. Zuma in a negative sense, and added their negative judgment. The Universe does not respond to the positive and negative judgments.

The Universe focuses energy on Mr. Zuma, and that is where his strength lies.

The same is now happening with the swine flu that originated in Mexico. There is already talk of a pandemic in the UK, and according to the media, in the past two days the number of patients with swine flu has "more than doubled" – that is from two to five individuals out of a population of about 61 million people.

There is talk in the House of Commons about massive preventative measures to keep the swine flu virus at bay, but no talk about people being and remaining healthy. Guess what the effect will be?

What is the solution to these issues?

It is so simple. When you are faced with an unwanted person or situation, identify what it is that you want, and focus on getting what you want. Do not spare any thought for what you do not want. Remember that the Universe gives us exactly what we want, and does not even hear the judgment that we express.

What would be the best countermeasure for swine flu? An action group that focuses on excellent health, and that sends thoughts of excellent health into the Universe every day.

What would be the way to get the president that you want selected in a country? An action group that provides unconditional support for the person that you want selected.

In these instances, face masks and court cases are excellent ways to focus on what you do not want, and to then get exactly what you do not want. Of course that provides something else – more to complain about, and more negativity to focus on.

Now you can understand why I go out of my way to not watch the news and get sucked into the mass hypnosis and propaganda that becomes most people's reality.

And that does not mean that I focus on not watching the news. I focus on creating slowly, step by step in more and more detail, on what I want for myself. That is a far more valuable way to spend my energy.

 Take a few minutes to reflect and make notes on what you have just read.

25 August

FH: I wonder how many people are looking for a business opportunity that provides backup and support in starting their own business. But we help people with more than that. There is also an opportunity for

- People who have been made redundant
- School leavers
- University graduates
- Women returning to work
- People in jobs they hate

…to not just start a business using the skills, knowledge and experience they have, but also achieve their life's purpose and getting the balance between spiritual and business. But instead of going "fluffy" as you say, say "No, fulfil your life's purpose and make money at the same time."

ES: Yes. Believe in yourself. Trust yourself and find your own hidden resources and use them.

FH: In these last few months I've changed the course contents considerably but noticed a distinct inactivity within The Water Cooler, and I am just wondering. I was questioning why the tap had been turned off and I doubt whether what I was doing was right or wrong and whether I was on the right path.

ES: My immediate feeling is that you are on the right path. You are looking at how you can again sell the 1% that you have already sold on The Water Cooler. You cannot. It is done. It is now about looking for the other 99% and getting that out into a much bigger world. It feels to me that you are at the top of a spiral at the moment. You have done an incredible amount of work with The Water Cooler. It has been so satisfying, it has been hard work. It has not always been easy, but you got to a point where you were really satisfied with that. You could look back and tap yourself on the shoulder and say "brilliant – you have done an excellent job". But that has changed into dissatisfaction with where you are.

I was looking at the poem "Gratitude without Attitude" you published last week where somebody commented and said "this is good, we want to see more of this side of you." There is a market for that as well.

FH: With the last couple of articles in The Water Cooler I have taken the concept of working for yourself, analyzed it and broken it down from a metaphysical perspective, and built it back up into the context of working for yourself. I have talked about cause and effect in terms of goal setting. I have talked about be, do, have – you need to be who you want to be from the outset, as opposed to try and have something that you just push away.

ES: Is the blog on The Water Cooler the only one you have?

FH: Historically I have been using The Water Cooler as a test pad. I've never been worried about money in my life. I just do what I do because I love to do it. I have just been testing things in The Water Cooler and people have approached me for more. I feel that I want to withdraw from The Water Cooler and concentrate on writing my blogs on my own site. My strategy until now was to write a blog on The Water Cooler, and when people contacted me, I would transfer the blog onto my own website blog and delete it from The Water Cooler after a couple of days.

ES: And on both blogs you speak with your own voice, but your voice is changing and so is your audience. You wrote to me that you were concerned about going cuckoo and losing everything that you have built up until now. That is not going to happen. Yes, your awareness is increasing by the day. I can hear that from what you say and the way you say it. This means that you will have a much richer product on the table for a much wider audience which is functioning at a higher level.

FH: I can relate to that as well. I am wondering – for me as an individual - what is my next step to start seeing the immediate benefit? What is next?

 Becoming aware of who you are, is not an overnight process. It is a journey of discovering everything that is not brain and body. Are you ready to answer questions you have not even thought of before?

ES: I have been feeling quite strongly since yesterday that I need to ask you about your dreams – the dreams you have at night.

FH: I have become conscious of not actually sleeping. I close eyes but my mind remains very active. I have no recollection of my thoughts during that time.

ES: So you don't go to sleep? You move into a different state? I would say just go with that for the moment. There is a lot of processing that is happening below the surface.

FH: I can feel that. That is a good way of describing it. When I go to sleep, I tend to – not drift - that is the wrong word. I am trying to push myself out so that I am not limiting myself in terms of my physical presence. I am trying to experience alternate realities as if they are happening now, but I cannot describe vividly what those experiences are.

ES: I understand. When you drift into a different state, you consciously leave your body. This results in a massive increase in your awareness. You will get to a point where you will probably feel that you have lost that focus. What you have now is the awareness that there is something cooking and it is just below the surface. You are impatient because you want to understand more of it and give more structure to it. Don't be surprised if, for a while, it all disappears completely and instead of having that amazing feeling of drifting off, you just feel a black nothing. When that ends, you will have a moment of complete enlightenment. That will not be a once off, but rather the first one that you will become conscious of. Just be patient. There is a lot happening at the moment that you cannot put into little blocks or into a questionnaire - that you cannot give structure to - but it is happening.

FH: I know you are right. The programme that I have developed is ready to go into the market, but I keep thinking that this is about working for yourself. The product itself was not ready to go to a wider audience.

ES: That is right. While you were doing the fine-tuning, you were already tapping into a lot that you were not necessarily aware of it. The product is there and it is perfect. You are now catching up to the product. What you have put on paper is very good. You are now learning how to present it. Did you at times, when you were working on this product, feel that you were not in charge, that you were just doing things and it was brilliant?

FH: On occasion yes. What I have noticed since I have made the changes to the programme is that the results people are getting this year are far greater than the results they got last year. Three distinct things have come out of that. I am taking the time in the first session to say "look, you need to put in the time and the effort." At the end of each session people are now giving me feedback. They document what they gained from the session, even before they do the homework assignment. They had proven to themselves the gain and benefit. Their confidence levels are up and they want to put their whole hearts into the homework and apply it.

ES: That makes sense. You are already getting people to look deeper inside of themselves and explore a lot more. You want to understand how and why you are managing that.

FH: The program was very commercial, but they needed to have the right mindset before talking about the business. They needed to be very clear as to who they are and what they have to offer before they could try and sell it.

ES: You have been able to put it on paper and take others through the process. But you are now back to square one. The process is fine, you have done it with a few people and you have seen the difference in the results. You are now going through the same process because you have moved a step up.

FH: I can see that. With my recent blogs on The Water Cooler the number of interactions has fallen dramatically. I am wearing two hats to interpret this. I think some people realise this is not my usual stuff. Others quietly take it away, contemplating and reflecting, and then implementing the various tactics to prove they work.

 What are your hidden resources? Yes, of course you would say "well, if they are hidden, I don't know". OK, we can try "what would you do if you only had 3 days to live", but that is not very realistic for most people. So how about this: think about the biggest challenge you have faced in your life so far. How did you overcome that challenge?

OK, you did that by using resources that you did not know you had. Now imagine for a moment that you have a license to brag like you have never bragged before. You don't need to prove anything, and you won't be expected to deliver on any of you promises. So tell me what you can do to make your life and this world a better place if given only half a chance. Go for it. And remember, you can keep going until your heart sings, because I won't hear you and won't stifle your creativity.

26 August

ES: Here are my comments on the article "You are not a Human Doing. You are a Human . . . "
I like your model of being, thoughts, words, action. This is how the creative process works.
Here is a question:

If being is the first step which then turns into thoughts,

- *Do you meditate and make space for your unconscious to guide you so that the thoughts can surface, and then you follow up on the thoughts and put them into action?*
- *If you do this, does it mean you understand that all your thoughts come from your unconscious anyway and you just need to open that door and allow them to get through, or does it mean you sit back and wait for the muse to visit you? Do you pull from your unconscious, even when it is not always rational, because that is the source of your creativity?*
- *Or do you focus on setting objectives and then let them materialize, while relying only on what is in your consciousness already (past experience)? If you do this, does it mean that you reinforce existing beliefs, or that you access your unconscious without even being aware of it? Do you push forward from where you are?*

FH: It's an interesting one. Personally I hate the term *meditate.* I prefer *contemplate*, but even then I'm lousy at sitting down closing my eyes and stilling my mind. I do tend to go into a room, sit down with a problem, challenge or predominant thought, and contemplate a solution, way forward etc., and lo and behold, a number of creative thoughts arise.

I have also experienced that by having a goal you can draw/attract/ manifest the necessary resources you need to accomplish that goal. It could be that while transmitting those thoughts others resonate with them, and get drawn to you to help you achieve your objective.

ES: How do you apply the Law of Attraction?

Consider the difference between "We have no . . ." This reinforces lack/shortage which is a reflection of many belief systems that focus on a limited pot and too many people wanting to share.

FH: Agreed - bad or negative mindset

ES: "We want . . ." but we will never get it, because as long as we want, we perceive a distance between ourselves and the thing we want. We can find many reasons to justify that want.

FH: As we tell our kids - "I want, never gets" in other words, don't demand, ask.

ES: "We are working towards . . ." indicates intent and that we understand how we create with our thoughts.

FH: Agreed

ES: When you dwell on the past, you confirm specific beliefs all the time. Those beliefs served you at the time. When you and your environment change, you may want to keep your beliefs the same. If the beliefs are no longer appropriate, you experience one world inside of you and another world outside of you. Over time this causes massive tension, because you need all your energy to maintain two different worlds that are in conflict with each other. The result is stunted growth, and dis-eases like cancer.

FH: Don't dwell on the past, or worry about the future, focus on the now.

ES: However, if you look back to your past experiences, and consider your self before and after the experiences, you become aware of how the experiences have changed you. If this results in any negative emotion (especially resentment, regret or revenge), you have not grasped the lesson yet.

On the other hand, if you understand how a part of you have become whole as a result of those experiences, you feel gratitude and get a glimpse into eternity. Then you can look back with only positive emotions, but you tend not to do that, because you have "become" or integrated the past experience and there is nothing to look back to. So maybe you should go back to the past, figure out what you have learnt from it, and then use the lessons for future planning. When you do that, you have to be very careful with how you word the lessons, e.g. rather than "avoid/do not do/be careful of", use "create/focus on/move towards".

FH: I can see the logic and reasoning for listing bad/poor/negative experiences in the past and acknowledging them for the lessons they've represented and how I've gained or benefited in real terms as a direct result of them.

How do you approach your career and the stuff you do? Is it "go, go, go – shoot now and aim later"? Is it "let me plan and think and plan more" – but no action while you chase your own tail?

Or are you able to ask a question, then still your mind and wait for the answer? When you do get an answer to your question, do you take note of the answer? If you never allow yourself that moment of stillness, you will take much longer to discover the richness of what you already have.

Your Business Start-up Plan

Many people wouldn't think of working for themselves in a spiritual context. Well, read this, complete the action points at the end of each step, and then craft your very own action plan for working for yourself. This exercise is very powerful, and very quickly will enable you to find not just the clarity you want, but also to create the action plan that you may need.

STEP 1: You are the sum total of your experiences to date.

By conducting a situation analysis, you take stock, and reflect on all the lessons you've learned over the last X amount of months and years. This process of reflection helps you to identify your achievements, your disappointments, the reasons behind those disappointments and what you've learned. Think about the journey you've been on with your business, the deals you've won, the successes, and some of the failures you've had and why. More importantly, retrace your steps and see how you managed to arrive at the position and set of circumstances you find yourself in today.

 It's time to summarize that journey you've been on in writing and describe exactly where you are in your life (and business) today and why certain results were or weren't achieved along the way. Write down what you've been doing and why, and what the net result and learning to date is.

STEP 2 - Desire, the human engine of possibility

Having completed step one, and reflected on your experiences to date and the lessons learned, then next step is to ignite the passion and desire within you. You know how you got to where you are, and some of the lessons learned en route, but now it's a case of deciding what it is you want to be, do or have next as you go forward. You have a desire for your heart to be fulfilled on a number of physical, mental, spiritual and financial levels. So it's time to set new goals. You need something to aim for.

 It's time to start creating new goals & objectives. It's time to listen to your heart, not your head. So, what do you want to achieve in the next 12 months? What do you want to "Be, Do or Have"? Make a list now. Get a sheet of paper, create 3 columns each with the heading "BE","DO" and "HAVE, and write down all the things that you want to be, do and have in each column.

STEP 3 - Know you life's purpose, better still articulate it, and live it

This is why creating an elevator pitch and unique selling point is actually so fundamental in helping you live your life's purpose. You need to fire up your levels of enthusiasm, and be 100% confident and true to yourself that what you're doing and the selfless service you provide to others, is resonating at the absolute core of your being.

If it's not, then change your job, change your career, don't just do it for the money - do it because you love it. More important, you need to articulate what you offer to others. You are who you are, offering the knowledge, skills and expertise you have accumulated during your time so far on this planet. In the history of the universe, you are unique, but it's high time you raised your energy levels and really started to believe in yourself and what you offer. Remember the last 4 letters of enthusiasm - IASM - I am sold myself.

 Write down who you help, what you offer, the problems you can fix, and the service or solutions you provide. Go on, do it now.

STEP 4 - Relationships are all about an exchange of energy

Having completed the first 3 steps, you've probably rediscovered that you are an oozing ball of energy, filled with desire and a passion to help others by applying what you've learned in your total experiences to date and applying the benefit of the lessons you've learned so far.

The last thing you want to do is to push others away or to be mistrusting towards you, so you need to target those you can help, and more importantly, those who want what you have, do and offer. Think of two magnets. Opposites attract. You want to target and locate those who need what you want. Having completed the first 3 steps, you have a much clearer sense of direction and purpose. Believe it or not, but prospects and partners who can help you reach your goals will be drawn to you and will resonate with what you say.

 Write down a detailed description of your target audience including role, organisation, size of employees, turnover, sector/industry and geographical area, or if you're in a B2C environment, think about all the different criteria you'd like a prospect to meet.

Some people say that **"Being leads to thoughts, leads to words, leads to action."** You being here and reading this is one thing. You've probably spent some time getting to this sentence. Now, if you're serious about your future circumstances, and creating the reality you want, then complete each action point in your own words on paper, and start putting it all into action. It's time to start manifesting the results you want from your working for yourself.

 Take some time out to make notes on what you have just read.

27 August

FH: Crikey, You are getting me thinking. I'm really noticing my change in approach and interaction with prospects and clients. I wrote about poverty consciousness in a blog today - and the people are beginning to like them too. I think it's attracting a whole new audience.

Refer to the article "It's always about the money". I've wanted to write about money and working for yourself in spiritual terms for a while as many people simply don't get it. I think it might just open someone up to the idea that there's a lot more to life than just finding the money for the mortgage every month.

I forgot to say....
I was taking my son to work yesterday morning at 05.45, and stopped the car to watch the sun come up out of the sea....WOOOAAAA, a huge golden ball of energy lighting up the entire sky - a Scotsman enjoying the wonders of a sunrise, whatever next ?!?!?!

Time to get all fluffy – yes, you too. Remind yourself of a beautiful moment you have recently experienced. Seeing the beauty in something small or in another person is part of opening up to yourself. It does not matter whether you saw a well-toned body, read a book that made you want to cry, or saw a glimpse of joy in the face of your loved one when you came home. Just be quiet for a moment and relive that moment of beauty. That is part of the richness that you already have.

It's Always About the Money

When it comes to working for yourself, people are always obsessed about the money. If they want the sales, then they need or want the money. They may even take the conscious step of creating a plan, but then wonder how they will resource the plan. They need or want the money to resource the plan.

Some would argue that there's never enough money in the world to compensate for a lack of fulfilment in what one does. Without a heart filled with a joy for life, even spending that which you make or earn becomes joyless.

With a lack of sales, a lack of pipeline and a lack of cash in your bank account come a **poverty consciousness -** the mindset that people tend to adopt when things don't go according to plan or simply aren't going well.

It's often borne out of a fear of lack and denial of self-worth. Many people remain in a poverty consciousness by the belief that individuals tend to be lazy and refuse to work unless they are made to by the fear of being poor. Many therefore stay in jobs they don't like, and are unable to show their true creative talents for years. For those working for themselves, these beliefs can often come across in their voice, their handshake, their writing. They can often come across as needy, desperate, and skint in the minds of prospects. Then prospects reading the unconscious signals consciously decide not to do business with them.

Others continue to do jobs that they hate in the belief that this is what they must do in order to survive financially. They actually continue to remain in a poverty consciousness, both in their own minds and the minds of people close to them. The truth is that the opposite is true. Once we recognize what we enjoy, and what we excel at and become aligned with our life's purpose, we tend to work all the hours of the day as an outward expression of who we

46

really are and because our expectations are not totally focused on money or financial matters, and when we detach ourselves from the financial rewards, and money begins to flow much easier. Money is simply an exchange of energy.

Yes, it can be a piece of paper, a coin or an electronic transfer with no actual value on itself. Paper-based money would probably end up worthless if we didn't all agree the value. Did you know it only costs 3p to make a £5 note? In a phone call to the Bank of England they also confirmed it costs 3p to make a £20 note and a £50 note, but we place a value of £50 on that £50 note. We all know how the banks have artificially increased their "value" by billions of £££ in recent years too. When money is transferred electronically it is a pure energy transfer.

There was no shipment of physical cash in a GPS tracked Securicor van from one bank to another, no briefcase containing precious gems or stones handcuffed to the wrist of a well-dressed gentleman wearing Top Gun sunglasses. No, you simply traded a certain amount of your own energy (service to others) in exchange for money (more energy) which ultimately will be exchanged for other goods and services (more energy.)

Many people value themselves based on what they have, and how much money they have in the bank. That is one way to look at it I suppose, but try and value yourself by what you give to others. Think of the energy exchange you give to others in the service you provide. Many people feel abundant, deserving - even flush when they have a lot of money, and they quite rightly spend it, some even waste it or squander it. When they have no money, many feel more inferior, weaker or maintain a lower self-esteem, and their creative output is much lower.

We get pleasure (short term energy gains) from the things we receive (one-upmanship, sex, alcohol/drugs, fame etc.), but we get/create longer lasting happiness for ourselves from the things we give, and that includes service of that which we enjoy giving.

If you're feeling abundant on occasion, give to charity. If you are in a position to give, then that must mean you already have. If you already have, then you are re-enforcing the **prosperity consciousness.** The amounts can vary, yes, but the principle remains the same. I remember watching a chap begging outside Euston Station. Everyone was walking past. All the commuters were trapped in jobs they hated. They were making the daily commute to maintain their own poverty consciousness, yet they looked down their nose at the chap who was perhaps actually experiencing (even trapped in) the exact same mental state as them.

Me, I was a visitor to the city, I was an observer as I watched the hundreds of people on the tube - none speaking or smiling, faces stuck in books, all glum unhappy people (probably having had to get up at 06.00 for a 09.30 start). No-one appeared happy, just half asleep - or maybe I should say, half awake.

Treat money with respect and gratitude, acknowledge the energy that went into creating that which you receive, but more importantly start respecting, and valuing what you have to offer too.

If what you offer and provide is less than the cost of the problem you can fix, then think of the impact and the true value of what it is you really have to offer. More importantly, start adopting a prosperity consciousness and start doing what you want to do, not what you have to do, and watch the returns starting being commensurate in direct proportion to the level of energy you put into giving selflessly.

My father once said, "You won't always find the job that you want, but you'll always find the job that you need". I replied, "I don't want a J.O.B. (to be just over broke), I want a life, I want to do what I want to do, and do it well, not just be told what I must do".

I love working with people, not for people.

And I have a funny feeling there are a lot of people who think like that too.

Later:

ES: With regards to the article "It's Always About the Money"

1. Judgment of others' experiences.
The celebrity culture which is so strong in this country and the US, says "Don't ask me what I want for myself, because I have such a low self-esteem that I would not dare ask myself what I want. What I am very good at is identifying another person who already has what looks good to me, and then I decide that is what I want. Whether it suits me or not is irrelevant, and I do not deserve anything for myself." What does it really mean to be individual?

I was just thinking about comparing yourself with your competition as part of working for yourself. It is necessary, but with what mindset do you do it? You could compare and fail on every point, completely negate your individuality, tap into the energy of your competition, and fail to do what they do because you use someone else's energy.

Or you could compare and realize what you have to offer and emphasize what makes you unique, and create your own energy – and see the miracle. But this takes self-insight and being grounded – it is easy to be so "unique" that you have nothing in common with your market.

This relates back to the concept of one-ness – of course we are One – but what does this mean in daily life? Should we be clones on all the visible stuff, or do we share the same invisible journey? Can you accept representing both the spectacular success of Coca-Cola for over 100 years and the spectacular failure of Dasani (bottled water sold by Coca Cola) in the UK? Are you happy to be both Hitler and Sister Theresa?

On the other hand there is a self-fulfilling prophecy where you "fake it until you make it" you draw the energy to you by going through the motions, and at some point you generate the energy rather than draw it to yourself - when you move from being student to becoming master.

2. Judging your own past experience and perceiving it as a bad experience
When is an experience "bad"? When is the experience "good"?

Are you familiar with your blueprint or life script?

What does the whole idea of judgment mean to you? This relate to the law of attraction again.

3. There is also the concept of timing.
You can do a perfect job and fail at it, because you do it at a time when it is not relevant. Does this mean you should never do it again? In 1993 I tried to start my own business – out of desperation and because I had no understanding. I did everything by the book when it came to working for yourself at the time and it failed – because I was petrified and not ready, and I knew it, and so did everyone I dealt with.

Does this mean I should not work for myself because I "failed" once? It would be like giving up driving the first time another driver cuts in front of you, or giving up running the first time you fail to do 100m in less than 12 seconds.

But more important, I think we get glimpses of our blueprints without even being aware of it, and at the time the glimpses do not make sense, and because we do not see the full picture, we "fail". On the other hand, if something is so alien to your nature that it makes you physically ill, you do not prove anything by being pig-headed and going against your true nature.

Are you doing something at the moment that is not in line with your nature at all? Why do you continue to do it?

4. *Something has worked for a long time and now it is no longer working.*

NLP refers to limiting decisions based on limiting thoughts. At a certain point in time you have a success and you think "this is the way to do it". Your thought results in a decision, which you base future actions on.

Nothing wrong with that.

The problem comes when you stick to that decision, no matter what, while everything in and around you change. The result is tension between your inner and outer world, and loads of emotions and physical reactions (very much like wearing clothes that are two sizes too small). When you let go of an outdated decision, you make space for "nothing", and out of "nothing" creativity is born. That "nothing" is the scary bit if you do not understand what is happening.

It does not really matter whether you meditate or contemplate - it is more about the awareness that you need to make space for "nothing" and allow the creativity to surface.

This is going to become quite important to you when you reach the space of "nothing" - to keep your faith.

By the way, a spin-off of that "failed" attempt at working for myself in 1993 was a life-long friendship with a crazy Portuguese woman who is still my best friend. What "failed" was a massive success in a completely different way.

What is it that makes you authentic? That is what shines through in your business and in your life. A shy person can make a good salesperson if what they sell is 100% aligned with their passion. An extrovert can come across as desperate when they are in a job or business that is completely against their grain. You may not realize it, but people buy or don't buy what you are selling about 10 minutes before you enter a room. We unconsciously send out energy waves that other people pick up, and we always have our "antennae" out, picking up waves from other people. What makes you unique and different from the billions of others around you? If you are not sure, leave it for now and get back to this page once a day until you can put your uniqueness into one sentence.

You are the sum total of your experiences to date

You may want to start a business or work for yourself.
You may want more **leads**.
You may want more **referrals**
You may even want more **sales**.

But wait.
Question is: **Why now?**
Why do you need them now?
What's gone wrong?
What have you been doing historically, or up until now, that's caused them to stop?

Hmmm.

If we are the captains of our own destiny, then it is up to us to stop and examine what we've been doing, how we've been doing it, and its relative success to date. Seems logical you would think. But how often do you actually stop, reflect, and examine your previous actions and experiences to determine what the learning has been, and to decide how you can apply that learning as you go forward to allow you to generate even bigger and better results from working for yourself?

- The world is changing.
- The world of employment is changing.
- You are changing.

Have you been dissuaded from trying new tactics because of someone else's bad or negative experience?
Have activities which have worked in the past, simply stopped generating the results you used to get?
Do you require more resources?

Have you been dissuaded from trying new tactics because of someone else's bad or negative experience?

Have you gotten lazy, apathetic or simply down heartened by the current economic climate?

I bet there are hundreds, probably thousands of people who might be able to benefit from what you have to offer. The problem is, you just can't seem to find or locate them, or persuade them to do business with you. They might be experiencing their own set of personal challenges at the moment preventing them from experiencing clarity and choosing you as their preferred solution. After all, wasn't it Arthur Robert Ashe Junior who said "Success is a journey, not a destination. The doing is usually more important than the outcome."

 Reflect and make notes on what you have just read.

Cause and Effect

Quite often when things don't go according to plan either in your business or personal life, it's because we are dealing with the **symptoms** of our thinking.

Now, on a slightly deeper level, it could be argued that your thoughts are the "**cause**" of the results that you have experienced previously (and currently) in your life. If you were to change your thoughts (or mindset) towards your life then the chances are that the effects (your experiences) will change accordingly.

Many people have been socially conditioned by their family, peers and others. Other's opinions have molded and shaped your consciousness and perception about your life. Some get to the stage where their ego takes over, and they actually think that working for themselves is beneath them. They end up treating those who are actively involved in the "black art" with the contempt they think those people deserve. Their thoughts of marketing or selling their wares conjure up images of second hand car sales men, direct insurance types or snake oil sellers.

Many people view the art of marketing as something beneath them, or a waste of their invaluable time and superior intellect. It's more common than you think, across many fields and disciplines - the actor who won't go to auditions, the out of job chief executive won't go to interviews, the athlete who won't train or practice, and the consultants who won't sell, are all being held back by their ego. You have to put your ego aside, and start re-considering your thoughts, perceptions and views towards working for yourself, for it's actually affecting the reality of your current sales and revenue.

Niels Bohr and Werner Heisenberg, two of the prominent names in quantum mechanics, presented the case that nothing is solid. Everything is a sea of never ending energy, constantly changing, and the actions (including thought) of the observer can vary the result, or create the reality that they experience. In other words, we can mold, shape, create and experience the reality we want by our thoughts. Everything starts with a thought.

Think for a second.

The phone rings with a prospect wanting more information about your products or services. That prospect was generated via a phone call, which was generated from a call to action, generated in an ad, which was generated from sales copy, which came out of a brainstorm of thoughts about what should be in the ad that came out of a brainstorm of thoughts as to what should be done to generate more sales.

The process started with a thought as to how to generate leads, and then focused on the thoughts of how to express or sell oneself in an ad, so the ad was written, and then placed in the paper. Over the years, advertisers have tried a number of innovative approaches to appeal to each of the five senses. TV, Radio, perfume Scratch cards, food sampling at deli counters, wine tasting parties, even social networking - you name it, they've tried it.

But as we take a closer look at each of the five senses, we know that each of them operates at their own frequency. We know that dogs can hear a whistle that is inaudible to humans; various animals can see or feel outside of the frequency range that humans can experience.

In other words your sensory perception is limited and interprets the messages it receives from a very limited standpoint. Quite often our sensory perception can be distorted. It's not always accurate because it's an interpretation. Your thoughts help to determine what the energy forms and how it is interpreted and experienced. This can help towards explaining such things as prayer, positive thinking, goal setting etc. Your thoughts are in fact molding the universe on a per particle basis to create your reality.

Look around you right now. Everything you see in the room you are in NOW started as an idea, a picture or thought in the mind of the person who created it. Look around you and identify that statement with the objects around you ... The seat you are sitting on, the computer you are using, the desk, the pen, the post-it note, the paper clip - all began as an idea or thought from the person who created them. That person's original thought resonated at a particular frequency and as it was shared and expressed, grew stronger and stronger, attracting other thoughts, and ideas, until it transformed into a physical object via a very simple PROCESS.

In short, you literally become what you think about most. Your reality, or the results of your thinking, acting and doing create the reality that you are currently experiencing. That manifests itself in terms of the sales and revenue you generated this week. **Your reality, and for this example, the results you want from working for yourself, become what you have imagined and believed in most.**

Quite often, however, the one thought that preoccupies your mind the most, is quite often the one thing that you have not acquired, accomplished or achieved. This continues to elude you because of your negative thinking.

For example, answer the following question truthfully....What is the one thing that has been the predominant thought in your mind today, yesterday or for this past week, or month?

 Take a minute to acknowledge the one thing you have been thinking about the most, and write it down. It may be anything at all. Go on, write it down.

Whether you work for yourself or someone else, there are times that you might feel overwhelmed by everything, or more specifically the results (or the effects) of your thoughts and actions. Sometimes you can become so preoccupied with the effects of negative thinking that you fail to achieve **your** working for yourself objectives.

Many become unsuccessful and fail to achieve **their** working-for-yourself objectives because they have lost their focus and concentrate far too much on the effects rather than the cause of their experience, which more often than not is their own negative programming.

Ever wondered why certain business situations keep repeating themselves until you undergo a major breakthrough?

For example, some people are always experiencing feast or famine. Some experience lots of appointments or no sales. Others spend hours online every day in the hope that their online marketing (if that's what they call it) will somehow miraculously start generating amazing results. Others are constantly experiencing serious cash flow problems. They have one bill paid, only to be faced with another unpaid one, and so it continues. In fact, one definition of insanity is to continually do the same thing while hoping for a different result.

It could be argued that all problems arise from believing in a false thought (or cause). Until it is changed, the effects of that thought (or cause) will keep coming back in different forms, manifesting those thoughts, when working for yourself, in the form of poor or negative results. It could be argued that all problems arise from believing in a false thought (or cause). Until it is changed, the effects of that thought (or cause) will keep coming back in different forms, manifesting those thoughts, when working for yourself, in the form of poor or negative results. Some consider the law of cause and effect as the number one universal law.

Throughout history, many spiritual and scientific teachers have reinforced the importance of this one law. Many have taught that you get what you give, you reap what you sow, or what goes around comes around, or every action has an equal and opposite reaction etc., but one thing is certain:

Things improve in your life when you improve your thoughts.

Whether it's health, wealth or happiness, the principle remains the same. You are the cause of everything that happens in your life, whether you are conscious of it or not. Becoming aware of and mastering the principle of Cause and Effect is vital to your future success because the results you generate from working for yourself are mirrored via your thoughts and beliefs.

How often have you been dissuaded from buying something simply because the person selling it didn't believe in it, or just assumed you weren't going to buy anyway?

Focus on what you want, not what you don't want. More importantly, stop dealing with the effects of your problems. Identify the root cause and address it head on.

 Reflect and make notes on what you have just read.

28 August

ES: I have some observations about the article "Cause and Effect"

    1. "Everything starts with a thought."

Does it? Or does everything start with a quantum vibration which we then turn into a thought?

    2. "Quite often however, the one thought that preoccupies your mind the most, is quite often the one thing that you have not acquired, accomplished or achieved and continues to elude you because of your negative thinking."

When you are on a spiral and you have no idea of what is happening to you, you have those really destructive on-going conversations in your mind while you chase your own tail. Is this necessarily negative thinking, or is it rather ignorance of the process?
And why do you describe it as "negative" thinking?

Is it just the thought that occupies your mind, or is it a whole raft of things happening in conjunction with the thought that makes you fixate on the thought?

    3. "Ever wondered why certain business situations keep repeating themselves until you undergo a major breakthrough?"

This does not only happen in business situations, and it is not necessarily cause and effect.

For example, why do some people have serial marriages or relationships? Why do some people have one health problem after the other?

Yes, cause and effect do play a role, but what if such people live a

*life script aimed at teaching them a specific lesson and they just
don't get it because they have no awareness?*
Can you explain the nature of the breakthrough that happens?

**Part of your growing awareness is assessing all your
past experiences and starting to see a pattern. Once
you see the pattern, you no longer need to repeat the
experience. Can you see some pattern in your past
experiences?**

4. "It could be argued that all problems arise from believing in
   a false thought (or cause). Until it is changed, the effects
   of that thought (or cause) will keep coming back in
   different forms, manifesting those thoughts, when working
   for yourself, in the form of poor or negative results."

*But what if every experience I have is part of my life script and I
am simply not tuned in to the meaning that the experience should
convey to me? Surely then nothing about it is false/poor/negative?*

*This raises the question of judgment again - why do we judge
things as true/false, good/bad etc.?*

5. 'How often have you been dissuaded from buying
   something simply because the person selling it didn't
   believe in it or just assumed you weren't going to buy
   anyway? "

*How do you know this about the person? Can you read a person's
energy field by looking at them?*

*Overall, I can see something happening here: you are excellent at
what you do, but you are changing rapidly - and in the right
direction.*

*There is a gap between your knowledge and your growing
awareness, and I can feel some tension as you are working on
bridging the gap. This is part of the process of moving from*

excellence to nothing, so that you can make space for a higher level of excellence.

And yes, the compliments you get are good for the ego, but also confirmation that your audience is changing with you and following you - which means perfect timing and synchronicity.

It is scary to move from what you know to what you don't know, so that you can again bridge that gap and move to a higher level of security and knowledge. If you look back at your life, you will see that you have done it before, and that you are in fact much more equipped to deal with changes than you give yourself credit for.

FH: I read your comment about energy fields. I have never thought about energy fields. However, my gift (if I can call it that) is I can instantly recognise/feel when someone DOES NOT like me (even though they are all smiles) and being nice. As a general statement, I have been proven more right than wrong.

ES: That is because you read the person's energy field. You do this intuitively.

Yes, it is a gift - you observe not just the person's face or body language, but the entire energy body - and it may or may not resonate with you. I mean resonate as in literally energy waves resonating (where a person likes you) or crashing against each other (where a person does not like you).

FH: Yup, it's a feeling, not a visual clue

ES: And do you need to see the person or be in their presence to confirm the feeling?

FH: Yes, I need to be beside them (they don't actually have to speak to me)

ES: How about this - you have never been beside me or met me in person?

FH: Hmm. So that feeling (finely tuned) can work outside time/space and is NOT a physical "feeling"?

ES: Yes, but it is also physical. When you are not aware you believe that you need to be in the presence of the person, but when you realize that time and space are not a factor, you move beyond the physical.

FH: I guess, I need to work on this "awareness" malarkey

 Note down some incidents where you became or were aware of another person without being in the presence of that person, and it turned out that there was a mutual connection. It may be as simple as thinking about a person and then getting an email from that person, or having a Facebook conversation with a friend you have never met. Or how about that classic where you think about a person for no reason and then they call you or someone mentions them in a conversation?

Your Unique Selling Point and Elevator Pitch

So you are thinking about wanting to work for yourself? Now, stop and think.

How long have you been on this planet? How many learning experiences do you think you've had in total to date? How many awkward, bad, negative or moments that you'd like to forget? Lots? Hundreds? Thousands?

Every single one of them has helped shape you, mold you into the person you are now. In the history of the universe, you are unique. There is no-one in the history of the universe, that has shared all the thoughts, and experiences you have, or endured the lessons you have, or mastered the hints, tips, techniques, and know-how collectively to offer what you can, to help your fellow man.

You are unique. You are an impressive, intelligent, cosmic wonder. Question is, how do you articulate all of that and be able to summarize exactly how you can contribute to others through selfless acts of giving and service, to help them grow and develop as they travel on their own personal journey of discovery.

 First thing you need to do, is write down who it is you help. What are the positions, statuses, or roles of the individuals you can help? Do you help owners of small business? Sales directors? Fleet managers? Hotel owners? Who is it you can actually help? Go on, write down a list of the types of people you can actually help and the industry or sector they belong to.

For example, perhaps you help IT Directors in the Entertainment and Construction Industry, or you help website owners of small online retail outlets etc. Who do you actually help?

64

Second thing you need to do, is write down all the problems, frustrations and negative experiences you've had and benefited from, or you can help others with. Other people are experiencing need, want, grief, problems, anxieties, and frustrations just so that you can shine, and help them doing what you do best. Problem is, many of them either don't recognize the problem because they can't see the wood for the trees, and they need you to do what you do best, or they're too scared to ask for help, and don't appreciate the impact of what's really going to happen, if they don't seek help sooner rather than later.

So write down all the problems people have that you can help them with, but more importantly write down what the signs or indicators are, so you can help others recognize whether they need your help. This will enable you to better qualify people in the future ensuring you're spending time with people who meet your criteria or who recognize they need your help.

 Getting there! Now thirdly, what are the benefits you can offer these people who are suffering from these specific problems, who now recognize that you can help them having now recognized the signs or interpreted their Key Performance Indicators? Give them an incentive or indication as to how you can help people with these problems, needs or frustrations. In other words, write down a list of benefits that you offer people who meet the criteria that you wrote down in step 2 above.

Some people refer to testimonials or case studies to help illustrate the point and drive the message home. But make a list of all the ways that you deliver value and service to your clients, and how they will realize and experience that value.

65

29 August

ES: I have thought about your article "Your Unique Selling Point and Elevator Pitch"

This is an interesting article about giving back. The way it is written hints at some assumption that you can only give back once you have done some living, which is true, but it also closes the door for people who do not have much life experience.

How would younger people identify what they have to give back - how would you advise them to word their elevator pitch when they are still "taking"? Or would they just rely on their youth and forge ahead?

Can you see a pattern of having taken and now giving back in your own life? If you have to see your life as a blueprint with two parts - taking and giving - what would you say are the major themes in your life? What are the things that you are passionate about (of course including working for yourself) that determined your life path? What are the repeating obstacles that you have become aware of?

To put it in a different way: people like to believe that their jobs or careers define them. The work you do to earn money does not define you, but is rather like a play happening on a stage, and you are one of the actors - sometimes the main one, and sometimes a supporting act for someone else.

If you have to describe your life in terms of the life lessons that you have learnt and the emotional experiences that you are still repeating, why would you say you are here? What is your life purpose? You might not have an immediate answer, but it would help if you could do some "life review" because it will help you to get through the next five or six months when things start to get tough.

I am sure you also know some of those people who get migraine where others get a headache, or they get the flu where others get a cold. On the same scale, what you have behind you will shape your future - but in a positive way. When you have some awareness of your life theme up to this point, the picture will become clearer sooner and you will have a compass to guide you.

 In for a penny, in for a pound. You can just read about Fraser's experiences, or you can play along and contemplate your own navel. What pattern do you see in your own life? What experiences do you tend to repeat? What do people often say about you? And yes, all of this relate to you personally and to your business. You are one person, not a collection of Lego blocks that can be taken apart whenever you please.

You are the Captain of Your Own Ship

Quite often when things don't go according to plan, it's because we are dealing with the symptoms or effects of poor or ineffective thinking. Now, on a slightly deeper level, it could be argued that your thoughts are the cause of the results that you have experienced previously (and currently) in your life.

If you were to change your thoughts (or mindset) then the chances are, the effects (your experiences) will change accordingly.

When things go wrong, who's to blame? Is it the Government? The economy? The banks? The noisy neighbor from number 22 and their loud music? No. it's your life. You make the decisions. You are responsible. **You are the captain of your own ship.**

Quite often when things don't go according to plan, we want to blame others for the circumstances or position we find ourselves in. But like any good "captain" of industry, leaders take responsibility, and learn from their mistakes. They create new plans, resource them, and simply crack on.

We need to set new goals or objectives after we reach a plateau, get a little lost or battle weary, or simply need some encouragement or some bright ideas for generating more progress in our life and business.

One of the first thoughts we should have when it comes to working for ourselves is: what is it we want? What are the objectives we want to achieve? At a deeper level, it's desire that drives us. Desire is the engine of human possibility. It is desire that defines us. It is our desires that drive us to do what we choose to do. **Yet many people simply drift through life reacting to each of the circumstances they find themselves in.** Others plan their journey and set sail and choose where they want to go.

"Terra Incognita" is a term used by 17th Century Cartographers to describe unexplored areas of maps. Some would simply draw dragons or sea serpents to represent areas of maps that remained unexplored. As nothing was known about them, depictions of sea monsters were used to instil fear into traveler's hearts and minds. In fact, at one time, nearly all of the Americas (the new world) - was **Terra Incognita**.

Are you courageous enough to explore and claim what is rightfully yours?
Or have you continually put off embarking on a new voyage or working for yourself because of fear of your own "demons"?

* **Are there areas of your life or business that remain terra incognita?**
* **Do you have "dragons" preventing you from venturing into New Worlds (or discovering new opportunities)?**
* **Do you have unidentified obstacles, challenges or issues that are holding you back?**
* **Have you calculated or estimated what the return on investment or "treasure" would be if you conquered this new "territory"?**

 A useful exercise is to draw 3 columns on a piece of paper, and add the headings Terra Incognita, Dragons and Treasure. Terra incognita is the area you want to explore. Dragons are the obstacles, issues and challenges you face. The Treasure, well, that's the upside or benefit of doing it. Now complete each column.

Everyone has undiscovered treasure just out with their reach. Some go exploring, others dig, and some never find it.

Have you got your map? Have you got the resources for your new voyage? I'm sure if you want it bad enough, you'll set sail, and reach your destination. Quite often we lack the resources to complete our journeys. We might even lack the resources to start our journeys. Some never make them.

Well one thing's for sure, with a bit of planning you can find the crew and talented team members you need to help you plot your course, resource your ship, raise your anchor, and set sail. (Some will even help you steer through stormy waters, and even help you dig for treasure.)

As to whether you find your treasure, well that's down to whether you're focusing on the voyage or the destination.

Many people want different things. Some just take each bridge as they cross it. Do your react to life's circumstances and what life throws at you, or do you seek the lessons to help you on your journey? What do you really want to **BE, DO** or **HAVE**? It's a serious question.

You probably don't recognize how much value you have amassed on your journey to date. This is value that you can share with others to help them avoid making the same mistakes you did. You are where you are, today, as a direct result of your experiences to date.

You should have already have acknowledged that, but now it's time to set new goals and objectives, to activate new levels of desire, to raise your energy levels, to raise your game, and take your life to a whole new level.

You're not done. No sir, you're not even close.

Desire is funny, for there's not a single human activity that isn't founded on some inner quest or urge requiring to be fulfilled.

Imagine this. You go to your favorite restaurant and you sit down at your favorite table, and you're very comfortable in your surroundings. You like it, and you're contented for you know your favorite dish is on the menu and everything is familiar to you.

Then it happens...

It's a new waiter - not your favorite that's on tonight. (But he's eager to please and help).

The waiter asks you what you would like. You immediate response is to come up with a dish that you saw on some morning TV programme and it looked delicious. The waiter says "Let me see what I can do". You then say "Oh, don't bother - it's too much trouble". He then goes off to the kitchen and comes back smiling telling you that Chef will make it for you.

You have your favorite starter - "Cullen Skink", a fish and potato soup. It is delicious and it fills you up. Now you're feeling a bit guilty as you don't know whether you can manage or appreciate the full benefit of what other people are doing or creating on your behalf. You feel guilty from enjoying one of your pleasures.

Your main dish is then brought to you and it is sculpted to perfection, smells delicious, and looks as though there's enough to feed a small army of jungle freedom fighters. Your eyes light up, you lick your lips, almost feeling a tad embarrassed that someone has gone to a lot of effort for you, (but hey, he offered) and you get stuck in.

Half-way through the meal, you're getting full. You're struggling, but you also appreciate the effort others have gone to help you to deliver on their promise to satisfy your requirements.

Finally, you clean your plate, and place your cutlery at "half past six" on your plate, and gently lift the serviette and politely wipe the corners of your mouth. "That was amazing" you tell your friends at the table. "I am stuffed. I couldn't eat another morsel." (You probably want to do undo a button, or go up a dress size at this point)

But desire is a funny thing.
We have different levels of desire, for we are consciousness in action. Once our minds expand in trying to solve a problem or engage in meaningful topics of conversation and insightful concepts round a dinner table (or any other situation of sustained thinking) they never contract to their original size. They continue

to expand... But you're convinced your needs are met. You've reached a new limit in your experience, you can't do (or eat) anything more.

You think you've reached your limit...
....until you spy the sweet trolley. Oh. Oh, watch those levels of desire rise again. Even when you know you're at your limits, you now see something you want - a new goal.

Yes, we can sometimes reach a limit to our appetite, but is there a limit to what we desire?
But it means more choices - Sticky toffee Pudding, fresh apple pie or Strawberry cheesecake, or a bit of all three. Just when we think we're done, or we're beaten, it's the activation of new goals and desires will take us to where we want to be. Have you noticed when you go for a meal with a woman, they see the sweet trolley, then they come out with the immortal line - "I shouldn't", but they do!

The ultimate objective of our desires is happiness, but quite often we tend to focus on short term gains or pleasures which can often leave us more empty wanting twice as much - (just like an hour after eating a Chinese meal - you're starving again.)

Many people remain constantly unfulfilled, not in their stomach, but in their life. They need a new diet of confidence, progress and results. They want to work for themselves.

There's no point in feeling guilty about desiring something. Guilt activates the emotions and feelings and creates a chain reaction which more often than not can and does manifest the result that you require. **(But just be aware, that with every choice, comes consequences – even if on this occasion we will forget about your lactose/dairy intolerance and your diabetes - you want that dessert).**

Do you want pleasure like cheese cake and the consequences associated with it, or do you want long term happiness and enjoying the healthy buffet that life throws at you? Just be clear on what it is you really want. The more specific you are, and the more accurate in your description, the quicker the universe will take your order to the kitchen and cook you up exactly what you ordered.

So, in terms of working for yourself, consider what it is you really want to **BE**, **DO** or **HAVE** now as you go forward. You may feel satisfied with where you are, what you're doing or what you've achieved to date, but **maybe you've just spied your own "sweet trolley"** - it could be a new car, a holiday, anything you want to be, do or have.

Whether you want to work for yourself or not, you need to set new objectives. You need to list exactly what it is you wish to achieve next, and the resources you require in order to resource the plan and get you there.

More importantly (and many people leave this bit out) - you also need to write down what it is you're going to GIVE in order to achieve your goals. It comes back to what you have to offer, and why people would choose you to help them take their game to a whole new level. Now here's the bit we all know - Your goals need to be Specific, Measurable, Attainable and Time bound (**SMART**).

It's time to raise your anchor and set sail to new horizons, but first, what's the next objective that you want to achieve?

 Take a moment to reflect and make notes on what you have just read.

Know Your Life's Purpose, Better Still ... Articulate it and Live it

What do you do? No, seriously, what is it that you DO and can offer others?
Now that you have said what you say you do, how does it feel? Does it excite you?
Does it make you feel proud, passionate, or does it do nothing for you at all?

Hmmm.

The irony is, you probably get asked that question many times a week, even a day at appointments, networking events, social events, or even down the pub.

But there's a greater, more profound message in writing or articulating your elevator pitch or unique selling point. Seriously, I mean it. It can ignite the spark of absolute essence within you. It can help you to discover who you really are, why you are here and what you can really offer.

For some, it can really help them to define their true purpose in life, especially if they are doing what they enjoy and love to do, and excel at doing it too.

If you don't totally come alive bursting with energy and enthusiasm in every single cell of your genetic makeup, when you think about what it is you do, then how on this earth, are you going to be able instil confidence and enthusiasm in others for **what it is you offer?**

Did you notice a slight subtle difference there? For that's the key - In answering the question, you don't want to get lost in process and activity in describing how you actually go about your business. The point I'm making is that it's actually all about getting you to ask yourself what it you OFFER others is, and what is the **VALUE** that they get from connecting and engaging with you.

It's Time for a Reality Check. People aren't actually interested in what you know, what you have or what you do or how you do it, they're only interested in what they will **GET** as a result of you doing what you do. **(Big difference!!)**

I remember meeting an accountant chap at a particular networking event at the Tower Hotel in London. I politely asked him "What do you do?" and before he'd finished telling me who they were, and what they did (not what they offered, and what I would get), I found myself very quickly losing interest, looking round the room to see who else I could mingle with, while they continued to do a "me, me, me, me". Now I don't want to appear rude, but I'm sure you've probably asked that question before at some networking meeting in the past in less than 1.3 seconds, but received a six minute monotone Shakespearean soliloquy in return, and became very bored, disinterested or simply convinced that the person speaking was coming across as needy, desperate or skint.

When people want anything, they often come across as "needy". When we are in a state of need, we tend to focus all our attention on one person...
...OURSELVES.

Quite often we can be so consumed in our problems, issues and challenges that any opportunity where someone shows interest in what we do, we rush in, desperate to pour out all these justifications and reasons why they should do business with us. **So what happens? You unconsciously end up pouring your heart out trying to sell what you have and come across as "selling" (something you yourself probably loathe and despise).**

You don't mean to, but unfortunately that's what's happening. When someone asks us what it us we do, we have a tendency to see the spotlight shining on us, and we think - "Ooh. Ooh, a chance to speak about me and tell others what it is I do."
NO.

It's actually the universe's way of helping you to arrive at yet another **opportunity junction** (as I call them). This is you being

75

tested to see whether you are in your flow, or are meeting resistance. **You are the sum total of your experiences to date.** You are who you are, having done what you've done, to learn what you've mastered in order to help and serve others.

On a teleconference call last week, I asked 7 people what they did for a living. Only one was able to articulate it in less than ten words. The rest took on average 30 seconds to just over two minutes to tell the rest of us what they did. How long does it take you to tell people what your passion is?

You need to live your life's purpose. You need to fire up your levels of enthusiasm, and be 100% confident and true to yourself that what you're doing and the selfless service you provide to others, is resonating at the absolute core of your being.

If it's not, then change your job, change your career. Don't just do it for the money - do it because you love it. More importantly, you need to be able to articulate what you offer to others. You are who you are, offering the knowledge, skills and expertise you have accumulated during your time so far on this planet. In the history of the universe, you are unique, but it's high time you raised your energy levels and really started to believe in yourself and what you offer.

Remember the last 4 letters of enthusiasm - **IASM** - "**I Am Sold Myself** ". You should be doing what you do, because you love it!

You need to start BELIEVING in yourself, and BELIEVING in what you have to offer.

The first breakthrough, the very first building block of a successful self-employment strategy is **CONFIDENCE**.

If you don't have confidence in your skills, knowledge, and solutions, (and have an excellent portfolio of testimonials from clients who have benefited from what you have to offer and have demonstrated their confidence in you), then how the heck can you build confidence in others?

Remember: CONFIDENCE leads to PROGRESS which leads to RESULTS.

What you really, really want, more than anything else in the world, is to find people you can help, and offer them the knowledge, skills, experience and value you have accumulated so far on this planet. You want happiness, contentment, and peace of mind. You don't want money worries, or any negative experience.

Happiness comes from giving, being true to yourself, and doing what you love to do. Stop focusing on what you have to get (or want to get).

STOP PRACTICISING SELFISH LIVING!

Many people have heard of the quote **"There is nothing you cannot be, do or have".** Many people tend to live the formula the wrong way round.

Quite often they are obsessed and consumed with frustration for the things that they DON'T HAVE. They become obsessed in wanting to HAVE or achieve certain things. But the mere act of wanting something actually acknowledges the fact that there is a distance between where you are and what you want, so you actually end up pushing it further away.

You need to focus on the BEING first. Be who you want to be, not who you HAVE to be. Then focus on DOING the things you excel at and really enjoy doing in order to get (or HAVE) that which you desire. Stop focusing all your attention on yourself, and start focusing on living your purpose. Start being that solution driven, results oriented person that can help specific people with specific problems that they HAVE.

 Take a moment to reflect and make notes on what you have just read.

Testing is For Life, Not Just for Headlines

In life, just as in business, we can be faced with many different situations - some good, some bad. What's interesting is that we learn the lessons from the bad times, not the good times. Yes, we like when things go well, but when we don't get the results we want, it pays to sit down, analyze and reflect on what worked, what didn't and why. We often need to stop dealing with the symptoms or the effects and need to look for the root cause.

In the past, I've ran identical ads on The Water Cooler's marketplace, except for different headlines. Some have outperformed others by as much as 300%. It's all about testing, testing, testing and sharing the methods and results – not just in business, but also in life.

I remember one chap who wanted to generate some more referrals. I offered a new approach for him to test, one that he wasn't totally comfortable with. I taught him to ask for referrals, but only after he had demonstrated or given value to a third party.

Reluctantly, He accepted my challenge and **in less than a week, he had generated over 100 referrals**, and several chunks of new business. I remember discussing with a property developer how much he paid to advertise in the national press on a weekly basis, and suggested he test a different approach. "It won't work, I can't see it working." He **got a £1500 advert for £150, then turned it into £13,000 worth of revenue following a very simple, but powerful, proven process.**

Many people throughout history have quit at the last post, and there are countless stories of those who tried, tried again, having faced adversity and tragedy repeatedly, and went on to astound many of their detractors by achieving their goal, objective or dream.

Thomas Edison did 10,000 experiments before creating the light bulb. Colonel Sanders approached 1000+ people before he could get someone to buy his chicken recipe. (And if you get the chance read about the adversity Abraham Lincoln had to overcome on his journey to become the president of the USA - a fascinating story of courage and determination.)

I was shot in the eye when I was 15. That was quite a harrowing experience in itself (believe you, me) but I used the experience to overcome my new-found fear of guns to then become a marksman in the .22, .303 and LMG. I was appointed the Lord Lieutenant' Cadet for Banffshire and accompanied Prince Philip on his official engagements up here in the "heelands".

How many of us got found on the search engines the first time we tried, or get the reciprocal links we asked for with the first email we sent? How many times have you stayed up all night preparing for a meeting or appointment, thinking "it is in the bag", only to return home next day, empty handed? Do you ever ask the question "Why?" Do you ever pluck up the courage and ask your prospects why they don't want to proceed, or do you spend time quietly asking yourself why you didn't get any new contacts from the networking event or exhibition you attended?

In many of my speaking engagements or workshops I start by telling people how I've failed many times in business over the years, and how I estimate I've made over 192,000 bad commercial decisions. (I also go on to explain how I reckon I've made 48,000 good decisions but that's another story.)

In her book, *"If life is a game, these are the rules"*, Cherie Carter Scott has a chapter entitled "A lesson is repeated until learned." Think about that for a second. How many times do similar or identical situations tend to appear or manifest themselves in our lives on a regular basis?

What about the businessman with the continual "feast or famine" syndrome, the politician with the negative news articles, or the individual with several failed relationships or marriages under their belt? If something doesn't work, treat it as a sign that the universe has better things in store for you and you're just not ready yet.

What's important from each lesson, or "trial" or testing period that we have, is not necessarily the outcome, but how we react to the situation that we find ourselves in. Controlling our emotional reaction, and channeling that energy into finding a better, more efficient or more profitable solution to the problem, can often pay thousands of percent more dividends than taking it out on the people, staff or partners close to us. One of the first instinctive responses we can often have is to lash out and look to blame someone.

I remember I used the mass mailing option on The Water Cooler when it first came out, and golly, did I make a right hash of it, but hey, I wanted to test it, and I was prepared to get it wrong in order to get it right. Many people are scared to try new things, test new things or stick their head above the parapets for fear of what others may think.

The way I view it is, if your intention is noble and you're being true to yourself, then even if things don't go according to plan, what really is the worst that can happen? You may have to apologize, or it may take a bit longer to find the right approach. Some people hate apologizing. Some view it as a sign of weakness. I'm human, I cry, I bleed, I eat, I snore. On occasion, I even get things wrong. I remember one of the best responses I ever got to an article was in response to me sending out that wrong mass mailing on The Water Cooler. I wrote a blog to apologize, and ended up generating business from several new members that read the blog that didn't even get the original email.

When various tactics don't work, they're only temporary setbacks, not life threatening moments of despair. The way I look at it, for every "no" I reach, or every poor or negative result I achieve in testing a new approach, it takes me one step closer to the optimum result I want.

We just need to do lots of testing, in small doses, instead of doing big one off projects that have the potential to have a major impact if they go wrong badly. Success is the culmination of repeating small steps every day.

Sometimes the daily grind can get you down, and perhaps you may even feel that you deserve more, or better. You quite probably do, but one thing is for sure - the payback that you receive will be in direct proportion to the amount of effort you have put in.

Apparently it takes about 10 years+ to become an overnight success in business. Oh, and one last thing - it's important. **In my experience, it can take up to five times longer to generate the same amount of revenue online than it can offline.** Don't necessarily believe all the spin - If your gut feel or intuition tells you it's too good to be true, then back off.

Don't convince yourself you're going to make millions online, for there is a strong likelihood that you will not. Many of the big money earners that you read about in those long copy websites in the USA belong to the same small circle of comrades that started out online about 10 years ago, and keep recommending each other to each other's list and at each other's events, slowly building and building up their lists. The results that many show you from their "last blog" or "last email" or "latest offer" didn't just happen. They are actually the result of many years of testing, tuning, and constantly refining the offer, the proposition and the process.

Next time you test any approach (whether it is in life or business), or if you are left wondering why someone responded or reacted to you the way they did, stop. Identify the lesson. I bet you a £1, when you think life is very unfair to you, or the universe is conspiring against you, it's actually preparing you for some amazing things to come.

Everybody likes a winner, but how often do you know how some of the people close to you are feeling when the chips are actually down, and they're experiencing some upheaval? How's their week been? What challenges and issues have they had to face this week? Quite often many people keep their poor or negative results to themselves. I think it's also true that a lot of people have many acquaintances, but perhaps only a handful of "real" friends.

I've learned on The Water Cooler that friends can be identified quickly when you ask for help. Having been asked for assistance yourself, recognize the fact that you might need assistance too in the future, when things don't go according to plan and you could find yourself in the same situation.

 What lessons have you learned in the last 4 weeks, and what are you going to be doing differently in the coming months ahead? Take a moment to reflect and make notes on what you have just read..

31 August

ES: Here are my thoughts on "Testing is for Life, not just for Headlines"

You refer to "bad commercial decisions". Such decisions always have other spin-offs like learning about abundance vs poverty, being confronted with a part of yourself that you refuse to acknowledge and own, handing conflict and division to the point of becoming integrated and whole, etc. If you can recognize what you need to learn from every decision, you can gain so much more from your "failures". Look wider than just what you thought you wanted to achieve with a decision. We tend to get stuck on the main purpose we had in mind and the so-called "failure", which was the real reason for the experience.

FH: I am totally sold on that – it's also strengthening my "awareness" to discover "why is this happening to me" while in the midst of chaos.

ES: The way people respond to us are meant to hold up a mirror to us. What do we see in the mirror? Don't ignore the lesson - acknowledge your "shortcomings" and work on them. E.g. a person complains about being ignored by others, but they do not realize that their energy field says "Leave me alone - I am hurting". Or a person gets bullied because their entire attitude says "I have no self-worth - please confirm that for me" and the people around them simply oblige.

FH: That has been an important lesson to me with some of my detractors on The Water Cooler - I can see now that I was becoming too much like them rather than the real me. Not only did they not like it, I've actually been fighting all the way unconsciously. With your help I've now recognized that, and started being true to me and who I really like being. Although I have no need to be like anyone else, some people appear to take exception with me just being me.

ES: You wrote about poverty consciousness and being needy in the article "It's not about the money". The opposite of that is knowing that there is enough for every soul in the Universe and you are entitled to as much as you want. Why then do people not get what they ask for or feel they are entitled to? Because a part of them still says "I am not worth it" or their ego still says "I have something to prove". What are you entitled to and why?

FH: We are entitled to whatever we desire if the intention and service is true. The focus should be on happiness, and not pleasure. We are here to evolve and contribute to consciousness and grow. We grow by learning, and create happiness from giving.

ES: On the one hand it is a good exercise to work out what you want to be, do and have. But that is still in one dimension - ignoring the world inside of us and focusing on the world outside. Carl Jung said "Who looks outside, dreams. Who looks inside, awakens." You can look outside and do paper exercises and get what you want, or you can look inside and develop your awareness and get what you are worth and deserve.

FH: I had a strange experience in a supermarket the other day - I thought the shop became very bright, and while I was losing a sense of focus on all the brand names in the shelves, the colors of the products were becoming very bright, intense and distinct - I can't fully explain it - it was strange. I've also been getting better at remembering my dreams each morning - bizarre though they are, nothing of any real significance or worth remembering - yet.

ES: You said "What's important from each lesson, or "trial" *or testing period that we have, is not necessarily the outcome, but how we react to the situation that we find ourselves in. By controlling our emotional reaction, and channeling that energy into finding a better, more efficient or profitable solution to the problem, can often pay thousands of percent more dividends than taking it out on the people, staff or partners close to us as one of the first instinctive responses we can often have is to lash out and look to blame someone."*

It is more than just controlling the emotional reaction. Emotions = e-motion = energy in motion. Emotions are an expression of the tension between our inner and outer world. The stronger that tension becomes, the more emotional we become. When you simply control the emotion without understanding the nature of the tension, the emotion will grow stronger and you will display behavior that could be destructive, e.g. have a tantrum or cry, or cut off your emotions because you do not want to / cannot deal with them. When you understand the nature of the tension, you will probably have the same emotion, but it will be much less intense and you will be aware of what is happening to you and let the emotion flow and resolve into feelings (which happen when the tension is resolved). This is where the spiral comes in.

 Read this again: "Emotions are an expression of the tension between our inner and outer world. The stronger that tension becomes, the more emotional we become." Think of how emotional you become when you believe one thing and the opposite is happening to you. For example, you believe that your marriage should last forever, but things happen that make you aware of the cracks.

FH: I need to think this through.

ES: You said "Many people are scared to try new things, test new things or stick their head above the parapets for fear of what others may think."

People who express fear of trying new things, still try new things as part of their lives, but they just do it without any awareness. I know many people who "never try new things" or are "risk-averse", when in fact they create low-risk experiences for themselves.

They often put a lot of energy into creating experiences which confirm their negative view of their worlds and keep them stuck in their feelings. Then there are other people who are willing to always create and try new things, because they put that same energy into resolving emotions and moving towards feelings.

FH: The majority of men I know get on really well with their wives, and women all tend to say the same thing - men are bad communicators. I can't shut up - I tend to want to speak about all sorts of emotional, spiritual topics - stuff that men tend to avoid.

ES: You said "The way I look at it, for every "no" I reach, or every poor or negative result I achieve in testing a new approach, it takes me one step closer to the optimum result I want." *When you think life is being very unfair to you, or the universe is conspiring against you, it's actually preparing you for some amazing things to come.*

To put it another way, for every action there is an equal and opposite reaction. For every electron there is a proton. To refer to the spiral again: fermions start off at a distance from each other and are compelled to move closer together. The closer they get to each other, the more tension they generate, because fermions do not share and always push other fermions away. However, fermions are destined to merge at some point. As they get closer to that point, they increase their resistance until they reach breaking point and merge. That is the moment of gratitude where fermions turn into a boson and we have a glimpse of eternity.

FH: This explanation I like. I'm going to re-read that last paragraph over and over until it "sinks in".

 Think of the worst decision you have made in your life. What did you lose as a result of that decision? I bet that is an easy one to answer – and probably a long one as well. Do you feel off balance? So let's restore the balance. Make a list of what you have gained as a result of the decision. I like to call it "school fees" – the price you paid for life experience and wisdom. First prize is if you have a real "aha" experience when you realize why you made the decision and how you in fact learnt a very valuable lesson from it.

Probable Futures

Nothing is set in stone when it comes to working for yourself. Everything is constantly changing - the market, the consumer, the methods of promotion. Even the solutions customers want and how you provide those solutions are always changing. This is especially true when people try to predict or forecast their future revenues.

Sometimes it pays in the planning process to understand what realistic outcomes can be. Quite often many individuals can set completely unrealistic expectations, and become very, very despondent about relative results that fall way short of their expectation.

Many people dwell on their regrets of the past, but continue to fear the future, yet do nothing in the present to change their future outcomes.

Many hire consultants and get despondent by the lack of results.

Everyone is looking for results. Some are demanding results, and many get results, but it is not always what they really want.

Some get so obsessed on attaining X amount of traffic, Y amount of Leads, or Z amount of Revenue, and are watching the metrics, analytics and weblogs like a cocaine addicted city trader watching his trading charts by the minute.

Quite often it pays to detach yourself from the end result, and to stay in the process. By remaining in the process of constant refinement, we can often pleasantly surprise ourselves with what we achieve. I also think it's important to complete each part of the process. Many tend to miss steps, or inadequately resource a particular aspect of the plan, and they wonder why the final result is different from the one they expected.

How many times have your actions in the past failed to yield the results you wanted? Remember that ad in the paper that failed to generate a single response? What about the tradeshow or conference you attended that didn't recoup the cost of the stand? Perhaps you spent over 90 minutes travelling to an appointment or networking event, and had the long lonely journey back after securing no sale, appointments or new confirmed contacts.

All future events are probable events. Many people get themselves into a right state, convincing themselves that certain results will happen because of a definite choice to travel down a particular road, and allocate resources to an activity after great deliberation. If you do one mailing and it doesn't work, it's not direct mail as a concept that doesn't work.

Is it? How can you possibly tell from just one attempt? Was it the list? The franked postage? The offer? The Price? The payment terms or method of payment?

Quite often there can be a number of variables that can determine the final (or potential) outcome of any activity.

Many people defend themselves, their behavior and their decisions when the results don't always pan out the way they want. This is natural, but I'm sure deep down they knew from the outset that they hadn't really given it 100% themselves. They were counting on, or praying for the other party to deliver on their behalf, despite the fact that they themselves hadn't done the preparation or adequately resourced the project or passed the correct resources at the right time to the person requiring them in order to complete their part of the process.

All events are probable events. There can often be a number of possible outcomes, and varying levels of results. The trick is to control your emotional reaction and use every opportunity to learn why certain outcomes were achieved, and the reasons for it. Working for yourself can be full of temporary setbacks, but never permanent failures. We need to re-evaluate our performance, take corrective action, and adequately resource the amended plan. If at first, you don't succeed, try, and then try again.

I remember a conversation with a woman from Birmingham - a market research consultant. She said "Online Social networking is stupid. It doesn't work." I thought that was somewhat ironic that a market research consultant targeting businesses would try a student and band euphoria network rather than The Water Cooler.

Don't suffer from analysis paralysis, and don't contemplate suicide from a lack of poor results. They are to be expected as part of the learning curve, and your journey to getting it right. Even, if you don't have the resources for a full national TV or radio campaign, or if you lack a large team of advisers, you will always have the benefit of hindsight by your side. There is a universal law called the Law of Compensation which states that you get what you deserve.

Now on occasion you may feel you deserve more than you've currently got (which is often true), but the return that you crave is usually in direct proportion to the amount of time, effort and resources that you allocate.

You can continue to do what you've always done, and continue to get what you've always had, or you can choose, today, to start thinking differently in order to start experiencing a completely different set of results.

1 September

ES: Ah, "Probable Futures", *now let me see . . .*
You said "Everything is constantly changing."

I don't know why this is relevant, but what immediately came to mind is the conflict between body and spirit that some people experience. They are quite happy to deal with change and will bravely take on anything and everything new, while they are doing their best to cope with things like arthritis, muscle pains, tense shoulders, all forms of cancer, high blood pressure, sore joints etc. - all indicating that the person is VERY scared of change and will do anything to NOT change. While their mouths say the right things, the rest of their bodies express their fear of change and resistance to change. This creates a tension between their inner and outer world, which is reflected in their bodies.

This dichotomy causes much pain and the conditioned response is to treat the pain with chemicals - create more imbalance and discomfort in the body for you to focus on, and you might be able to continue ignoring the cause of your pain and tension.

You said "Many people dwell on their regrets of the past, but continue to fear the future, yet do nothing in the present to want to change their future outcomes."

Very true. People have no understanding of their own power to create. They create their daily experiences without even being aware of what they do. But ask them to create a future for themselves, and they would happily leave that to someone else - a boss, politician, medical doctor, church minister, celebrity etc. because they have a learned helplessness. They claim that they cannot create their own future, but have no idea how others do exactly that for themselves and for everyone who wants to follow them.

People fear their future because they have no understanding of what they needed to learn from the past. They look back and just see failure (for which they blame others) or success (for which others get the credit).

But they create their own future anyway, even if their decision is to follow someone else. So it is not quite true that they "do nothing" to change their future outcomes. Even "doing nothing" changes the future outcome from being spectacular to being average at best, or mediocre at worst.

This is why visualization is such a powerful tool - if you can see something in your mind's eye or imagination, you have in fact retrieved that something from the quantum vacuum, and this is the first step in letting it materialize and become concrete. Anything that prevents you from letting it materialize is a limiting thought which forms a barrier between "problem" and "no problem".

You said "Quite often it pays to detach yourself from the end result, and to stay in the process."

If you can manage to detach from the process as well, even better. Have you ever tried peripheral vision? Think of the biggest problem you have at the moment. Then focus on a spot on the wall in front of you until your vision gets blurred. Become aware of things in the room that move, without looking away from that spot. Become aware of things happening outside of your field of vision, 360 degrees around you. Then think of your problem again. When you are in that state, you move beyond any emotion, time and space, and you achieve a clarity that gives you a complete solution.

You said "Many people get themselves into a right state, convincing themselves that certain results will happen because of a definite choice to travel down a particular road and allocate certain human, technical and financial resources to a working for yourself activity, task or tactic after great deliberation."

As your awareness grows, you learn the difference between what I call a deep sense of knowing and a motivational plaster of "If I say it will go well often enough, maybe it will!" So in fact they get themselves in a "wrong" state based on a mixture of fear, desperation and lack of trust.

 Have you ever experienced that "deep sense of knowing"?

You said ". . . you get what you deserve".
Do you really? How good do you need to be and for how long, doing what? And when you don't get, what did you do wrong? Who is punishing or rewarding you? Who or what is judging your actions? Do I sense some religious remnants and fear of punishment/guilt for being "greedy" here? (OK, I do not score high on tact at times.)

About your experience in the supermarket:
That is a version of an out-of-body experience, which indicates you are aware that you are not your body. Your body is a container for your soul, and such experiences raise your awareness. It is very real, even though it would not make for good conversation in the pub. And you are safe, because you are grounded - with your family life and ordinary demands, and because you are cautious and questioning rather than gullible and desperate to escape "this bad world".

Re your dreams - I like your description of "bizarre".
Before you go to bed, ask in your mind to remember them, and keep a notebook next to your bed. When you wake up from a dream, make a note of the objects in the dream and your emotions. Then look up the symbolic meanings of the objects (there are loads of websites that provide explanations) and go with the meaning that resonates with you. These dreams are an early means of communication that will be fine-tuned over a period of time and continue when you are awake. It is an exercise in tuning into the vibrations that you are receiving.

You are right, not many men feel comfortable with openly discussing spirituality and emotions.

They often do not have the vocabulary (especially if they do not like reading) and they have this cultural view of associating "soft topics" with being weak. As a result they become quite lonely.

If there is one thing you can change in your life, what would that be? Since nobody else is reading this, you can be truthful with yourself. What is the one thing that you would want to change overnight if you had the power?

OK, now ask yourself what prevents you from making that change. What do you feel in your stomach? What does your head tell you?

Now decide on one thing – no matter how small – that you can do to bring you half an inch closer to that dream of yours. Don't worry, half an inch is a start. And notice how you feel in your stomach, your heart and your mind.

You Will Need to Manifest a Budget and a Plan

Have you recognized the need for a new approach to start manifesting the results you want from life? You need to take the conscious step of creating a business plan, but are probably wondering how you will resource the plan. Fear of the unknown and of failure, (and in this case, fear of being unable to resource or create a plan) can often prevent us from adopting an abundance mindset.

All you need is a little more faith, and belief in who you are, what it is you offer, what it is you desire, and a plan of action to make it all happen.

So, if you're looking to find start-up capital or allocate a budget and find the necessary resources (and "buy in") for your plan, then you might just find the following of interest…

You and your business are unique, and so is the process of creating abundance and justifying a plan to get the results you want. You and your business are not the same as everyone else in your field. Don't adopt a herd mentality, for the majority of businesses tend to do the same as everyone else when it comes to creating a plan and trying to justify the budget. YOU MUST NOT DO THIS.

Here are five quick tips advising you what you should <u>not</u> do when trying to create a plan and coming up with a budget.

- Don't just take last year's figures and add on X% for good luck
- Don't make the classic mistake of knowing how many sales you need, but not knowing how many leads you need
- Don't try and set a budget without having done a plan.
- Don't try and write a plan without having done an audit.

- Don't invest in new activities if you lack the skills or knowledge in existing areas.

Having said all of that, to help you justify, find and get the budget you need, read the following:

1. Everyone in your team needs a new level of awareness - They need to read the signs and symbols of prosperity.

Quite often different departments compete for budget, are protective or secretive about their own reporting, and do not like to be held accountable (or justify their existence) to others - but it's a team effort, involve everyone, and measure everyone's performance.

Let them know what they need to be monitoring, counting, or measuring to prove to them (and you) that you're creating the reality you want. If leads aren't generated then there are no sales.

If there are no sales there are no customers. If there are no customers no invoices are raised. No invoices means no cash coming in, which means everyone could be out of a job pretty soon, **and that means everyone ends up adopting a poverty consciousness** - and you don't want that!

2. Ensure the need for sales drives the working for yourself budget, in other words "accept the reality of your situation".

Bit obvious really, but essential - don't just think - "Oh, I'd like to try a stand at an exhibition". Let the needs of the market dictate your product development, and let the needs for sales determine your working for yourself approach and budget. What's the logic behind the thinking? More important, what's the science behind the numbers? Allow your lack of abundance to focus your mind. You want to reduce your cost per sale and your cost per lead, and increase the life time value of your clients. Many of your competitors don't know the answers to these questions, and haven't conducted an audit to find out what else they don't know, or what their situation really is. **(Believe me, ignorance is not bliss!)**

3. Remember the answer is in the "lessons".

If you suffer from "feast of famine syndrome", or you are not generating the results you want, then one of your first priorities is to complete an audit. Remember that you are the sum total of your experiences to date, and that the answer lies in the lessons learned from poor or ineffective working for yourself. You need to take stock and conduct an audit, and brainstorm ideas about what needs to be done. Once you know what's wrong, the next step is to follow through and plan your new activities, and then implement them.

Being leads to Thought, leads to words, leads to action, leads to results. Simple, really.

4. Make "Intention" and "Expectation" your allies not your foes.

Return on Investment is often one of the primary metrics in helping you to decide the plan. Management, finance and your shareholders will want to know. More than likely your life partner will want to know how much money you need, how you are going to get it, and what the payback is if you do get it. **Always remember, it's better to under-promise and over-deliver, than to over-promise and under-deliver.**

5. Waste not, want not - Sack non-performing sales staff.

If you have to find a budget it could come from sacking non-performing sales staff or terminating non-performing contractors. You cannot afford to "carry" anyone. Every member of staff must contribute to profit rather than become a burden and contribute to cost. A recent company was wondering how to find a £12,000 sales training budget, yet five out of 14 sales staff had failed to reach their targets for the last four months - at a cost of £3000 + car + expenses, each per month. You do the math. You can't afford that to happen. **Perception and Reality are not the same, but many salespeople don't see like that.**

6. All for one and one for all - Give them Clarity.

If different departments agree the milestones, metrics or KPIs to create an integrated reporting system and common objectives for the organization then why not create an integrated budget by combining elements of each department's budget. We all "rob Peter to pay Paul" on occasion. Formalize it, legitimize it, and make it happen. Give everyone clarity so they know where they stand, and what is required of them.

7. Prioritize the "must haves" against the "nice to haves".

Don't fool yourself - turnover is vanity, profit is sanity, but cash is king. If you've got cash, keep it, don't blow it on extravagance, or it will bite you in the bum later, when you really wish you hadn't spent it. Again, one of the best exercises you can do is an audit to identify what's preventing you from achieving the results you want and calculating your return on investment if you address those issues, challenges and obstacles head-on. Focus your activities on what you need, not what you want. (That comes later.)

8. Focus on results, not ego stroking or platitudes.

In other words, demonstrate in your strategy that the majority of budget will be spent on results driven activities, not flag waving or brand awareness. And never buy big stands in the middle of an exhibition hall or tradeshow - always go for the outside. **All your activities should do one of two things - Build your list, or generate sales. That's it.** If they're not, then you're doing it wrong. It's time to start adopting a prosperity consciousness and to start focusing on increasing your levels of abundance.

9. You need to Return to "Source" (Best Source).

It's unbelievable how many people don't know where their leads come from. Ensure you always ask leads, prospects, enquiries and referrals how and where they heard about you, and log their response. If you know your best source of leads and sales, then logic dictates that you allocate more resources in leveraging that source to your best advantage. Chances are, you already have thousands of pounds of sales opportunities for your products and services waiting to be discovered in your spreadsheets, databases and CRM systems. Sometimes we simply don't see the wood for the trees. Sometimes it's just a matter of physics - for every action, there is an equal and opposite reaction. You need more action, even if that simply means doing more follow-ups or identifying what worked in the past, and repeating it.

10. Plan the work and work the plan.

A business without a plan is a ship without a rudder (and remember - you are indeed the captain of your own ship). When you know what's wrong, fix that and you're making progress. Next you need a plan that gives confidence to everyone, including stakeholders. Next you need to implement the plan. Having a means of reporting the progress and results you will generate will let you allocate adequate resources.

Don't forget - a plan will only work if it is adequately resourced with the correct resources.
…and now you know how to get it resourced.

What's your plan, and more importantly who's in your team? After all, when it comes to working for yourself …

…**T**ogether **E**veryone **A**chieves **M**ore.

It's time to give thought the plan you want to start generating the results you desire.

 Take a moment to reflect and make notes on what you have just read.

2 September

ES: I sensed some contradictions in the article "You will need to manifest a budget and a plan"

You wrote "Waste not, want not - Sack non performing sales staff" *and follow this up with* "All for one and one for all - Give them Clarity".

"Waste not, want not" means there is not enough of what you need, or there is not enough for everyone, so work sparingly with what there is. People like Bill Gates believe that there is enough of what you need and there is plenty for everyone - all you have to do is believe that and you will see it happen. They focus on creating abundance for a purpose and they do not allow anything to dilute their energy.

"All for one and one for all - Give them clarity" *I agree with this, but it works better if you bring in personal value systems as well. When people have similar values, they all work in the same direction because they are fired up by the same passion. There is no need for identical value systems - you do not want to be surrounded by clones, but if you really want a strong team I would say at least 3 of the top 5 values for each person should overlap.*

When this is the case, you retain variety, but the team focuses their energy in the same direction with the same vision. It is very much like a marriage - you want a good balance of similarities and differences. The similarities should be in the things that really matter for both, and the differences allow each person to have their own space.

When the team/company has clarity on a shared vision, the synergy is amazing. Also those people who do not share the vision go elsewhere. You can freeze them out of the company because they "do not contribute", or you can help them clarify their values and vision and accompany them out of the company, and they

100

become ambassadors for the company who treated them well right onto the sidewalk.

So the logical flow would be "Give them Clarity", then "Let go of non-performing sales staff." There are times when you have to leave people behind so that you can move forward. At times it is really hard, but at other times it is a relief for both parties. Either way, the more Love you apply to the separation process, the more energy you have to move forward - no matter whether the relationship is personal or business.

You wrote "Sometimes it's just a matter of physics that for every action, there is an equal and opposite reaction." For everything that fails, at that precise moment there is something that succeeds, but we have been conditioned to be so judgmental that we focus only on what "failed" and we miss what had succeeded at the same time. The Universe is in complete balance.

Start looking at your disappointments and failure and identify firstly what you needed to learn from it, and secondly how each one of them got balanced out **in that moment** e.g. on the day when we agreed to work together, (a massive high) a woman whom I regarded as my best friend for a significant part of my life told me that she never wants to hear from me again because "I scare her" (a massive low because I realized that she is incredibly destructive and in fact our paths separated years ago for reasons that have only in the past year became clear to me. I know I can help her but she would rather live a life of misery than give me the time of the day.). Your offer and her email reached me at about the same time!

On the surface the incidents were not related, but on another level both incidents confirmed for me that I have entered through a gate that was waiting for me. I now love her even more for holding up a road sign for me saying "Keep going, even if it means past me". Even if we never have contact again, I will always be grateful to her for the way she behaved to me over the years, because most of it resulted in introspection and realizing significant truths. She

101

has been one of my greatest teachers, and I have in the past week had two really pleasant dreams about her which tells me it is OK to leave her behind.

We do not live our lives in compartments. Everything relates to everything else. When you start looking for the balance, it is a real eye-opener.

You wrote "It's time to start adopting a prosperity consciousness and to start focusing on increasing your levels of abundance." *It is interesting how inner abundance is often expressed in the form of money. The more you grow spiritually, the more your view of life changes, and the more you create outer abundance.*

Who are the people that you have left behind? Think about work colleagues that you got on with very well but no longer have contact with. How about friends that you fell out with or drifted away from? Did you outgrow a relationship that once was beautiful? Are there family members that you wish you could get that past closeness back with?

As the saying goes "sometimes you need to break an egg to make an omelet". In hindsight, can you now see that you personally gained from leaving those people behind, even where the circumstances were sad or unpleasant? And trust me - they all eventually catch up with you again when they are ready.

Everyone has a need - you just have to find it and fill it

Ever wondered why some people appear to lead a charmed life, where everything always seems to fall into place, and they don't appear to be facing any "challenges", "issues" or "obstacles" in their life or business like you do? I bet if you look a little closer they have probably been on an incredible journey to take them to where they are now. Some realize it, some don't.

- They've probably had to stop and evaluate where they are on occasion, and learn from the lessons they've had to endure up until that point.
- They've probably had to reevaluate what it is they want, and had to set new objectives to help them grow and develop.
- They've had to revisit who they are, redefine their offer and articulate their elevator pitch and unique selling point as they continue to follow and implement their life's purpose in giving service to others.
- They've probably tested lots of different ideas, concepts and approaches to find the one approach that works, and they've come to recognize that testing is for life, not just for headlines.
- When we become aware of the lessons that the circumstances of life (and business) throws at us and of the different results we generate from our different approaches, we want to take control, to look out for the signs in advance, and take the appropriate course of action.
- Once they've become aware of the lessons they've learned, and how to avoid, reduce or eliminate future negative experiences, they've probably formalized their thinking, and resourced their own plan of action, the question is …

Who needs what you have to offer?

More important, as you realize your own dreams living your life's purpose, **through your own business**, you need to consider not just what you offer, but WHO you can help with what you offer, who wants what you offer, and where can you find them.

Imagine that you are the "leading actor" in a play. In fact, imagine you are the director, producer and scriptwriter as well of the same play. The world in effect is your stage. All the other people you interact with are also actors, but they don't have a copy of your script and each experience, set or circumstances, or event in your life is a scene in this play.

You can (and do) often change your roles as you plan and perform in this play. Each of the other actors brings something to the play, to help add value to your performance, but because you don't yet know what it is (and neither do they, for they don't have a copy of your script), you all still ad lib, feeling your way, trying to bond, build rapport, even help each other. You give encouragement and cues when needed to deliver a great performance - even if that means some critical feedback or constructive criticisms (or reviews) on occasion.

Sometimes the props and scenery around us appear so real, we convince ourselves they are real, often forgetting that we only imagine they're real (a bit like our fears). They just serve their purpose helping us through a particular scene. Once that scene (or experience) is past, they've served their purpose, just like the other actors (friends, associates) who come into our life randomly (from the wings) on occasion to contribute to your own play called "life". Some would argue that you've been here before. Some would argue you've visited this "world stage" many times (over various lifetimes) and been involved in various productions. Perhaps you've been a different character in a different play, set in a different setting, country, or time period.

Sometimes, just sometimes, we recognize fellow actors or think we know them "from somewhere". Has that ever happened to you? Someone walks on from the wings, into your life with a definite purpose. You don't know why they're in your play, in this scene. You have no idea of the message or lines they have to deliver. Quite often people enter into our life with a message for us, or they contribute in their own special way, to help us stay focused and get on with the show. Sometimes we think we've seen or met them before.

Déjà vu?

 Have you come across a situation like this, before?

But what about your audience?

What are they looking for? Why have they come to see and listen to you? What is so special about your performance that will encourage them to pay and listen to you? Of all the other actors and shows in town, why should they give up their time and money for you? Why should they give it you? Who can benefit from what you have to offer?

You now need to describe an ideal client. You need to write down everything you want a client to be, have and do. You need to create an ideal client profile. You don't want to attract (or work with) just any old client.

You don't want to attract (or get referred) someone that's going to steal your ideas, or get you to work for peanuts, and expect you to work until the early hours of the morning, then take 3 months to pay you. Do you?

No siree.

You want some harmony and balance in your life.

You want to live and lead an abundant lifestyle.

You want to work with people you respect and like, and not for people you hate or mistrust.

The energy has to flow both ways in a client/supplier relationship. It has to feel right for both parties. Each one has something to offer the other. Each one should be respecting the other, and the value they offer or bring to the table. Both parties should be holding each other accountable to ensure both give each other what they expect and when. Different people do different things, and behave in different ways. They all have different pains, needs, problems and frustrations. You need to consider how you can help those people, but more important, where you can find them.

I remember one of my coaching calls, working with a life coach who wanted more clients. I asked her who she wanted to work with. She said "Everybody needs a life coach". We were on a group call at the time, and I asked the other four people on the call. None of them said they needed a life coach.

Hmmm.

It reminded me of that old story about four people named Everybody, Somebody, Anybody, and Nobody who worked in a business.

There was an amazing product had been devised by R&D. Everybody was sure that Somebody would want it. Anybody could have wanted it, but Nobody did. Somebody got angry about that because they thought Everybody wanted it. Everybody thought that Anybody would want it, but Nobody realized that Everybody wouldn't want it. It ended up that Everybody blamed Somebody when Nobody bought what Anybody could have had.

In other words, not everyone will like you, your products, services or solutions. So you need to ask yourself:

Are you "product led" or "market led"? Do you think your product, service, idea or solution is good, or has the market told you it's good? More important, has the market told you it needs your product, or do you just *think* they need it?

Who needs it? Who wants what you have to offer, what's been their feedback to date, and do YOU listen?

Not everyone will have a need or a requirement for your products and services, so you need to focus on those that have a need. Quite possibly many people won't even have recognised they have a need, until your message makes them aware of that need. Let's focus on who wants or needs what you have to offer. The trick is to identify them, find them, communicate with them, and convert them into paying clients at the price point you want.

You need to focus on those who have a real need for your products and services, who recognize that what you offer solves a specific problem for them. They also need to recognize the value in what you offer, and that the cost of your solution is less than the cost of the problem they have.

- What problems do your prospects and clients suffer from?
- What is the root cause of these problems?
- What are the symptoms or effects of these problems?
- What is the financial, emotional or physical impact of that these problems can have?
- What is the remedy or solution for these problems?
- Why should they pick you over everyone else in your field?

More important, where do these prospects live? Can you target them online? Can you target them offline by geographical region? Localized Google AdWords advertising might help. Local business directories might help. What about micro television advertising focusing in on a particular TV region (or county)?

Some people only do one form of advertising in their local yellow pages, but is that where your prospects or prospective clients turn to, to find a solution like yours? Think of a magnet for a second. Two magnets are attracted by their opposite "poles", a bit like your prospects - they have a need, you have a solution.

So what are their needs? What are the problems, issues, and pains you can fix? More to the point, how can you describe who these prospective clients are? If you were to buy a mailing list of prospective clients, which criteria would you use to create your list?

Which fields or segments of data would be relevant to you and help you to identify the prospects you need to speak to?

Do they

- Have a phone?
- Live within a particular post code?
- Represent a house, a branch, or the HQ of a particular firm?
- Have relevant turnover?
- Have the desired number of staff?
- Own the required number of vehicles?
- Earn the required joint salary or household income?
-

You need to write down and create a prospect profile of who you want to work with.

Remember, being leads to thought, leads to words, leads to actions.

Once you know what you want, and you create a written prospect profile, you can start giving that to other people to help manifest and create the opportunities you want. You could give your prospect profile to mailing list, tele-list or email list brokers to see how many people or records they have that match your criteria and requirements.

You could use Google Blogsearch (http://blogsearch.google.com/) to find blog owners who match your criteria and target them as potential JV partners to do endorsed mailings to their list. But you now need to think how your prospects think, and where do they go. For birds of a feather flock together. There must be places online and offline, where prospects who meet your criteria congregate. Out of curiosity, what newspapers, magazines or journals do they read? Which websites do they visit, or directories do they use? Which networking clubs or business clubs are they a member of and when do they attend their monthly meetings.

Start thinking how you can reach out to your target audience, and how you can start resonating with them, by talking their language, and understanding their problems. You need to engage them, and start doing some real research by gaining real feedback, insightful and honest feedback about what you offer, and whether they actually need it or not.

It's time to create a prospect profile of who your ideal clients are, and where they are located.

It's time to give that prospect profile to your best contacts and advocates, so that you start receive good quality, qualified referrals at the level you want to accept, not these half-baked, unsuitable referrals you've been receiving because you never did tell your advocates exactly what it was you wanted or who you could help, yet they thought they were doing you a favour.
(It's not about taking my word for it, or trusting me - it's about finding the REAL you, and trusting yourself).

 Take a moment to reflect and make notes on what you have just read.

Know, like and trust

What is your perception or understanding of the term "know, like and trust"? The following might throw a slightly different perspective on all 3 terms to help you to start generating some real progress and results when working for yourself. Reading the following is one thing, but if it resonates with you then perhaps its time for you to start experiencing a few breakthroughs of your own.

Know / Knowing

Are you trying all sorts of weird and wonderful tactics and strategies such as networking, SEO, blogging, even attending workshops or exhibitions, in an attempt to get known for what you do and what you have to offer? Many people know that there is a problem with their life – **they just don't know what it is or why**. No matter what they try, it just doesn't seem to work. Quite often they are having more arguments with loved ones, and quite often about money (that elusive commodity many use to falsely decide whether we are in a prosperity consciousness or a poverty consciousness.)

Is something not working for you and do you KNOW what it is?

Quite often we are simply dealing with the symptoms, or effects of bad, poor or selfish habits, instead of the identifying the root cause, and addressing the issues, challenges, and obstacles that hold us back and are preventing us from achieving the results we want. I had an accountant chap who came to me for advice. He said he was unsure why his business wasn't working. **Now the funny thing about accountants (and most service based professional) is that many of them think selling is beneath them.** They tend to treat sales executives with the contempt they think they deserve.

When we identify the resistance in our life or business, and are able to address or eliminate the root causes, it permits an incredible new flow of energy to be released. This new flow of energy can manifest itself in a "eureka" moment.

You begin to trust your intuition or gut instincts better, some amazing revelations appear before you, and you have a greater sense of knowing what you should be doing and why. Identifying the issues, challenges and obstacles that are holding you back and preventing you from manifesting the results you want, can often result in much needed clarity. In some cases the individual begins to realize they haven't been on the right path, doing the right things, or doing what they want to do.
They've been doing certain things in certain ways just to survive financially. With fire in your belly and a new lease on life, you will want to fire up your levels of desire and set new objectives.

A few pointed questions can help them to realize they haven't been in their flow for a long time, and that they have been focusing on all the wrong things. Many people begin to sense a bigger picture, or vision of what they really want to be, do or have. They begin to experience a sense of knowing, a sense of purpose and that they must change in order to change their circumstances.

That sense of knowing can often be interpreted as feeling they have something much greater to offer, as part of a bigger picture.

Alas, many people are stuck in the daily treadmill of life, and don't take time to ask these questions. They don't experience that new inspired, fired up feeling of enthusiasm, belief and hope for the future, or how they can contribute in their small way to the much bigger picture or **recognize the phenomenal amounts of opportunities that exist now, in real time in their reality.** These opportunities enable them to excel at what they offer the world.

They remain trapped by their ego, oblivious to the real issues that keep them in their poverty consciousness. **They have no sense of knowing** who they really are, what to do, or why they're here.

Like
Many professional service providers often have worked for many years in corporate life. They're often very technically minded, very analytical, and have a very strong academic background. They are often from a middle management background, used to having their leads provided for them. They have a full expense account, and many never having been held accountable, being allowed to float through their career. **They don't like to be challenged or be held accountable, and dare I say it - they like to have an easy life.**

Quite often their values are completely different from that of their customers and prospects, and quite often they don't actually know what their prospects and clients really like or – more important - want.

Many don't know simple things like the Life Time Value of a customer, Cost per sale, cost per lead or which low cost or no cost offline and online tactics they could use to generate leads, enquiries, referrals and sales. Many are simply ignorant of such matters.

The feeling of not liking the idea of working for yourself can often be reflected in the way they market themselves on appointments at networking events, and becomes apparent via their lack of enthusiasm, and passion for what they offer. It gets worse. That lack of enthusiasm is not only picked up and interpreted by potential prospects and partners, it is magnified by the fact that they actually need more business, **and is now making them come across as "needy, desperate or skint".**

They need to like what they do. They need to love what it is they offer, and they need to ooze enthusiasm and passion for what they offer. If they don't, no amount of money is going to make them happy. They need to like themselves, and be comfortable and happy doing what they want to do. If they're doing what they do for financial reasons, then perhaps it's time to ask some serious questions.

Quite often, when we don't like something or someone, it's down to perception or our own set of values. We have a bad habit of comparing people, situations, and events. However, many potential prospects, partners or associates that we come across in our daily prospecting can act as a mirror, and we have a tendency to mistrust or not like them. Like a mirror, they reflect what we need to accept or change. We can identify something in them that we don't like, which is more often than not a weakness in our own skill set or behaviour set that we know we lack.

In other words, people we come across in business can unwittingly amplify our failings and weaknesses without them having to say a word, and we don't like it. When we don't like someone, it's perhaps the universe telling us that there's actually something in ourselves we don't like, and that something may be the key to unlocking some major breakthroughs in our life or business, as we may be lacking a particular skill or behavior. A quick way to fix this is training to acquire new skills and knowledge to fill those gaps.

Trust

Ah, this is an interesting one. Prospects often mistrust potential suppliers because they may be unknown or lack confidence. Stop and think. Maybe the trust isn't there because there's something they don't like about the supplier. Maybe the supplier does something that reminds the buyer of something they don't do or perhaps need. **Perhaps the buyer is reminded by the supplier of a weakness they have, and they don't like it - and that's the real reason why they mistrust.**

We can often mistrust others when we don't understand why certain people behave in a certain way and we question their motives or intention.

Once we understand the intention behind someone's actions everything becomes clearer, but quite often we simply don't give

113

people the opportunity or we don't take enough time to try and understand their intention. Sometimes it's not about taking someone's word or about trusting them. Perhaps it's all about you, finding the real you, and what it is you really want.

Perhaps it's about knowing and trusting yourself to do what you want to do, and recognizing what you need to do. Perhaps you need to have more faith and belief in your own knowledge, skills and solutions so that people will trust you. Maybe the problem is inside of you - not them. We don't like looking in the ugly mirror, and sometimes potential suppliers can scare us or un-nerve us, for we know that they speak the truth when they tell us how big a problem is or how much it will cost to fix it. We sometimes don't like hearing the truth.

Sometimes we need to hear the truth from someone who has a fresh perspective on a situation. Sometimes we need to listen to the person that can look in objectively and explain the true reality of that situation. Again, it's perhaps the universe trying to tell us that it's time for a change. Sometimes we need to trust our intuition, and simply just know that it's time to make a decision to work with others, and prepare for the breakthroughs we need in order to take our game to the next level.

Confidence is associated with trust. If you lack confidence or have a low self-esteem because business has been slow recently, your credit cards are at their limits, and your life partner appears to be picking fights about money, **then perhaps you need to start trusting the universe, and recognize the lessons it's throwing at you.** Perhaps you haven't taken a step back to objectively reflect on the journey you've been on, and where you are on that journey. So when it comes to "Know, Like and Trust", don't just think of others, start thinking about what do you really Know, Like and Trust about you, your business and the solutions you have to offer.

 Take a moment to reflect and make notes on what you have just read.

3 September

What if you slept, and what if in your sleep you dreamed, and what if in your dream you went to heaven and there you plucked a strange and beautiful flower, and what if when you awoke you had the flower in your hand? Oh, what then?
--Samuel Taylor Coleridge

 Like I said earlier- take note of your dreams at night. You have reminder dreams, prophetic dreams, and symbolic dreams – all sorts. This becomes clear when you start to write down your dreams and then notice the synchronicity between those dreams and what happens in your life.

7 September: That Damn Cat!

ES: A physicist called Schrödinger had the question: if you put a cat and poisoned food in a box, what do you have in the box? A dead cat that ate the food, or a live cat that did not eat the food?

FH: You won't know until you open the box.

ES: Yes, and even when you do open the box, you will see either a live cat or a dead cat. At some point the cat will be alive, and at another point the cat will be dead. The two states of the cat will be in complete balance, but at different times.

We have all kinds of life experiences, and we only see one side of that life experience. That one side of the life experience is typically like Schrödinger's cat. You have a fantasy of your first love and how it would have been if you had married that first love. Then you meet this first love again and he has a stomach that frightens you, he doesn't wash and there goes your fantasy – and you are down in the dumps.

Or you have a nightmare about an experience, but eventually you realize that it was just the way you looked at it at the time that turned the experience into a nightmare.

It is like putting a 3-year-old on a roller coaster when they are not ready for it at all. Throughout our lives we carry only one half of the equation and that shapes our reality. It is only when we understand that there is another half of the equation and what it is and how we can benefit from getting that balance that the fantasy or the nightmare disappears and we get balance.

FH: This is a good example of how many self-employed people or those wanting to become self-employed worry about their future plans and probable/possible outcomes unnecessarily.

Remind yourself of situations where what you expected was the opposite of what you experienced. Often we build up expectations, only to discover that the reality is not even close to expectations. This can be "good" or "bad" experiences – either way, it is about building up a fantasy and then comparing it to reality.

You and your Time - Do you Exchange it for Money?

We think of time as past, present and future. However, is there only the present?
Can we actually experience the past, or can we only remember" it?
What about the future? Is it not just something we imagine in our mind's eye?

Do you focus your attention on the past, the present or the future?

Will people buy from you what you have learned in the past, the solutions you make available now, or do they pay in advance for what they will receive from you in the future?

Albert Einstein wrote: *"...for us physicists believe the separation between past, present, and future is only an illusion, although a convincing one."*

It is the present that is always changing - not the past, or the future. The future hasn't occurred yet. You imagine it, you do not experience it.

The same could be said of the past. We may relive the past or play it over and over in our minds, but are we not simply just recalling our memories and playing them over and over again like a DVD player?

I've written previously how we can often allow the past to cloud our judgment or allow past or previous conditioning to affect our decisions in the present, and how certain judgments and assumptions in the present can affect our future outcomes.

But sometimes we can become obsessed with time, or should I say the illusion of time, and its effects upon us.

Think of all the different ways time (or the illusion of time) can affect us, how it can increase our stress levels or blood pressure. There are many ways in which time can affect us when working for ourselves:

- Appointments
- Delivery Dates
- Clocking In
- Project Deadlines
- Extended lunch hours
- Product Launches
- Sales Cycles
- Advertising Deadlines
- Payment Schedules

The Egyptians, we are led to believe, invented the sun dial to help us understand the direction of time, or how to quantify the passing of time. **The problem was that Sun Dials don't work at night**. We had water clocks, but the flow of water can change based on the temperature of the water. We then tried sand, which has proven to be very reliable for everything including the art of boiling eggs.

The oldest mechanical clock in the world, built in 1386, is in Salisbury. We've had cuckoo clocks, digital watches, even atomic time pieces (out by 1 second in 10 million years) all designed to tell us we should hurry, we must do things quicker, we must not be late.
Supply chains are getting shorter. Shareholders want bigger results - sooner. Consumers want by yesterday what they were promised now, for if a web page takes longer than 3 seconds to give us the information we want, we are off elsewhere. To think, people used to rely on pigeons or runners for their information.

The earth spins at a speed of 1670 km/hr (or thereabouts) and takes **23 hours, 56 minutes and 4.06 seconds** (see, you've been wishing 3 minutes, 55.04 seconds of each day away, without realizing it) to complete one sidereal day or one revolution of the earth on its axis.

While some business owners sleep, they have partners, staff or suppliers working on their behalf on the other side of the planet.

Many of us exchange our time for money in business. The question is: will you? All service-based businesses get paid for implementing a service, in other words they exchange their time for money. **This should be the LAST thing you do, not the first**. Put another way, this should be the most expensive part of your product offering. If people want you to do a job they must be prepared to pay you what you're worth, and recognize the value that you bring to the table. So how do you get people to recognize the value you offer, and your true worth, with the time you have?

It's simple. You start by offering something of value for FREE. At £0. (**Just ensure that it is NOT your time.**)

You don't want to start by offering to implement a service for people as your only product offering. What tends to happen then is that you go to sales appointments or meetings and give your ideas away at the meeting, or you end up documenting your ideas in a proposal for people to steal them and not engage you.
Worse still, they agree to use your services, and they screw you down on margin, not paying your true value or worth, and you end up working longer hours for less to deliver the end result for the client.

You must begin by offering something for FREE and not be bound by your time. As part of working for yourself you will start by offering something for FREE. This will be something that you can use as a lead generator in your business… Something that can demonstrate your knowledge, wisdom, experience and the true value of what you really bring to the table. More important, your FREE item of value helps you to build your list and to generate qualified leads.

This item could be an e-book, a white paper, a CD, a DVD, a pod cast, a FREE Report. It could be a video, a FREE consultation, or anything that you feel comfortable in offering that can help

FRASER HAY & ELSABE SMIT

demonstrate that you are an expert in your subject, and have a thorough understanding of your prospective client's problems, pains or needs. You need to demonstrate you have KNOWLEDGE they want.

As you acquaint, interest, and finally sell additional and often higher priced items to your customer, your profit margin will increase. This approach works very well, whether you are working with a brick and mortar business or going strictly with an online presence. In both instances, the task involves winning the confidence of the prospect, identifying entry level products or services that will be of interest to the prospect, selling the prospect on the goods or services, and then continuing to offer additional products or enhancements that will make life even easier for that former prospect that is now your customer.

Your **FREE** Item of value should not only demonstrate your knowledge, wisdom and experience. It should also act as a qualifying tool using criteria that you set to determine whether you want to work with the prospect (or not.)

Wouldn't that be great?

To have a system that involved no cold calling whatsoever, and every prospect who calls you is pre-qualified using criteria that you know determine whether they will buy from you at the price point you want to deliver value and service to them?

Think how powerful that could be.

You need to productize your knowledge.
Providing additional goods or services that are in a similar price range will be another way to increase your profit margin. This is sometimes referred to as lateral selling. Simply put, you are not really pushing items with a higher price tag, or even enhancements to services you have already sold which would increase the profits. You are simply broadening your current situation to include more

of the same, from a charge perspective. The more value you offer, the more you charge.

You begin by productizing your knowledge and then sharing your knowledge with prospects, **BEFORE** you share your time with prospects.

How many times have you attended meetings or appointments just to give your ideas away, or to be told that the prospect has no money?   Or worse still, can you put your ideas in writing and they'll get back to you?

You may even suffer from feast or famine syndrome, and have to experience a drought while you wait for those bigger consultancy deals to land. Now you can productize your knowledge, and offer different solutions and price points to help you generate cash flow via your list of people who requested your FREE item of value, **while you select which clients you really want to work with and spend your time with.**

Whatever your perception of time, perhaps you should consider changing your perception of how you market yourself?

 Take a moment to reflect and make notes on what you have just read.

11 September: No Time Like the Present

ES: I have thought about your article "You and Your Time". *Interesting question: Can we actually "experience" the past, or can we only "remember" it?*

FH: Technically, we can "experience" it via different sense (if those senses – clairvoyance, clairaudience and clairsentience - are activated). Many dwell on the replay and so cloud their judgment and prohibit themselves from seeing the full picture.

ES: But you can also experience the past again by means of recalling those memories so that you can recreate the situation for the purpose of seeing the other side of the same memory.

FH: I feel as if for the last 3 months I've been in the middle of a creative drought, but now I'm holding a high pressure hose in my own 1 million gallon reservoir of ideas/content to "hook" new prospects/audiences with to really benefit from what working for themselves is all about.

ES: That gives me goose bumps - that is exactly what you are doing. You are shaking off the imitators and attracting more people who understand their own power.

FH: I really think my difference in the marketplace is that I'm helping people to discover, define and profit from their life's purpose (not just their products). It's got far greater meaning and purpose, and appears to be resonating with many people questioning where they are and what they are doing with their life and business.

The timing appears to be right, because the concepts I'm writing about are the things they are playing in their own minds and the topics are the questions they are already asking and pondering about, wanting answers (and a plan of action).

ES: But what they do want is inspiration, motivation, wisdom and encouragement.

 What do you think makes you, your business or your product unique? Don't use your mind to answer this question. Use your heart and feel it in your stomach, and then put it into words. You would be surprised at the result if you leave your mind and logic aside and feel the answer rather than think it.

13 September: The Destructive Power of Being Judgmental

ES: We pre-judge other people on a daily basis without even being aware of it. Either a person is like us - good - or unlike us - bad. We do not even consider for a moment that we are all images of God (or whatever you want to call that Force), and that therefore rapists and the World Trade Centre bombers and Sister Teresa and that monster from Austria who kept his daughter prison are equal representations of God.

Here is where the difference comes in - and this is my understanding, and not a judgment - I think. Can you really say that a spiritual world leader like Barack Obama and a beggar are equal? I say no.

They are equal in the sense that they are both in human bodies, and this indicates that they are both separated from the Source.

But their degrees of separation are different. Barack Obama is far more whole than a beggar, and this is reflected in what he says and how he lives his life. That does not mean he is perfect - he will have to deal with some horrific decisions over life and death and moral issues while he is president. These issues are part of his journey, and as he grows spiritually, he will become even more integrated.

The beggar also has challenges, and he will also have to make decisions, but these decisions will be far less complex - he will be concerned about his own life and survival, whereas Barack Obama will be concerned about the survival of the planet.

In quantum terms, one is working on an intricate, complex series of spirals within spirals, while the other manages one spiral at a time.

If this is being judgmental, then saying that a custard tart is less solid than a loaf of grain bread is also judgmental.

The judgment comes in when you start to see yourself as morally above another person, to the extent that you discard the other person as second-hand.

In one of our conversations you said ". . . all mind is one mind." *I just had an interesting thought. If all mind is one mind, then you and I and the people we work with are one mind. We have access to the same information and we can all do the same. Then how come do people want to learn what we know, and why are we in a position to teach them? Is it because every person that we take on as a client in fact represents an aspect of the obstacles that we put in our own paths when we want to access this one mind? So if I want to help spiritually confused people, my own spiritual clarity increases every time I help a person. When you help a person with a "working for yourself "issue, you in fact help the person with a personal obstacle that is expressed as a "working for yourself "issue.*

This has two implications. One is that we help people to remove their own obstacles so that they can access the mind, and the other is that every client reflects our own obstacles in their own way, and we resolve our own obstacles by helping other people to remove similar obstacles, so that we can access the mind.

*I recall you also saying that "*The Universal mind is static or potential energy". *Is it static? I wonder. At school we were taught that the planets have specific orbits around the sun. More recent research shows that these orbits are not that specific. If they were, it would be possible to predict their paths with greater accuracy. However, as someone described it, each planet moves around the sun at more or less the same radius, but like a drunken fly, i.e. backwards and forwards in various intricate patterns - more like a crocheted table doily than a pencil line. Add to that the fact that everything around us is a wave, until we consciously find the wave and turn it into particles. Add to that the fact that when a proton and electron split, they can be at infinite distances from each other, and they can combine at any point to form quantums of light. All that sounds like a lot of very active energy to me.*

I remember you questioning whether "Human consciousness consists only in the ability of man to think". *I cannot agree with that. When we think we use our brains, and our brains are only capable of processing a very limited number of thoughts at the same time. And there are so many things that we experience without thinking. The ability to think is for me equal to the ability to press the buttons on a complex computer. If you can press the buttons, that does not mean you can program the computer - you only manipulate the existing program in a very limited way.*

As for "Mind is static energy, thought is dynamic energy". *The implication is that mind is part of time-space (i.e. static), when mind is in fact beyond time-space (i.e. neither static nor dynamic, it just is).*

You also asked if ". . . it is essential that you control your thoughts so as to bring forth only desirable conditions." *This is the basis of the positive thinking industry. If it was true, life would be perfect as long as you apply positive thinking, but that does not happen. When you control your thoughts, you create what you want - and whatever you want have both a positive and a negative side, and you can escape neither. If you focus only on the positive, then the negative catches up on you, maybe in an area of your life that you think of as unrelated, but it will be there. So the quickest way to get what you want is to manifest it with both the positive and negative sides present. Then you will not be elated about it, and you will not be depressed about it.*

It would be like eventually finding a gorgeous, rich, considerate soul mate, but accepting that they come with earplugs for their snoring, vanity procedures to remain gorgeous and the frustration of never being challenged because they always agree with you. If you include it all in your order, you will be not happy, but content - because happy implies you refuse the sad which comes with it. (I think I can make a stack of money in marriage counselling).

Have you ever looked for the balance in your life? Let me give you some examples. Is there a black sheep in your family? Of course, I hear you say. Have you ever thought how that person contributes to everyone else feeling good about themselves in comparison? Do you have colleagues or clients who are always willing to try something new, and others who will always fight any changes?

Is there always one part of your life that is perfect (e.g. your relationship goes well), while another part gets out of hand (e.g. you have stress at work)? Look for these contrasts. If you only focus on the bad parts, they drag you down. If you only focus on the good parts, you could become one of those neurotic "positive thinkers".

14 September: Coming out of Slumber

FH: I've come to the realization that those who I'm working with need to pull their socks up, start working correctly and appropriately, or we need to review whether we terminate. I think it is about authenticity. I've been authentic to myself. I am now asking others to be authentic too, and if they are not going to be authentic, then I would prefer not to deal with them.

ES: You have quickly grown into your new skin and you are comfortable with that. If there are people that are not comfortable with that, you cannot change them and it is OK to leave them behind.

FH: That's fair. In terms of the last few weeks, I think my wife believes I am on some drug! I am taking it all in my stride. Little things like the colors in the shop - I was in the car yesterday to pick up my daughter from work and I thought "Let's just see if it is going to be exactly the same" and it wasn't – it was not the same experience at all, and I became aware of the difference.

I was reading about connectedness, unity and wholeness. Everything is connected – I can accept and understand that. Each little sign or symbol that is given to me or that I become aware of during the course of a day is serving a purpose as well. I just need to recognize the sign and try and understand its place in all of this.

ES: It does take a while to get used to it. For example, sometimes it feels like my body is transparent. My neighbor's front door would close and I can barely hear it, but I can feel it in every cell of my body. Does that make sense? It's like I'm here, but I am also being aware of stuff that happens sometimes up to 100 yards around me.

FH: That is something I have been trying to experience consciously as well. I work at my desk in the office, but quite often when I am thinking about something I go to the other room to contemplate. When I am there I become aware of sitting on the leather settee and looking at a particular window. It is like taking three steps back and keeping the same perspective. I am looking at myself from outside the window. When I start playing with that, it is as if I can see something or somebody moving at my extreme left or extreme right. Round the mirror there is a beveled edge and I become aware of the trees 20 yards outside the house while I think of something completely different.

ES: You have allowed all this energy to flow freely and your body vibration has changed. You are settling down into that as well. It will become more and more important for you to protect yourself, to ensure that you don't just experience this ability, but you master it and can switch it on and off. You also need to protect yourself against other people who are aware of what you can do, and want to latch on to you.

FH: I am at a stage now where I am acknowledging the progress I have made, and becoming more aware of the signs, symbols and occurrences and to readily accept them in advance of them happening to heighten my awareness when they do. I am also introducing the gratitude element that we first spoke about. Of all the people that have wound me up this year, I have now viewed it as a lesson to help increase my emotional sense and awareness levels. I have accepted each of the individual lessons and thanked them and I have moved on. It is like a burden that has been released. I am like a kite that has had an extra 100 feet added to the string.

ES: That's right. It is amazing what happens when you start looking for those lessons that people teach you about yourself in the way they behave towards you. The moment you grasp that lesson and understand how they have helped you move from where you were to where you are right now, it is like an electrical spark – that moment of gratitude, of consciousness. That moment actually also changes your entire body. If you go back to physics, that spark is where a proton and electron would clash and become one and form a quantum of light. Every time that happens, your physical body actually becomes lighter.

FH: We're off to Italy at the beginning of next month – the entire family. At the end of last month I had a whole host of unbelievable challenges. I said to Wendy "Trust me. Go with the flow, have faith. Everything is as it should be. I am neither up nor down, and we're going to have an absolute blast. All the things you are getting concerned or stressed about will all be sorted out. Just have faith." She gets all wound up very easily about all sorts of situations and things. I used to, but now not as much.

ES: Yes. It is difficult to describe it to people who have not experienced that yet. That is the massive difference between an emotion and a feeling. An emotion is energy in motion. It is literally the proton and electron fighting against each other, resisting, like opposite poles of a magnet. They know they will eventually get together, but they will put up a hell of a fight before it happens. The closer they get together, the bigger the fight gets, the stronger the energy gets, the more irritation, frustration, anger, excessive emotions there are. Then they become one. Once that happens, it does not matter what people say or do. It seems people have lost the ability to press the button, or the button has disappeared.

FH: I thought emotions and feelings were the same. I can understand emotions as being energy in motion. How would you describe a feeling?

ES: Can you recall the first time you held your eldest child in your arms?
FH: Oh, I cried like a baby.

ES: That was a feeling. It was totally unique, completely different from what anyone else experienced in the world, it placed you above and beyond space and time. It is something that you cannot put into words. The effect on your physical body is complete

131

lightness and release. It is not easy to put it into words. That is a feeling.

FH: Here is something that I have noticed and tried to hide. In watching the X-factor, I get so emotional for the people who come out and astound themselves and the audience. I really feel for them in terms of where they are, their motivation and their aspiration. I really feel for them in the recognition that they have done well and where they are. Some of them perform exceptionally well, and I want to cry tears of happiness for them.

ES: That is a feeling. It is even more than happiness. What they do and the way they do it touches a place inside of you that you cannot really point to. But you know it is there and it opens up and you cannot put into words what you experience at that moment.

FH: I want to control this. If this becomes more intense as I go forward, I really want to condition myself to recognize the signs and symbols and become aware of it so that I can manage that and channel it appropriately.

ES: Yes, and recognize the difference between an emotion and a feeling. When you get the tears in your eyes, is that because you have a feeling that is beyond words, or is it utter frustration and anger that you find difficult to express because it is so strong?

FH: For myself, I think emotions are more anger-driven and feelings are more happiness-driven.

ES: That is one way of looking at it.
Men in general tend to stay away from anything related to feelings and most things related to emotions. They only associate with their male energy and they deny their female energy. This is why when you start talking about spiritual stuff, most men will change the topic, and most women would want to talk with you.

FH: I can relate to that 100%. If I was to look back at all the friends and companions I have had throughout my life, I got along 100% better with women than with men.

ES: You will notice as you go along that there will be particular men that you will probably feel much closer to than before and you will feel comfortable with it. When my step-brothers get together they would kiss each other. My two brothers would not kiss each other even when they are on their death-beds – it's just not done.

FH: It's very much an English custom to kiss each other on the cheek. We Scots are a bit more "hands-off". Sometimes when I meet a female, I feel uneasy with that quick gesture of hallo. I can relate to that quite a bit. It does not concern me. I wonder if I sometimes appear stand-offish rather than approachable. It's funny how we recognize these things on occasion.

Something that has been really weird - in the last 2 days I have had this pulling – not yearning - towards America – as if I was going to do business there or something like that. I am thinking it can't come from the website. I have not done anything different with my business. I have been using The Water Cooler to fine-tune my proposition before I get going on the new site. But it is as if my instincts are telling me that something is already in play as a result of the changes that are happening and I am about to get a proposal – something about me doing the new stuff in America very shortly. I don't know whether that is wishful thinking or dreaming.

ES: It is all of that. It's definitely wishful thinking, it's definitely dreaming, it is having access to another dimension which is called imagination –which is totally underrated. Are you familiar with the visual technique where you see loads of dots appearing until you can see make out the image?

FH: Yes?

ES: That is what's happening. You create all of that. You create your entire future. Your thoughts don't just appear in your brain.

They surface from – shall we say the collective unconscious - and only by the time they surface do you become aware of them. But they are there long before you become aware of them.

That thought from the unconscious is slowly starting to materialize. And the nice thing is the more you recognize it, the quicker it will materialize. When you are afraid of something, exactly the same process happens.

Here is something interesting. Have you ever been made redundant or been dismissed from a job that you really disliked? Can you recall the emotional turmoil that you went through at the time? And look back now. Do you think it was a good or a bad experience?

You will probably tell me that at the time it was pure hell, but afterwards you realized it was the best thing that could have happened to you.
Was there another time in your life when you thought the world was ending, but in fact it was a lovely new beginning? Like a divorce or the end of a relationship that made way for happiness with another person?

What you went through at the time was pure emotion – and you can imitate it whenever you want. What you feel looking back with insight and gratitude is a feeling – you cannot imitate it, but you can remember it once you have had the experience.

17 September: Stop, Look and Listen

ES: I get a very amusing picture of you dancing through what looks like a minefield, with dogs running after you and trying to bite you. Sorry, I should not laugh, but it does look funny, especially if I look around and see what it is all about.

FH: After our chat, I think I can understand that. I have challenges ahead/around me, but I also am surrounded with people letting me down at the moment. I think the lesson is that I have allowed them to leverage my good nature, and I don't mean that in an egotistical way, I've simply allowed them to get a away with murder and not honor their contractual obligations - I suppose I've been too much of a nice guy (too laid back).

ES: You are being pushed forward from all directions. You are not totally willing to go forward, because there are specific constraints that you have put in place. You have very good, valid reasons to justify those constraints, except that all those constraints belong to the era of the transistor radio. They were very valid at the time, and perfect for what you wanted to achieve. However, so much have changed.

FH: I'm curious as to what those constraints are? Do you mean self-imposed rules? Terms of Business? Modus Operandi etc.? Are you saying my outlook on the way I market myself/manage my business is outdated? Are the constraints my limited beliefs in myself? When you say "being pushed forward from all directions", do you mean on various personal development fronts, or do u mean on a personal, business, emotional, financial, mental fronts etc.?

ES: At times you feel you are being torn apart when you see what people do, because what they do is just so wrong in your book. This is a reference to practical issues, nothing moral. You have put practices in place which have over time become the cornerstones of your business.

These practices are no longer needed, but you are in phase where you are not completely sure of your footing. As a result you want to hold on to the known until you are totally familiar with what is new to you.

FH: Is this a "control" thing? I think I've pinpointed this down to the reporting systems I have created, as I have clearly identified that the primary reason for many of them not generating the results they want is because THEY ARE NOT DOING THE RIGHT TASKS to help them promote their business. Many of them come up with all sorts of excuses and reasons, and some even try to point the finger at me. At the end of the day, the truth is they simply haven't done the tasks they need to in order to make progress.

When you say "*these practices are no longer needed*", do you mean that my own behavior is changing, and that I don't need to carry out the tasks I used to until now, and that I have to revisit my own set of behaviors in order to develop me/the business further? Can you expand on this?

ES: *That is not how it works. This is a time to let go of the known, so that you can make space for the unknown. Does this mean that you will lose everything you have built up? On the contrary. You will retain everything that is solid and can stand the test of time. You will lose everything that is holding you back for whatever reason.*

FH: I feel as though, another line is about to be drawn, and while for example I derive a reasonable income from those I'm working, I feel that perhaps now is a crunch time with regards to revisiting my own model and where I want to take what I do further. This will mean revisiting the people around me, and whether they are truly committed to going forward or not as the case may be.

ES: You are concerned about financial issues. Could it be because you still have a one-dimensional view of finances and your earning ability? What if you let go of some constraints that no longer make sense to other people? What if they are simply ignoring your constraints and they are using their behavior to tell you to let go? And no, this does not mean let go of the money and let them get away with what is yours. On the contrary.

FH: In other words, they are taking advantage of my good nature (as opposed to owning up and taking responsibility for their own actions/ contractual obligations or inactivity)!

ES: This is the time where you need to apply your energy to obtain what is yours. You are excellent at using your energy to create, as you have recently shown to the world with great success. When you did that creation, you completely trusted and allowed out energy to flow through you.

When it comes to money, you want to still apply the same rules which got you where you are, like a learner driver imagining driving a Ferrari on a motorway, while being overly careful on the village high street.

FH: Money has never been my motivator. It's rather been doing what I want/love to do. However, I suppose I have allowed myself perhaps to undervalue what I offer others, because I love it so much. Perhaps I have missed the true value of what I offer in terms of cost/value to others and their situation.

ES: Somehow you still believe that with your work, which is your passion, it is OK for you to drive a Ferrari at full speed, but when it comes to money, you need to stick to just below the speed limit. Do not doubt your own power. Use it. Learn to apply it in all areas of your life. And do not be afraid of it.

FH: I think I relate to that, as above, in terms of having the confidence to charge what I think it's worth in terms of the value I offer. It will attract the correct people who need, value and respect what I have, instead of trying to appease or keep the status quo with those I have attracted previously to me. If they believe in me and the product and the modus operandi, then the true results will come anyway if they do the tasks. Question is, is it time I change my behavior (and beliefs) in a new direction, and if so specifically what?

ES: All those people are testing you to see what you will do. They are challenging you. Use your inner power, not against them, but to prove to them what you are capable of.

FH: Are they taking advantage of my good nature, and using it against me, knowing that I wouldn't want to cause a storm in a tea cup, then again, if they are blatantly disregarding their contractual obligations, its time I have "that chat" with them

ES: How do you do this? In old terms we would have told you to apply your mind, but you now know that this has a different meaning. Use the new meaning.

This is also a lesson in resolving emotions. First resolve your emotions, and then speak to each of those people, one at a time. Do not prepare what you want to say to them, because you will base that on emotions. Be willing to trust, and listen to what comes from your mouth. There is an important lesson to each one of them as well as to you in everything you will say to them. You will not need to say much, but what you say will touch them in the right places. They will become aware of your power, and they will do what needs to be done. About the people who "let you down" - be firm where you need to, and let go where you need to. All this is part of a cleansing process.

FH: I think in every instance, each of them already know they have let themselves and me down, by not doing what they said/or committed to do. It's not my fault or problem – it's theirs. Aha! The G word - "GUILT"! All I need to do is to get them to admit that it is their problem and what and how they will remedy it, and if they choose not to, I will have to remind them of the five year contracts they have signed and the implications of not adhering to the contract. This may cause one of several responses:

- They terminate, and refuse to go further. I sue/claim for the balance of the five years
- They negotiate an exit deal with me or
- They simply give themselves a good shake and start becoming more serious about their future and mine.

ES: And you want to know about your next products? All we can say right now is prepare for a massive surprise. Keep your awareness up, and trust us. By the time you return home from your holiday, your next step will be crystal clear. Your next product will flow like the previous one, but on a larger scale.

FH: I think I'm getting an inkling that it has got something to do with unemployment and starting a business, helping people to become aware of why they are here and to recognize their life purpose and turn it into cash.

The emerging market of rising unemployment I think gives me a backdrop and excellent opportunity for PR to talk positively about unemployment (as no one can in the media at the moment - it is all doom and gloom).

This could be leveraged, explaining that people don't want to work for others in paid jobs. They want to work for themselves and do what they love, and get compensated for the value they offer. I think everyone is here to contribute and leave a legacy. I also think that everyone is here to do something different and that includes their purpose and their business. I also think that you and I need to spend time with people who have something new to offer or are trying to find that something new. I don't think we are meant to be working with just another hairdresser, accountant, training company etc. I think our biggest challenge is to attract the people who want to create and offer something new who are also trying to find us.

139

Can you recall the last time you have gone through massive changes in your life? It is not easy – it can be compared to walking from a ramshackle house to a new palace through a dark corridor. You feel vulnerable and often the temptation is there to just get back to your old habits.

However, you then discover that the old habits no longer make sense to you, and you have nothing to replace them with yet.

For example, you grew up with happily married parents and want the same in your life. As things happen, you have a disastrous marriage and your self-image takes a serious beating. You then know that you will never be married to the same person for 40 years – unless you have a death wish. Time to change your thinking. But what to? What is your new measure of a successful relationship if it is not 40 years of happiness in your first marriage?

FH: I want to discuss our recent exchange. Financial issues – what do you mean that I am one-dimensional?

ES: It seems to me that you have particular ways of dealing with finances and some of these ways are based on "I'm insecure, I'm not sure of myself, I don't want to step on people's toes." This is saying do what you want to do, don't hesitate. You're not hesitating anywhere else, why are you hesitating with this?

FH: That's true. Relationships tend to fall out because of one of two things – money, and a complete lack of communication. I always try to make sure I am on a good note regardless of whether the relationship finishes or continues. There is a grey area and I suppose with some people I prefer to maintain the relationship, rather than ruin the relationship because they owe me money. In hindsight I have actually been giving my power away by being Mr. Nice Guy.

One of the things that came out from our last chat was that I am strong-willed and capable in certain areas but when it comes to money I'm too much of a nice guy. I should be holding people more to account.

ES: But there is a reason why you hesitate. That reason relates to some emotion that keeps coming to the surface.

FH: I don't know what that is. I can only assume I don't want to rock the boat. I like the relationship, and don't want to lose it.

ES: Why?

FH: I don't know. If I look at it from a fresh perspective – I ditch the non-payers and it makes room for something else to come into their place. I think maybe that's where the hesitation has been. Do I terminate the arrangement because they haven't been paying, and I have a choice of consequences? Now that I am speaking to you, I realize that I haven't actually followed through with the consequences with a number of people. Maybe it is time for me to do so. I have done everything I said I would, and they haven't done everything they said they would.

ES: And the reason why you are holding back and not following through is some belief which is outdated. If you do follow through the world will keep turning.

FH: One of the things at the back of my mind is that three of the people who have failed in their contractual obligations to me are on The Water Cooler. I suppose it's that need to be liked and the preservation of my personal integrity that is perhaps making me cautious in terminating relationships in case they go out and say something that is not correct or true and that could potentially damage me in the future. I don't know.

*ES: You said two things that, in your mind, may be contradictory. You want to be liked and you want to preserve your personal integrity. It is not a contradiction. You can and will preserve your personal integrity even if **other** people choose not to like you. As long as you choose to like yourself, it does not matter whether other people choose to like you. That will give the right message.*

FH: I think I get that. You said these people around me were testing me to see what I would do. I can see that as well. They know I am a fairly nice, open, relaxed chap, and they are trying to get one over me. My father said to me when I was about 10 or 12: "Fraser, you are consistently inconsistent. When you are older that will save your bacon, because nobody will be able to second-guess you". Maybe my father's wisdom might be put to a test imminently. People are testing me because they know what is due to me and their contractual obligations but they are just not delivering. I really have been unsure – I have talked to them about it and they have said "I will get it sorted" but they do nothing.

ES: There are a number of universal laws. One of them states "Say what you do, and do what you say." If you say what you do, it is clear to people. If you then don't do what you say, you are sending out the opposite message to those same people.

 Think of the message you send into the world. Is it consistent in terms of this Universal law? For example: when you agree on a time for an appointment, do you ensure you are on time? When you promise to meet a deadline, do you keep that promise? These may be small things, but if you are inconsistent in small things, it becomes very easy to also become inconsistent in bigger things.

What you sow, you will reap. In other words, it you are inconsistent, you will receive exactly that back. Scary thought ...

FH: You are right. I have been Mr. Nice Guy for too long. I want to change – I have held back.

ES: I have just noticed the first sentence about dogs running after you and biting you. A dog is the symbol for loyalty. Your loyalty is biting you.

FH: Hmmm – interesting. A lot has been happening today. Half of me says I'm going to fire all the coaches that are there now. I want to say "Look, you either meet your obligations, (you have signed a five-year contract which is worth a chunk of money) or stop." I would prefer to have someone dedicated to it as opposed to someone swinging the lead and taking advantage of me.

ES: And using your reputation for it.

FH: It is not about the money, it is about initiating the process. I have been in hibernation and focusing on what works, but that has inhibited my growth. It is now accelerating in a number of different ways. It is like "Drop everything that is not contributing to going forward and it will soon be replaced by everything that needs to be".

ES: The people that you deal with help you in your agenda – without you or them realizing what it is that you are doing.

FH: A chap, Hans in South Africa, was supposed to pay me every two weeks for five years. It's been a bit spasmodic and now the activity has stopped. The contract even says what activity he should be doing, but he clearly hasn't done it. I had to laugh when I read "Don't prepare what you're going to say, just say what you're going to say."

ES: When I wrote it, I realized what it was all about. When you think of this South African and what he does as opposed to what he should do, how to you feel about it?

FH: The way I view it, I say to them "You only need to apply 12 hours per week on this business to make anywhere between £2000 to £5000 minimum per month." I know they are not doing it because they are doing other things.

ES: How do you feel about that?

FH: I am frustrated. I know the system works. They have got the complete system. They contractually agreed to compensate me for that. They are not living up to their end of the deal. I know it's not me. It's definitely them. We've just not had that frank chat.

ES: If you prepare, on the basis of this frustration, what you want to say to him, you will remain stuck where you are. If you can find the space where there is no frustration, no other emotion, and don't prepare, but just say what comes through your mouth, it should be very interesting.

 Ensure that before you have an important meeting (whether it is business or personal), you get rid of all the emotion and act from a place that is above emotion. Read the section below on how to do that.

FH: The Scotsman in me says "Do I sever a revenue opportunity of tens of thousands of pounds or do I cut my losses?" I've always had the philosophy that a fight is not a good fight unless you know you win it. Even if you win it, you don't want to enter into that fight, because there are all sorts of negative aspects to a fight and it can drain you.

ES: That's right, that's where you are stuck in emotion. Emotion runs up and down and sideways, and you don't know what to do next. Try this. Think about what this guy is doing, the effect it's got on you right now and the emotions you feel right now.

FH: OK

ES: Now find a spot where you can fix your eyes until you get cross-eyed and don't look away. Now become aware of the room you are in. Become aware of what is happening elsewhere in the building. Now become aware of what is happening outside of the building.

Now put the problem into words. What is the problem?

FH: The problem? Am I making it a problem? (Laugh)

ES: Where's the problem?

FH: Yes . . . I see what you mean.

ES: Before you call him, first get into that state where the problem disappears. You take away the emotion. Then call him and just allow the words to flow and see what happens.

FH: I will try that.

ES: When you make the call, record it, so that you can listen to it afterwards.

FH: With 90% of the people I have helped this year, it was always about straightening them out first, and then focusing on the rest. That is re-enforcing the "new start" idea. Nobody is doing this on a national basis.

ES: I have noticed that. I market myself with everything I think and say and do. You help me package it. If I didn't know what I am marketing, I will go out into the world and people will say "What is she doing? This woman is confused". I'm not confused. I'm clear on what my passion is and what I want to do. People pick up on that.

18 September: It's never too late

FH: I got money in this morning from someone due me since January!

ES: *Just because you changed your thought process and expectations -- you did not even need to do anything physical. We have such power, and we are too scared to use it.*

FH: I was very matter of fact (no emotion), and he paid by return via BACS!

This is not only about money. Imagine the change process as a kind of Pavlov conditioning carried out by an invisible hand. You notice just a glimpse of the hand, then you touch it, and then you discover a sweet in the hand – and it is all yours.

Awareness is about noticing things that you would ordinarily not notice or maybe not attach any meaning to, and slowly steering into a direction that you would not have considered before.

20 September: Excuses, Excuses

FH: I recognized earlier this week that some of the coaches are really not doing what they should be doing. So I put together a document to say to them what they should be focusing on. They know what they should be doing. I've got a means of measuring whether they are doing it or not. I am perhaps inhibiting myself by spending a lot of time musing over their inactivity. These are the tactics that they should be putting into practice on a regular basis.

ES: If they do these tasks, what will they get out of it?

FH: They will get clients and do business.

ES: Would they have goals other than income and lifestyle that they can achieve?

FH: Yes, if they have gone down deep enough to question and write down exactly what they want to achieve. But again I suspect they would not have set their goals. They are not doing what they should do. I know what I tell them to do works, but they go off in their own way.

ES: There is some constraint that you have put in place for yourself. These people are telling you that you need to change. The more you work with them, the more you will discover what you expect of them where they are not complying yet.

FH: So they are doing what I am not doing?

ES: Yes. They are letting go. They are no longer controlling their business. You are trying to get the control back in place on their behalf. You want them to toe the line, but at the same time there is freedom available to you and you are not embracing it yet.

FH: Some are claiming poverty because they have no sales and no prospects. The reason for this is that they are not doing what they should be doing. Therefore they are not making progress and not getting the results. That can lead to doubt in their mind that what they do does not work, so they stop the tasks and the payments as well. They create a stalemate.

 Remember what we said earlier about stress being the difference between your inner and outer world? When you get stressed out, your outer world will not change to please you. You need to change your inner world to be more aligned with your outer world.

ES: What are you doing about it?

FH: I can remind them of their obligations. I do make myself available to them. It is their business, and they make the decisions. They decide how fast or how slow they want to go. They can use me as often as they want. I am their cheapest resource ever and very expensive if they don't use me. I am almost asking them - do they want to call it a day or not? If they do, every decision has consequences. What are the consequences for me if they do quit? It will give me more freedom because I am holding myself back by wanting to help these guys who don't want to help themselves. What about the consequences for themselves in terms of their obligations to me if they do quit?

It's not for me to terminate the contracts. It's for them to admit that they haven't done their bit and it's very unlikely that they will. We need to negotiate an end or termination to that agreement that makes sense.

ES: That's right. It comes back to "Say what you do and do what you say" – not just for them, but for you as well. If they say what they do and don't do what they say, why should you bear the consequences?

FH: Yes.

ES: And you do put more and more stuff in place for them to do what they say.

FH: But they are not doing what they say.

ES: That's right. So instead of you trying to change that and help them and take on their burden, maybe you should just give it back to them?

FH: Do you mean saying "You have an obligation, you have a contract, what do you want to do about it?"?

ES: Yes.

FH: Interesting. Every time I want to pull them up on something, I tend to give them something – like giving them a compliment before I ask them why they have not used the previous stuff I have given them.

ES: What is it that makes you hesitate every time you want to confront them?

FH: I don't want to lose the income. Yes, they do pay me, but it is very spasmodic and I really
have to be on their case.

ES: So they are playing the game according to their rules and not yours?

FH: That's a fair assessment.

ES: *And they are taking a lot of energy from you and not giving anything back.*

 Who are the people in your life that are taking a lot of energy from you? You will know who they are because part of you feel you owe them something while another part of you feel they are taking advantage of you.

FH: Yes. I've honoured my agreements. I've gone out of my way to negotiate favorably for them to give them what they want. I've continued to be available to support and help them. They either did not pick up the support or they don't do what is required of them to get the returns they want, or they simply don't pay as per our contract.

ES: *And every time it gets very, very close to a confrontation, you give them something else to help them.*

FH: That is an honest and fair appraisal in hindsight. You are giving me a big stick to start whacking them with, aren't you?

ES: *You've got the stick already. You just don't want to use it. Something is holding your arm back and you are saying "I can't do this."*

FH: Yes. I suppose I don't actually see myself as a . . . as I said in the email I think they are leveraging my good nature against me.

ES: *Yes. And there is nothing wrong with having a good nature. That is just the way you are. But a good nature does not mean avoiding conflict at all costs.*

 Conflict makes us grow. What do you do with conflict? Do you avoid at all costs, or do you fight back? Or have you succeeded in becoming both a spectator and a participant?

FH: I think you're right. Hmm. I sent an email to Hans in South Africa. He had actually missed a payment earlier in the year and I hadn't picked up on it. I noticed he hadn't said anything to me. He's avoided the e-mail altogether and has not communicated in two weeks.

ES: *". . . you are in a phase when you are not completely sure of your footing and as a result you want to hold on to the known until you are totally familiar with what is new to you."*

FRASER HAY & ELSABE SMIT

FH: I think I do understand it now. As I go through this transition, do I keep what I already have and manage it as best as I can, or do I sever connections with them all and embrace the new as it comes in? It is as if I am trying to stop a flood putting my finger in the hole in the wall, as opposed to just hammering through the wall and letting the water come through?

ES: That's right.

FH: Hmm. But then that makes me think about all the stuff that I have been creating in terms of the website and the offering. A phenomenal amount of time, effort and money have gone into the new site that the people on board aren't going to use, so I will not see the return on that.

ES: If you put another five or six things in place to help them, will anything change?

FH: No, I think you are right. They are not changing their behaviour, regardless of what I give them.

ES: And if you don't put anything else in place but rather say to each of them "How do we move on"?

 With any change process, you get to a point where your inner voice shouts against your habits. Do you listen to that inner voice, or do you drown it out by doing the same things over and over?

FH: The worst will be them saying "Huff puff, I'm not going to do it anymore". I will say "Fine, what do we do about the agreement, because you now owe me x amount for five years. That now comes into play. How do you wish to address that?" They will have to negotiate an exit.

ES: And how would you feel about doing that?

FH: Half of me says I don't really have a problem with that, but I would have to definitely follow through and enforce it. I need to give a clear signal to say I do follow through when I say I am going to do it.

ES: That is the key. Half of you says "Yes, I can do it", and the other half says "No, I can't really do it."

FH: You're right. That is where I am. Are you saying I should be a kick-ass bad guy and really wind them all up and say right, this is it?

ES: Would you feel comfortable with that?

FH: No, because it is not in my nature. But what I would be comfortable with is saying "I think we've got a problem. No matter what I do, you're not doing it. If it is not working you don't come and discuss it with me. You don't want my help. You prefer to stick your head in the sand like an ostrich. I get the impression that you have given up. I accept it, but there is still the matter of the contract. How do we get to a sensible conclusion?"

ES: You have two halves that must become a whole.

FH: Half of me says that regardless of what I do, they still don't do what they should do. The other half says it needs to be resolved: either they leave and negotiate an exit, or they pull their socks up and start doing what they contracted to do.

ES: Let's try this. Put your hands on either side of your laptop, palms up. Put the part of you that says "I have do this" on one hand, and put the part of you that says "I can't really do this" on the other hand. Let's start with the part that says "I can't do this". If you have to turn that part into a person that you know or feel familiar with, who is the person?

FH: It's just me.

ES: And the part of you that says "I can do this"?

FH: That's me as well.

ES: What is the purpose of the part of you that says "I can't do this"?

FH: I can't really do this because this is the constraint that's holding me back. It needs to be done because it is holding me back from where I should be going. The fact that I am not doing it and not addressing it is allowing it to drift, so "I can't really do this" . . . it doesn't actually exist!

ES: Are you saying the part of you that says "I can't do this" does not really exist?

FH: It's really funny – it's like a set of scales. As I said it, that hand fell and the other hand went up!

ES: So the part of you that says "I can't do this" fell down and the other part went up.

FH: Yes.

ES: What does the part of you that says "I can do this" do for you?

FH: That hand tells me that it needs to be done. They have been given the opportunity, not once, even three times or five times, but multiple times and they failed to deliver. I want to say "Look, it is definitely not working, I think we just stop and I crack on".

ES: And what does that do for you?

FH: It feels right. This is the tiny little doubt that I have. While I may be honorable in everything that I do and in what I've done, they and their perception might relay an untruth to other people that could affect perceptions of me. That is the only doubt. Things have been said about me in the past that I really dwelt on and that was not true. I really value my integrity. It is not so much the confrontation, but I want to avoid a bad or negative perception of my integrity.

ES: So the part of you that says "I cannot do this" is the negative perception of your integrity.

FH: Yes!

ES: And what is the purpose of that? Just say what comes into your mind.

FH: I really don't want people to have a negative perception of me at a critical point when I am building the business, and I don't want to waste the time, money and effort that's gone into creating what I already have, to allow people to say it doesn't work purely because they haven't done it. People don't always tell the whole truth. They tell a part truth, saying "I signed up for this and it didn't work". What they really mean is that they did not follow the instructions.

 To what extent do you allow other people's views of you to dictate what you do, even if your actions do not feel comfortable?

ES: Having that part of you that says "I can't do this", what does it do for you?

FH: It is holding me back. Having it in my mind is preventing me from going forward to what should be done. I have to acknowledge where I am at and allow them to acknowledge that as well. I am ready to go to the next stage.

ES: And what does that do for you? To confirm that you are ready to go?

FH: I almost give myself permission to say "Stop messing around, crank up the engine, fasten the seat belt and let's just go."

ES: And what does that do for you?

FH: I suppose it gives me the confidence to know that yes, it has to be done, it needs to be done, and once it has been done, it will fall by the wayside and allow me to go to where I need to go. It brings balance, it gets me into my zone, it gets me to where I think it should be.

ES: On the other hand, you have "I'm OK, I can actually do this". What's the purpose of that?

FH: I can get rid of what no longer serves a purpose in going forward. It hopefully unleashes the power within which is held back by other people who are not actually doing it. Because I have not told them formally, it continues to perpetuate itself into a stalemate position. It frustrates me.

I have to think about it, to come up with a decision - one way or the other – break the frustration, let the energy flow and go forward. It gives me peace of mind. It gives me FREEDOM!

ES: What happened to your hands?

FH: I want to clap my hands. I want to rub them together like washing my hands.

ES: They came together?

FH: They did!

ES: So what's the problem?
FH: Oh, tomorrow is going to be a busy day! I will be speaking to all of them!

ES: Being the "bad guy"?

FH: No, the chat is long overdue. I am fairly confident about having the conversation. My only question is when we talk about the contractual obligation, whether they will try to weasel out and attack me and throw it back at me. I want to negotiate with each of them. I need to decide what I am prepared to accept. I don't think I should let them get off without any consequences. Their inability and their inactivity have held me back, but they will not view it like that. They will take a much more simplistic view on it. The contracts will stand up in court but they won't be able to afford it. Many of them will take the obstinate view that they don't own anything of value and for me to want to pursue it further will be a futile exercise.

ES: Does that make you the bad guy?

FH: No. But that is what has happened on The Water Cooler. Someone's perception of me led to another person not doing business with me. The perception was wrong and I don't want to fuel the wrong perception. Interesting. I'm almost making it worse than it is.

We live in an amazing world where the people closest to us work the hardest to guide us towards our own wisdom. We tend to have a view of "me, myself and I", and we get upset when the people around us distract from that wonderful picture by differing from us.

When you become aware of that and you focus your attention away from yourself, you discover this wonderful dance that you do with your family, friends and colleagues. The more you become aware of the actions of other people, the more you appreciate what they do rather than defend your own corner.

Think of the people you interact with every day. What do they do that you really want them to stop doing? And if they don't stop, what can you learn from them? Because believe me, you will not change them. You can only change yourself.

156

21 September: Blame and Denial

FH: The way you simplify complex matters has enabled me to question, gain an understanding of the mechanics and how it works. You simplify it in common and layman's terms so that everybody can understand it. I think that's the biggest challenge that most people have.

I've got a confession. After we finished the other day Wendy took the kids to practice. I felt wound up but I said "No, I'm very calm".

I went through the agreement of my coach in Germany and I said "I can't call him, its Sunday, it's wrong." Then I said "Why is it wrong? He is not a religious person". I then said "I will do it tomorrow". I was arguing with myself.

Then I said "No, no, no, don't put it off again".

 Notice how Fraser recognizes his two internal arguments and make them one decision to act.

I called him and he said it was good to hear from me. I said "Why? I have not heard from you for quite a while?" He told me how bad the world was. He said "The economy is so bad in Germany. My mind has been all over the place." I said "Well, I have a problem. I wonder if you can help me." He said "Yes, I'm always here to help you".

I said "It's about you. Is there anything that I've done, or that I've promised you and not done?"
He said "No, you make me feel bad, because I haven't done what I had to do."
I said "Pardon?" on purpose so that he could become aware of what he was saying.

He said "I feel so bad. My mind has been on other things. I feel terrible. I have financial problems here in Germany with my investments. I've had to do all sorts of changes. Now that you're phoning me I feel as I am letting you down".

I said "It's not about letting me down. It's your business. You decide how much or how little you want to make. I just hate to think that it's anything that I have done."

He said "Oh no, no, no, it is me, I feel so wrong, I feel bad. I must fix this, I must get you over to Germany to do a seminar and we will do this before the end of the year. I will organise it. I will get people to the seminar. I will get the local media as well. We must do this.

I said "That's excellent. I would hate us just to talk about it and nothing happens. I have the agreement here which you signed back at the beginning of the year but unfortunately, as much as I love you and as much as I think you are the best guy ever, I've got a problem with it."

He said "Fraser, I promise you, you have taken the first step and it's good you have woken me up to my situation. I need to fix it. I will be with you on the coaching call tomorrow night. Let's get things moving. I must do this, I must."

All that happened in about 20 minutes yesterday afternoon. I did not actually say very much. He did all the talking. He admitted he had not done what he was supposed to do.

I think guilt took over. I didn't get heavy with him. I was very polite and matter-of-fact. I didn't get heated and emotional about it. I was also looking for him to come up with suggestions to remedy the situation. I gave the problem to him because it's his problem.

ES: That's right. And how did you feel about his response?

FH: I felt he was genuine. I think the intent is there but whether he is able to follow through remains to be seen. I think he will be on the coaching call tonight. I think we will expand on it. I allowed him to take control of the subject and come up with the way forward.

ES: And were you prepared for conflict with him?

FH: If it arose I would happily have dealt with it. But I put my emotions to one side.

ES: And you were still a nice guy?

FH: Yes. I kept pulling him back to our contract. He agreed to fix it.

ES: *You were no longer afraid of being rejected. He felt it. You did not need to say it and he responded to that.*

 This is what happens when you recognize the two sides of an inner argument. You rise above both and that part of you becomes one.

FH: Now that does make sense.

ES: And that is what is so beautiful. You are in different countries. You don't even need to see him. Even before you called him, on some level he knew "Something is different and I had better respond to it."

FH: I think you're right. In fact, what you've just said - it's fear of rejection that I had. I suppose we all want to be loved. You did not mention fear of rejection yesterday but it makes perfect sense now.

ES: You became integrated and you no longer need to deal with it as a separate issue, because it's part of you.

FH: Got you. That makes perfect sense.

Your Fear of Rejection: How Much is it Really Costing YOU?

The following illustrates synchronicity at its best: Paul approached me yesterday, because he's had problems with a client not paying.

It's a client that's been with him for five years.

However this client hasn't paid him for four months. Paul didn't know what the problem was.

- He had done a good job
- He and the client get on well
- There had been no fall out
- The client simply hadn't paid him

We spoke for a while, and a couple of things came to light.

The client was using Paul's own "energy" and power against him.

Paul and the client have gotten on well for five years, and the client obviously knew Paul's very good nature. He knew that Paul didn't like confrontation and was using that to his advantage by ignoring the fact that he owed Paul money and knew Paul wouldn't fall out with him.

I asked Paul how much the sums involved were, and would it matter a great deal to him of he lost the client. "Well, he's been good to us and given us a lot of business over the years." Paul said.

That's because you've been his bank, giving him interest free overdraft facilities for up to five months at a time allowing him to decide when he could pay you.

YOU ARE NOT HIS BANK !

"I don't want to lose him as a client" he said.

"Well that's daft" I said.

"You want to keep a client who out of 60 months, has taken up 30 months to pay you for just six transactions. Your mindset is wrong. You don't want confrontation. You don't want to come across as Mr. Nasty and as a result your client is using your own power against you." I said.

"Take the emotion out of the situation. Be professional. Be YOU, call them and discuss it with your client. Give him until the end of the week or you will have to refer it to your credit control department" (Linda - his wife).

I'm writing about this now, because Paul came back to me this afternoon - elated. He had received BACS/CHAPS payment today from his client.

IT WORKED!

Quite often in business, we can still be nice and polite, but we don't need to fear rejection, because many people leverage that power against us.

I should know, for it's happened to me too.

Optimism is great, but you have to put it to good use.

Don't allow people to slow you down, or affect your future plans and growth because they are operating their agenda instead of sticking to the agreed agenda with you. Many people have a deep seated fear of rejection. This can stop many from cold calling, going on appointments, chasing money etc. etc. It can often come from negative experiences in the past, and the wanting to be loved or the need for approval.

The main difference I have found with successful people has nothing to do with ability. It's about "energy" and their ability to recognize and understand the dynamics and flow of that energy, and how certain people manipulate that energy to gain control over people and situations. How many films have you watched when the hero says "I know it's crazy and a one in a million shot or chance of it working", then he goes and does it, saves the day, big finale and the end credits come up.

Sometimes we have to recognize the personal power we possess and use it ourselves instead of giving that power to another person and then have to struggle to get it back. Some people want money, other people just want the power. Some want respect or love, some just want to save the world, and hey, that's fine. Knowing what really motivates someone is the key to understanding them, dealing with them, and how to generate the results you want. After all, wanting what you've got requires contentment, but getting what you want takes ambition.

Other people's motives, like the truth, are rarely pure and never simple. So wanting to do good, I think, is a powerful motive. Wanting to do it to others can be also powerful and dangerous. Many people will tell you throughout the course of your life or business "It's stupid. Don't do it - Give up." That's probably because they don't like to see anyone else with a firmer sense of purpose than their own. So don't fear rejection, recognize it, and leverage your own power to your advantage to stop others taking advantage of you.

Sometimes we need the "emptiness" that comes from making a decision as the result of a negative situation, in order to fill it with our next creation and next positive situation. For every action there is an equal and opposite reaction.

When I was a boy my father used to say - "You are consistently inconsistent", and that he could throttle me on occasion for not doing certain errands he wanted me to do. (He also said that when I grow up it would probably be one of my greatest strengths.)

I've come to reflect on that over the years and have since concluded that its people who are the most uncertain in their hearts, are the most dogmatic in their minds. I also think that no one wants your advice unless they're paying for it. If they ask for it, give it carefully. If they don't ask for it, keep your mouth shut and your eyes and ears open.

Remember, Fear stands for FALSE EVIDENCE APPEARING REAL. Sometimes we need to experience negative situations and learn from them to have a breakthrough and take us to a whole new level. And don't forget, a kite flies best against the wind. Don't undervalue what you have, and don't disrespect yourself by allowing others to take advantage of your good nature. Respect yourself and what you offer, and you'll never need to worry about rejection ever again.

 Take a moment to reflect and make notes on what you have just read and think of a time when someone has taken advantage of your good nature.

Wakey, Wakey.

Many people struggle through life not aware of the opportunities around them. When they do become aware, they react to the circumstances that life throws at them, instead of creating the life they want. By becoming more aware of everything around you, you can become more perceptive, more alert. You also become intuitively aware of your emotions and feelings how you can better channel them to positive effect.

- Are you questioning many things at the moment?
- Do you tend to notice things or "lessons" after the event?
- Are you spending time on things that are not essential or don't matter?
- Are you struggling to find solutions for problems at the moment?
- Are you facing resistance in key areas of your life at the moment?
- Are you constantly engaging with new and exciting people?
- Do you recognize where you are on your evolutionary path?

Is it time to stop, reflect and practice becoming more aware of where you are, what it is you're doing, and what it is you want?

If you stop and think for a second, how often have you become aware of:

- What's happening in your marketplace, and the trends affecting your market?
- How your body feels, and what it's trying to tell you?
- The energy dynamics when you engage with people (face-to-face)?
- Things you are guilty about
- Things you are passionate about
- What really motivates you, and makes you tick

- What is missing, and what it is you really want
- Why people are "attracted" to you
- Weird coincidences and synchronistic events happening on a regular basis

Stop and listen - Contemplate, and give yourself some "me" time more often.

 Take a moment to reflect and make notes on what you have just read.

24 September: Is Positive Thinking Flawed?

FH: Refer the article "Wakey, wakey". I want them to read, think, and I think by getting them to reflect on what they read they will become even more aware in seconds. This is sort of activating themselves and really getting them to think.

ES: Definitely - and you push their boundaries without them even realizing it.

Victims of "positive thinking" make the right noises and have no clue that the universe requires balance rather than only accepting heads on the coin and rejecting tails. Positive thinking means you accept only coins with heads, because you do not need tails in your life. So you throw away all the coins with tails, and see what is left.

FH: So positive thinking is flawed. You need to acknowledge the downside and learn from it.

ES: Yes - the entire universe is in balance - why should people be lopsided? We were born with two legs rather than one for a reason. Do you want to turn your life into a complete mess? Become a positive thinking guru - the Universe will sort you out.

 How do you feel about forcing yourself to only have positive thoughts?

Have Positive Thinking Gurus got it all wrong?

Focus on the positive and you will be rich!
Focus on the positive and you will be healthy!
Focus on the positive and you will be famous!
Blah. Blah. Blah.

Hmmm

Call me a cynic (or maybe a realist, even Scottish), but....

By focusing on one side of the coin, we can often forget (even neglect) the other.

I think that becoming obsessed with POSITIVE THINKING can be a negative thing.

We need the bad times and negative experiences so that we can learn from them.

While I agree that a healthy optimistic approach to life can be an asset, some coaches I've met recently preach "positive thinking" ike a Texan Evangelist having swallowed 2 acid tabs.

Is life not about balance?

It doesn't have to be all gung ho, ra ra ra ra ra ra. Does it?
Do we not need the dark to appreciate the light?
Do we not need the bad times to appreciate the good times?

Do we not need chaos on occasion to appreciate harmony and balance?

Even on my coaching programmes and workshops I prepare people for some things they won't like. They will feel uncomfortable.

They will feel challenged, even overwhelmed on occasion, and they must be prepared to get things wrong.

By getting things wrong on occasion and managing in such a way that the impact is minimal, the lesson can be substantial and for many can be a real breakthrough.

We need to experience the other side of the coin, to keep us in check and to give us a good grounding and grasp on reality. Yes many of us like our egos stroked occasionally with compliments, but if we got compliments all the time, and no constructive criticism, would you not begin to sense that something was wrong?

I think I fall into the category of "pragmatic optimist".

What do you think? Is "Positive Thinking" over-rated?

Do "negative experiences" (or should I say reflecting on them) help us to grow more than our positive experiences?

 Take a moment to reflect and make notes on what you have just read.

Later:

FH: I think I'm getting a better grip on all of this now as I look back on events this summer and try and put it into context:

- We are all part of a whole.
- We come to earth to experience "life" and evolve and contribute to "others" to help them evolve
- We forget where we came from.
- During life we experience various events to help us remember where we came from, and why we are here.
- Many people unfortunately let ego and "life" get better of them and distract them (conceal them) from the TRUTH.

- The journey in life is recognition of this, and how we can evolve, and help others and we seek to be loved by others to help us "integrate" back into the "whole" once that is done, then the journey completes and we return to "source"

ES: Exactly spot on. Which is why, when you leave a sick body behind, you failed to integrate and you return for another go at the same issues. We are meant to leave a healthy body behind as proof that we "passed" this leg of the journey.

 How has your view of the world changed since you started reading this book?

26 September: Expansion and Awareness

FH: Here is something interesting that happened.   Last week I bumped into an old friend, Colin. After Wendy and I got married and moved down south for a few years, Colin and I lost contact. He and his family now stay about seven miles from us. Of course we said things like "we must get together to catch up", but I did not feel that either of us meant it, and I forgot about it.

Last night Wendy and I went to our local pub for a meal, and there were Colin and his wife Margaret. We could not be rude when they asked to join us. Despite that, we had a terrific evening. Around 11pm Wendy and Margaret wanted to go home, but Colin and I still wanted to chat. The women left.

Before I could even say "so, how's things", Colin started telling me about an affair he was having. I first thought that it was the beer speaking, but Colin was really pouring his heart out.

Margaret is a sales representative and her job takes her away from home for most of the week. That leaves Colin, a school teacher, taking care of their two boys. It now appears that Colin has been having an affair with a fellow teacher for three years.

This was where the real AWARENESS thing kicked in. Even though I had a few drinks I became aware of him being OPPOSITE me, telling me about how him and his wife not getting on and how guilty he was feeling.

The more he spoke, the more I recognized and valued my position and relationship with Wendy.

I was an observer and listener, and able to see the massive contrast in what Wendy and I have.

ES: Interesting how one moment you are part of a situation and then suddenly you become aware that you are detached and you see/hear/feel so much more, and you know it is a process which happened suddenly over a long time. It gives you a different perspective on time and space.

It is different, and it helps you understand that you are not "better" than others, just different. And it is true - it does give so much more depth to what you have.

FH: Colin poured his heart out for the next 90 minutes. I didn't comment, offer advice, or JUDGE him. I think he wanted a reaction, but I couldn't comment or offer advice as I felt that I was in an opposite position.

ES: And you did not judge him because you have reached a point where you understand and practice unconditional love.

FH: It really helped me to realize how much I love Wendy and how many roller-coasters we've been on, and how we give whereas Colin and Margaret don't give. Their attention is on themselves. It was a real LIVE LESSON in AWARENESS and APPRECIATION OF "MY" WORLD if that makes sense. I just recognized the value of the incident, as if to practice all the skills learned to date that you've shared with me.

ES: It does make sense. It is a different feeling - where your emotions are in the background, not because you are pushing them away, but because you have mastered them. Interesting how you start to see "through" people without even trying.

 Now that you have realized that the people around you are your teachers, do you see them in a different light?

27 September: And the Day Came .
. .

ES: "And the day came when the risk to remain tight in a bud was more painful than the risk it took to blossom." Anais Nin

1 October: End of a Spiral?

ES: Somebody wrote this morning that only a courageous/totally crazy 16-year-old would tackle what I am doing now - she meant it as a compliment.

FH: I know the feeling. It feels as though I'm climbing Everest carrying a small car on my back, but I "feel" the spiral - and sense it around me (if that makes sense).

ES: It does. But you love every minute of it, even when it is scary. What difference does it make to your experience - knowing about the spiral?

FH: It helps me to visualize/conceptualize the workload/resistance will get easier, and why/where I am in the development of the current phase. It's interesting though, it keeps alternating from wide base to small pinnacle and from small base to wide pinnacle - if that makes sense? Do you envisage the spirals with a wide base going up? Or like a tornado with a small base winding up outwards?

ES: It is both. The spiral with the wide base and small pinnacle is more about becoming aware of some duality in you, and then you fight against yourself until the tension becomes overwhelming and you "snap" and become whole. The small base and wide pinnacle is the result, which is creativity exploding from that wholeness – an amazing experience.

 Think of your own intense experiences. Go back to when the experience started with an insignificant issue that grew and became a real problem for you. To give a true example: a British couple went on holiday in France and had an argument about following directions on a map.

Three years later the wife stated that incident as the

starting point of the decline in their marriage and her reason for obtaining a divorce.

Plot your experience on a spiral, considering the intensity of your own emotions along the way. Can you see how the two conflicting parts inside you became stronger and made you more emotional until it was finally resolved?

2 October: Escape and Evasion

FH: Hans in South Africa appears to be avoiding me, not returning my calls or emails or Skype messages (and pleading poverty). He appears to be choosing to ignore me

ES: Here is a lesson from my mineworker days: grab him where it hurts and his heart and mind will follow. You have to do that with some people - and this guy has no poverty except in spirit - he just bought a new car and is counting on you being in a different country.

FH: He mentioned two months ago he was going on holiday in October - I bet he's forgotten he told me.

 There are times when letting sleeping dogs lie only delays the inevitable. What are you putting off, knowing that you are only making your own problems worse?

Who's your Hero?

I loved my Dad.

He was amazing.

He showed me how to play snooker and Billiards. (Oh, the power of a "cannon")
His trick shots were fantastic. The one with the 3 balls and a match still earns me the odd free pint now and again.

No-one can knock that match down - it's funny.

As I reflect on him, I don't think I ever saw him drunk - ever.

I remember his self-winding watch - boy, did I want a watch like that when I grew up.

He could draw like Rolf Harris and Tony Hart and inspired me to draw too.

My Dad also had a passion for wood work and crafted the Queen's coronation coach and coronation throne out of wood - they were stunning.

He taught kids how to do the same, at our local community center, and he even sent off two scripts to Disney to be turned into movies, but alas, they were not to be.

He'd do anything for anyone, and had a dry sense of humor.

He died of cancer when I was 19, and he was 57, and I miss him - lots.

I got married to Wendy the following year, and we now have five kids. I wish he'd met our kids, he'd have made a great grand-dad, and the twins would have adored him.

He was my Hero.

Now, I took my son out for a few pints last weekend - our first "boys night out" together.

Scott's 18 and me, well I'm forty something.

We had a blast.

We played pool, sank a few pints and talked.

We talked, talked and talked.

It was refreshing, it was insightful and we laughed, and laughed, and yes, dare I say it, we got a tad tipsy.

At one point he just spontaneously came out with something that almost brought a tear to my eye, and I'll tell you about that in a moment...

But first...

I actually forgot about that comment until earlier this week, when I asked someone on a coaching call, who their HERO was. As it can often pay to emulate someone you look up to as a role model either in life or business, I'm sure you probably model yourself on some captain of industry, or there's someone in business you admire, you may even have gone to one of their workshops or bought their book or whatever.

Don't you? Haven't you?

Many business owners actually model their management style on a particular individual. Many coaches recommend you model yourself on someone successful in your industry who has created a successful business, or has found a unique and proven approach....why not apply that concept of modelling to other parts of your business, or life too.

Find a proven system or process that you see others implementing and working, and apply it to your business. Find a mentor, or a coach that can help you, support and offer guidance and help as and when you need it.

Do you want to know what Scott said after that 4th or 5th pint?

He turned round and said...

"You're my hero, dad".

Gulp. (That wasn't the Magners talking either.)

It was the first time he'd ever said anything like that to me, and I asked why?

"You just are".

(Now I wasn't going to push it, I was chuffed to bits he said what he said, but he was still going to pay for the curries later.)

Sometimes we all need someone to look up to, myself included. I know I've had my share of teachers, mentors and coaches over the years, and they've all made a special contribution in helping me to mould and shape who I am, and I immediately think of 4 – Angus Jones, Stewart Chalmers, Marcus Cauchi and dare I say it – Elsabe Smit.

I thank you all, and the many others I stumbled across here on The Water Cooler.

When we have a weakness or a need, you can bet there is someone out there who has a strength or solution for us.

 Take a moment to reflect and make notes on what you have just read. Think about who your hero is or who your heroes are.

1983

Let me take you back to 1983.

- Apple released their Lisa computer. IBM launched the PC XT
- Lotus 1-2-3 was launched
- Red rain fell over the UK (due to sand whipped up from the Sahara, apparently)
- Michael Jackson did his moonwalk (and later that year launched THRILLER)
- Margaret Thatcher got back into No 10
- Flash-dance and Return of the Jedi were huge box office smashes
- Pioneer 10 left the Solar System
- Red Hot Chili Peppers launched their first album

And my life was to change forever.

One Saturday in April, 1983, I was playing with friends on a beach near my home, when...

...BANG.

I felt an intense pain in my left eye.

I had been shot by a high velocity air rifle.

The blood was warm as it poured down my face, and I began to feel very, very tired, my other eye closed down, and I couldn't open it.

I had one problem. (In fact I had several problems)

- I was about 2 miles from home. (Along a rocky beach, and no transport)
- I had to get myself to a doctor quickly

- I was losing blood, lots of it – fast

The next thing I remember waking up on a hard surface unable to open my eyes, and my head all bandaged up.

Then it all went dark.

I awoke to Doctor Charisma and his immortal words:

"Good morning Fraser, your eye was bloody well mangled, and we've extracted it...

...it was a tad touch n go, and you got us all a bit excited at one point, but you'll live."

Gee thanks Doc, I thought.

I guess that was a turning point for me in more ways than one. Instead of thinking about going into the army, I had a radical rethink as to what I wanted to do with my life.

What year had a major "impact" on you, or your life?
Take a moment to reflect and make notes on what you have just read.

5 October: Say What You Do and Do What You Say

*ES: When you ask people **when** they will start up the business, this is where they often feel fear. They have their eye on "someday". For example "I want to do this when I finish working" as If starting your own business is not work. "I don't want to do it now in case I fail". Part of "when" is addressing particular fears.*

The creative process brings you a level of frustration that you've never had before. You think "I must be doing something wrong. This is not how it works" and then suddenly-you are not even aware of it-it is there, it is in place, and you can't keep up with what you need to do.

FH: Wendy picked up an article in a newspaper on Friday. She said we were talking about unemployment and there is no good news about and it is affecting the businesses in Scotland. I was surprised that she said that.

Hans in South Africa is a really interesting one. Instead of three months behind, he is now in for 57 months. Instead of owing £1 500 in back money, he now owes £60 000 under his contractual obligations. However, I will tell him tomorrow "Look, it is up to you whether you wish to proceed or not but I strongly recommend that you bring things up to date, because I've bent and twisted the conditions, I've revised the contract, and I have actually let slide the 30 day clause on three occasions. However, give me a proposal on how you want to continue, how serious you are and how you are going to do it. Or I'm prepared to negotiate an exit from the £60,000, five year contract."

ES: I was just wondering about you letting slip the 30 days clause. How does that affect your legally? Can he say "You've done it before, therefore I can expect it again"?

FH: No, because it's at my discretion. I have permitted it on the understanding that he was doing certain activities that he's not done. The money becomes irrelevant. I just want to work with people who are prepared to roll up their sleeves and get stuck in. If they do the tasks, they make progress. When we ooze confidence through everything we do, we attract business.

He keeps pushing it back to me. He said "What is the solution? What do you suggest, how do we deal with it?" He is making it my problem when it's his problem.

I'm saying "No, this is it. If you want to continue, tell me how you're going to do it. If you don't want to continue, you can negotiate a way out." I think that's fair.

ES: You negated a universal law that says "Say what you do and do what you say". If you apply this law, nothing can go wrong because then you are true to yourself.

 Here is that law again. How many of your problems have been caused by you saying one thing and then doing another thing? And yes, there are times when you need to compromise. We are not talking about that. We are talking about you getting clarity in your own mind about what you want to do. Even a "wrong" decision is a good decision because it steers you into a direction.

FH: That's very logical and very true. A number of other people don't do what they say and yet they appear to be free from any ramifications or get pulled up for it.

ES: It might not happen in the way you think or the way they expect. Let me put it this way: they think they get away with a business transaction, and they have no idea how that impacts on a relationship that breaks up - on the surface there is no link between the two incidents. Or they have a car accident and they don't relate it to a business transaction. Or their children do something incredibly stupid and they don't relate that to the business transaction. There is an irrational logic in what happens to us.

 Your life does not consist of compartments. Everything in your life relates to everything else. You cannot escape that. Can you think of your own examples where you took a brave step in one area and got rewarded in another area of your life?

There are two levels of planning in life. There is a plan that you can put in place - the business plan, the marketing plan, the financial plan or whatever plan - with its targets and objectives.

You will meet all of those and think you are brilliant at planning and you have no idea why it is that your life falls apart. Whatever happens in your life that you experience as "negative" has got to do with a plan at a completely different level.

When you do plans and targets and objectives on paper, for example, you apply your mind and use your brain. But when you live your life, you use your heart and your soul. People might think "I am getting away with murder in business" and they would have no idea why a completely different area of their life is falling apart.

FH: I can see that. With a number of people that have been around me this year, I have noticed their reason for being around me has not necessarily been for the benefit of a two-way relationship. They've been somewhat selfish.

This is an interesting journey as I put my little plan together. It's beginning to not only grow on me, but it is becoming more of a reality. People are coming into my life to test me, for want of a better word. I keep looking to see what they are contributing, what is the benefit, what is the lesson. Those are the two things. They are either helping me to get closer to my goal or they are helping me to get further away from my goal. And if they get me further away from my goal, why? And if they help me closer to my goal, I'm hopefully helping them recognize the value of what they are offering, so that they can offer this to other people as well.

ES: Think about the time lag. On the one hand you get better at recognizing how things happen and why they happen as they are happening. On the other hand, there is a necessity for you to live and experience an entire situation, and then look back, rather than get the message while it's happening.

 Life is about first living it and resolving the emotion. This is frustrating because we go through experiences that we feel make no sense, and we would love to fast forward and "get" the lesson or wisdom, then get back and make the experience easier for ourselves. What experience are you currently having where you don't understand the sense or reason for it?

FH: Well, I've certainly lived and experienced lots of negative stuff over the last 41 years. I've definitely done a lot of reflection as well. I think you become more aware of the lessons.

You need to live through the experience and learn from that and apply it to the next step. It's almost as if you're walking across a bridge and the bridge is only being completed with every bloody footstep you are taking. That is so frustrating because I'm a guy who goes "Ta, ta, ta, ta, ta, okay fine, bang, let's go"

ES: Yes, it is frustrating when on the one hand you want to just be at peace and be yourself, right in this moment, and you know that the future is something you are still creating, and you know that the past is a memory that you are putting behind you, which means right now is important.

But old habits die hard, and now that you've got new knowledge, a new approach, a new awareness, you are getting more and more keen to know what's in the future. It's a bit of a contradiction. And it's frustrating that now is far more important than the future.

FH: I recognized this when we spoke on Saturday morning. Two things have been significant. One has been my accident when I lost my eye and the other is my father. These two things are either in my dreams or I go off and I wonder and contemplate for a split second or maybe a fraction of a minute when I am contemplating other issues I am dealing with. I keep being drawn back either to my accident or to my father standing with a snooker cue in his favorite blue jumper. I'm just curious why these two metaphors keep appearing nowadays.

ES: And both of them relate to a particular time in your life which was a transitional time for you?

FH: Yes. That is fair to say.

ES: So they are taking you back to that time, but also reminding you that where you are now is different from that time. There are similarities and there is a difference. You are becoming aware of that.

FH: I understand that. It is almost referring back to the point you made earlier that we need the memory to recall the experience - it's almost like a before and after. We need to do the comparison from the old to the now to acknowledge the progress from the past in the now in order to help mold and shape our future in going forward.

ES: Yes.

FH: So by doing the comparison and recalling the memory of my father or my accident, I am defining the lesson.

ES: Yes. The experience is saying to you "Can you remember when that happened? What space where you in at the time? How did you feel at the time? How did you look at yourself, the people around you, the future, the past, at the time? You are in a similar

185

space now but compare what you were there to what you are now. There is a point of reference for you".

FH: I feel a lot more integrated, a lot more whole, than I was then. I don't say that lightly, I say that because I reflect back to the experiences that I have had over the last 20, 30, 40 years. Without those experiences I wouldn't be who I am now. I would not have shaped myself to be where I am now, but it makes me who I am.

ES: That's right.

We live our life in cycles. Each cycle consists of a phase of complete insecurity while things take shape, then security where we know exactly what to expect, followed by insecurity while we approach the end of the cycle and the beginning of the next cycle.

These cycles last for 7-9 years. Looking back at your own life and the major changes you have gone through, where are you in your cycle?

6 October: Action and Reaction

FH: I feel really low, down and crappy today after my chat with Hans in South Africa on Skype early this morning.

ES: Why do you choose to feel like that?

FH: Two things.

This is what he said: "Basically leave things where we are at the moment."

I said "My concerns are that under the terms of the agreement, £9 600 is owed up until end of September less the £3 600 you've paid = £6 000.

The revised cash flow payments that I agreed to help you with by reducing the £1 300 to £400, there are still 2 months owing on that (excluding October) = £800.

I'm suggesting you bring that latter up to date BEFORE you go on holiday, and then we can decide after you come back. I'm sure you'd prefer to pay £800 as opposed to £6 000 - I'm trying to help you here.

If you wish to continue thereafter, we need to stick to a firm plan of action, or if you prefer I'm happy to negotiate an exit."

He responded "Sorry I am having connection probs. I will think about over the holiday and chat when I get back."

I said "I'm confused. So are you saying that you want to go on holiday without paying what's owed, and then decide whether you wish to continue? If you were me, what would you do?"

ES: *Convenient connection problems!*

FH: In all the correspondence he wants me to find a solution to HIS problem, so I sent this:

"Hi Hans

Further to our Skype chat earlier today, I'm disappointed you want to leave things as they are without resolving them before you go on holiday, and thus further increase your indebtedness.

We had an agreement in place. Despite repeated requests to bring payments up to date, my offer to ease your cash flow and to save yourself added expenditure, as of today's date (6th October).

I would also like to draw your attention to Clause XD on page 12 which I am entitled to exercise under the terms of the agreement.

Despite my continued support, you are in breach of the agreement by virtue of failing to pay monies due.

I look forward to your proposals/payment to address the above no later than 9th October.

Failure to do so, will consider the agreement terminated, and the matter will be passed to my legal team.

Yours faithfully

Fraser J. Hay"

ES: So you gave his problem back to him.

FH: Yup, but I feel crappy, as I hate "bad blood" and pride myself on my relationships with people. I don't think he's going to just roll over and pay me (and I don't think he's going to WANT to continue, as there will be ill feeling from his side) but I genuinely think I've given him enough assistance and opportunities to come good and he chose not to.

(I'm also a little concerned that he might try and damage my brand in South Africa as a revenge thingy or that he well p****d off, but it is all of his own making) - it is just not sitting nicely with me, before I go off on holiday. I've done everything in my power and as per the agreement to help the guy, but it appears he saw me as a meal ticket who would do everything for him, and I suspect he feels I haven't done what I'd said I would - CLEARLY NOT THE CASE, but I still feel flat about it all.

ES: What would have been the outcome if you had gone on holiday first and then dealt with it?

FH: Probably the same, except the amount he owes me would be more.

ES: So would the timing have been better for you if you did this sooner or later?

FH: He chose the date and time to speak today, yet said it was inconvenient for him to talk, and then chose to have connection problems, so he is avoiding discussing the core issues, and I felt enough is enough.

ES: Now here is a question. You say you feel crap about it. Where does the feeling come from? From him aiming bad vibes at you, or from inside of you going out at him? It is only tricky because you would not normally ask the question, and your answer is the key to how to deal with it.

FH: It's certainly not the commercial aspect of it. I think I'm questioning too why I feel bad when he brought it on himself.

ES: Don't think about the why. Think of the where in your body and the how. Is the centre of the feeling inside of your body, or is it outside of your body? I.e. is it like a wave coming at you, or like a wave originating from you?

FH: I think I feel crap because whichever way he goes now or whatever step he takes, the relationship is now in effect over as the mutual trust has gone and the faith in each other appears to have gone too. He won't want to work with me because he feels uncomfortable with the situation he got himself in and will blame me. So I don't see him as being a good advocate for the business either if he has the wrong frame of mind, won't follow the system, and won't honor his obligations - all wrong signals to give off to someone you're trying to build a business with.

ES: You are hard work!

FH: Do you mean hard to get along with?

ES: Not at all hard to get along with.

FH: Or hard work and effort to achieve the things you want/I offer?

ES: Not that either - stop feeling guilty - you do that to yourself.

FH: But I think that he saw me as a potential meal ticket and that I would provide the solutions for him. I think he was looking for a magic pill, and didn't realize just how much effort is really required in it all, and I suspect that is what he has to face up to now.

ES: I mean stop using your head and tell me where you feeling is most intense - where in your body, and is it a wave of emotion coming at you or going out from you?

FH: I think it is mainly my head and shoulders.

ES: OK, and coming at you or going out from you?

FH: Going out - (I think)

ES: OK. Jeez - that was hard work!

FH: I just hate creating bad blood between people.

 No matter what we do, we cannot avoid conflict. That is part of our life blood, and the reason why we are alive. We can only improve the quality of our lives by acknowledging that and working with rather than against the conflict. Which conflict situation have you been avoiding or delaying?

ES: If you experienced the waves of emotion as originating from him, you would have needed some protection. But the waves are originating from you and that is easier to deal with. So here are some options.

Focus for a few minutes on breathing - when you feel like that, you tend to forget to breathe. All the oxygen goes to your upper lungs and the rest of your body goes without oxygen. You are not even aware of it, but it keeps your body tense. You can breathe in as deeply as you can, and then breathe out everything. A few of those breaths will take you to a different state of consciousness where your body will start to relax.

Or you can try something else which really works every time. Write him a letter - preferably by hand. Forget the business tone etc. and spell out to him in detail - I mean as much detail as you want and can manage - how you feel about him, his work, his performance, what he has done to your mind, body and soul, and everything you would want to say to him if there were no boundaries at all.

Once you have written down everything, decide what you want to do with the letter - burn it, cut it in tiny pieces, flush it down the toilet, whatever – as long as you don't mail it.

FH: I did that at the weekend in preparation for my call to him today, but thought it too long and emotional - but was brilliant for getting it all out my system.

I like our chats, because you go the extra mile by demonstrating a thorough knowledge of the subject. And the more I get to know you, the more I can see similar topics/subjects that you are well versed in...Quantum physics, spirituality, Christianity, kabala, etc. And you have well balanced total perspective on things free from religion, dogma or conditioning or forced beliefs. You have come to your own conclusions based on your own perceptions, observations and experiences because you lived it, and experienced it and UNDERSTAND it – you are not avoiding the explanation (which most people do).

The more I think about it, the more relaxed I'm becoming with Hans in South Africa as I have done nothing wrong. He was trying to get me to solve his problem, and I have in fact reminded him it's his problem. This is one of the few times in my life where I have the upper hand, and I think I'm putting myself in his shoes (wrongly) as I've been there so many times before.

 Giving problems back to the owners of the problems sounds easy, but take courage. Which of your issues are with you purely because you chose the lesser evil of carrying that conflict and passing it back to its owner?

This is especially the case where we allow people to use emotional blackmail because they are in an emotional rather than a business relationship with us.

7 October: Drawing the Line

FH: This is what Hans in South Africa sent me this morning:

"Hi Fraser,

The last thing I want is to part on bad terms.
I always have and still consider you to be a mentor and a positive source for me to achieve my financial goals. So after giving my predicament some thought today I have come up with an idea.

What if you could refer two coaching program clients to me each month.I could then conduct the coaching program for each of these clients, with you retaining the full fee for one of the clients and myself retaining the fee for the other.

This would achieve a couple of things.

- *The fee that you retain for the coaching course that I conduct would cover my monthly fees.*
- *I would also retain fees for the other course which would generate an income for me.*
- *The training and confidence that I will develop over time will eventually lead to me being more proficient and self-sustainable*
- *During this time we could work a lot closer together and develop the South African arm of your business and in return my business.*
- *It is the actual closing of the sale that I think I am having difficulty with, and I am confident this can be resolved.*

I do not understand your apparent anger towards my current situation. Yes I agree it is a setback and creates problems for yourself, but at no time have I downgraded or lost faith in your business. It is purely the fact that my lack of cash flow is causing difficulties with my family life and the development of my business.

I get the impression that you think, that all I am doing is trying to rip you off, this is certainly not the case. I want more than anything for all of this too succeed, But I just cannot afford to keep throwing money at something that is not working.

I am happy to keep working with you to come to an agreeable solution, but my current financial situation needs to be taken into consideration.

I look forward to moving forward and further developing our working relationship and friendship. Please do not consider me as an enemy. Because I am not.

I do appreciate everything you have done and want to pay that back, but I just cannot do it financially at the moment.

I look forward to hearing from you soon.

Kind Regards,

Hans"

He is now irritating me by not only making his problem mine rather than finding a solution for himself. He wants me to be the solution too. Putting the money issue aside, I've really been trying hard to see the lesson in all of this.

I've just drafted a reply to Hans's email. It's been hard not to get heated or "lose it" as I've written this.

"Hi Hans

Many thanks for your email.

I'm sorry, Hans, but it appears that you want to me to provide the solution to your problem(s). It also appears that you want me to do the work to help you pay off the money you owe me. Unfortunately, I'm not prepared to do that.

I have always been fair, open and direct with you and you have confirmed this many times in our email exchanges over the last few months.

You now want me to refer coaching clients to you eight months into an agreement which you signed to use the skills, tools and resources you've had access to (that I would also use) to generate the leads and sales you want and need to repay the monies owed to me.

You have also confirmed that it's not me, or the systems, but that you lack the ability and the resources to meet your obligations or to maintain the terms of our agreement.

It's on that basis that I terminate the agreement forthwith.

The basis for terminating the agreement is simply a business decision, nothing more, nothing less. You have confirmed that you are unable to honor the agreement, and it would be foolish for both of us to continue under the circumstances.

You state that you have reached a point financially, where you can't carry on. I too, recognize my commitment to you, and the investment I have continued to make, but I am not prepared to continue to act as your "bank". While you state you do not wish to end our relationship or terminate the agreement, by virtue of your non-compliance with the agreement, I now terminate the agreement forthwith.

I still like you and I know you will honour the termination clause to ensure there is no ill feeling on either side. I look forward to your proposals for repaying what it is contractually owed under the full terms of the agreement.

Failure to do so will result in the matter being passed to our legal representatives in Johannesburg, South Africa.

I also write to formally request that you cease promoting my company in South Africa and online, and enclose an "Undertakings" agreement to be signed and returned by the due date.

Thank you in advance.

Yours faithfully.
Fraser J. Hay"

I know I've been right, but I felt really uncomfortable about the whole thing - not so much because of the financial aspect - I liked Hans. I thought I trusted him. But as Wendy says, I've been too nice, not on one, two or three occasions, but all the way back to January. She says he's continued to take advantage of me. He hasn't proven his willingness to go the extra mile.

ES: That's right, and it's not your problem.

FH: I have another lady, Catherine, who is based in Dublin. She signed up and paid me every month, regular as clockwork. She's been really, really good with payment, but she's done nothing. She phoned me about half an hour ago to apologize because she was now taking the business seriously.
I said "Don't apologize because you want to take it seriously. Before you say anything, do you mind if I say something that might offend or upset you?"

She said "No, carry on."

I said "You signed up for the opportunity because the existing business relationship you are in is not good or strong and you wanted a backup and a back door in case your existing relationship went haywire. You have the agreement with me, you have kept that on the back boiler while you worked on the existing business but it got to such a point that you recognized that what I have is bigger and better than your existing business and now you want to make amends. That's great, but my concern is that you come up with this great bash of momentum over the next two weeks, and then it falls flat again. You need to convince me that you are the right person for the job."

I could not believe that I was saying it. It was almost like an identical situation to Hans in South Africa whereby one signed and paid all the time and has not done any work, the other one has done some payment and some work and not taken it at all seriously.

The other guys are just cracking on and doing it.

I was trying to be dispassionate. I was trying not to let my emotions get the better of me. I spoke with absolute clarity on a whole host of issues that I probably would have brought up as part of my emotions. I just could not believe how I was able to pick up on all the points and issues, and she agreed with everything I said, and apologized unreservedly.

I have just sent her an e-mail confirming our conversation and some action points that she's got to do.

As for Hans in South Africa, he just sounds like a right chancer, the more I think about it. I think he's got three other businesses as well. I can only suspect that the other business interests he has as well are not going too well either.

I think my response to Hans in South Africa is going to be very short and very blunt. I am not going to give it more thought until I come back from holiday.

This lady, Catherine in Dublin, phoned me up out of the blue. She had a Eureka moment where she has recognized the power of what she's got. She's just got eight people signed up. She wants to apologize for not doing what she had to do, and I am thinking bloody hell, this is weird.

 Each one of us generates our own energy. We each have the innate ability to do that. The more we believe in ourselves, the more we master the ability to create our own energy and determine our own future. If we allow people to be dependent on us rather than use their own energy, we don't do anyone a favor.

We may think we do good by helping people, but often we make matters worse, not only for ourselves but for those people as well, by doing things on their behalf.

Who are the people that take energy from you because they do not trust themselves, or because they believe you owe it to them to do things for them that they in fact can do for themselves?

What can you do to spend some time getting these people to help themselves before you move on and focus on your own life again?

8 October: Shaking the Tree

FH: It would appear Hans in South Africa was only tip of the iceberg and the others have just come about very, very quickly in a matter of days. You couldn't make this stuff up! But you are right. They may mutter under their breath and call me whatever when they put the phone down, but they are all eating humble pie. I advised my solicitor to follow through with each of them, giving them seven days to sort stuff out in time for me to come to back to see who's in and who's out.

I had no idea my week was going to be this chaotic, and I certainly didn't plan for it, but one thing appears to have led to another. They each synchronistically contacted ME about their position - almost like a GROUP GUILT thing - very weird.

And the solicitor says I have a 100% cast iron case. I guess this shakeout was long, long overdue. And you are right, it's got nothing to do with my integrity – it's theirs, but they are using my good nature against me. I'm learning – slowly.

ES: *And I am watching you climb up the spiral - the last part is always most intense. And it is great when you reach the top and feel that calmness where you can think completely clear - like a rubber band snapping and the tension is gone. Enjoy your holiday!*

 Are people using your good nature against you by taking you for granted? When you become aware of your own value, it becomes easier to remind others of what you are worth and how much you are prepared to give.

18 October: Reminder of Gratitude

FH: The holiday actually gave Wendy and me loads of time to catch up as we both lead very busy working lives. We spoke and spoke and spoke all week.

In retrospect, I used the holiday to see the Colin/Margaret incident as the catalyst for me to appreciate everything I have and to recognize the romantic setting as an ideal situation to feel gratitude for the special relationship Wendy and I have.

I also told Wendy about spirals. I think that I've just climbed a mountain that was symbolized by being on top of Montecatini Alto. Looking down Tuscany Valley, I felt I was ready for the next climb, more-so because the week before I had to discuss everything with Wendy about dealing with people that owed me money. The break helped me to get rid of, or more specifically to DEAL with stuff I was avoiding.

I also did a drawing of the leaning tower of Pisa – the first time in twenty years that I felt like drawing, and the finished item was pretty good, even if I say so myself. It also made me realize that when working for yourself, it is very easy to forget what you really enjoy.

ES: Wendy and you are tied with what I see as a "silver cord" - what happens to you, also happens to her - she is changing at the same rate as you - maybe a step or two behind. You got it right - a lesson in what judgment is and is not. Judgment is discretion - decide what resonates with your true loving self. Judgment is not judging other people whose path is different from yours.

 Let me give you an example. One person is in a marriage relationship that has had its lows and highs, but the marriage is still solid after a few decades.

Another person is in stable love relationship but twice divorced. Which one is right? Or rather, which one is right for you?

What if the person in the long-standing marriage relationship is dishonest in business, and the twice divorced one is always honest, even it if it painful?

ES: Discretion means deciding which option sits well with you based on your personal values. Judgment means deciding the one who does like you is right and the other is wrong because it is the opposite of what you believe and value. This is a VERY difficult thing to understand because we live in a society that is based on judging others - but you now understand what it is about.

The other interesting thing about you drawing after 20 years - we grow up, then make life choices that take us to a dark place, and then we reach a turning point and wake up and see the light. Then we go back to the point where we made the life choices. We remain the same person, but we are "awake" and quite different. For some people like your friend Colin that life choice was getting married and he is probably now at the turning point. For you it was not about getting married - you made other choices that had you with your back against the wall, and you woke up and are now back on your path.

And the very difficult thing is to know this and see your child make that dark choice. You have to respect it and stand by with the plasters and tissues, because there is nothing you can do to prevent it. If you do try and prevent it with your good intentions, you mess up your relationship with the child and you just delay their inevitable path - but that is another lesson in love.

 What life choices have you made that have determined your life path? Looking back, would you have made a different choice? Would you want to take the experience of making life choices away from others based on your life?

19 October: All Choices have Consequences

ES: I can spend a whole day explaining how stupid it is to "try" and do things. When you try things you don't do anything. You don't do it, and you don't not do it either. You just shoot yourself in the foot all the time.

FH: When you try to do something, you don't do it?

ES: Yes, but you also don't not do it.
If I have my mobile phone in my hand and I hold it out to you and I say to you "Now, try and take my phone" what would you do?

FH: I would take it.

ES: Then you did not try. You actually took it.

FH: I am not getting this one. Are you saying that when we use the word "try", we limit the outcome?

ES: Yes. I am standing in front of you. I have my phone in my hand. I say to you "Fraser, try and take my phone". You have three options. You can either take it, or you can not take it, or you can do nothing. When you do nothing, it means you are trying, because you have decided that you won't succeed.

FH: Fascinating. In terms of many parents, when the kid is in the swimming pool and the parent says "Come on, try," it is not a case of trying, it is a matter of "Just do it".

ES: Exactly. Believe and then expect.

FH: We like new ideas. I was reflecting on that while on holiday. I was daydreaming and looking across the Tuscany valley and I thought wait a minute, we have beliefs about things. Our imaginations come up with ideas. We then add our feelings to these ideas and our imagination to cement them and bring them into manifestation. However, quite often the emotions are incorrectly charged-we have negative emotions which then affect the solidity of the manifestation. We need to be consciously aware to stop thinking negatively and to start thinking positively because the prior conditioning of our beliefs affects the manifested world that we are creating on a regular basis.

ES: That is spot on.

 What have you tried in your life and failed with? Can you now see why you failed? How about you stop trying and just do it? What obstacle can you remove first?

FH: Colin and I have known each other for years, but we have never been that close. He called me last night and I said "Have you told your wife?" No. I asked "Are you going to stop the affair with the other woman?" He said no.

I have observed that Margaret is also very selfish. I thought they were right for each other. I said to Wendy we don't need to judge them or do anything or say anything to alter the path that they are on. They will come to that point themselves, by virtue of their own behaviour, and they are creating their own reality with their own lessons to learn. Even if it does result in a split, that split has been predetermined by their actions. No matter what I do or say, I don't think it will have a material difference or effect on the outcome.

ES: It is true. I would not be surprised if he comes and talks to you again later on just because of the way you dealt with it. People come into this world totally innocent and they believe the world owes them something. They grow up and expect their parents to provide everything for them. When they become adults they make their life choices.

Without any exception, every person makes a life choice that takes them to a very dark place, whether you marry the wrong person or decide that you will define yourself by means of illness or you choose to have an accident or you fail in business, or whatever you do, you make that choice deliberately in your early adulthood.

In many areas of your life you remain true to yourself, but in that one area of your life you become totally untrue to where you are. You literally go to hell. Its only when you can't get in any deeper that you think "There has got to be more to life than this". This is where you reach a turning point. This man is probably very close to the turning point from the hell that he created for himself. Somehow he sensed that you have the ability to help him come back to his true self again.

 Have you ever listened to another person talking about their problems without judging or giving advice? Observing the person's struggle with their two opposing inner voices is fascinating and far more constructive than attempting to resolve their issues or telling them where they have gone wrong.

FH: What he kept saying was how strong his feelings were for this other woman and they get on so well and there is a buzz between them.

I kept saying "what about your wife?" And he said it is not the same. I asked him what was missing. He said it was all the fun and excitement.

I said "Are you saying your wife is boring?" He said no, it is not that. I asked what it was then. He said the other woman is more exciting.

I said "So you've got something that you don't want to let go of but you also want something that is even more exciting, so you want both?" He said yes.

I said "Well then, don't you have a decision to make?" He said "Yes, but I don't want to make that decision. I am not prepared to make that decision."

I said "I am not here to influence you one way or the other. You have to live with the consequences. You have to decide in your own time. But everything you do happens for a reason. The reason tends to be that we need a bit of introspection. We need to reflect on our actions and what we do and how it affects other people. You may be thinking about yourself and your wife at the moment, but you also have two sons. You may want to think about that. I'm not trying to hold you back or force you. You can do whatever you want. Decide for yourself. You are in control."

When I said those words, "You are in control", they really resonated with me. His wife works away from home all week, coming home on a Friday night. When she is away, he has his own routine. He is in control. When Margaret returns home after being away all week, she is in the house for two days, and then Colin does not have that control. He has had this continuous black and white cyclical pattern of doing his own thing and not being able to do his own thing.

 Notice how Fraser gains insight by not judging, but reminding Colin he is in control of his own life. When you give another person the freedom to make their own decisions, you learn from the experience yourself.

He loves her because of their lifestyle (Margaret's job pays well) and the control he has, but he resents her when she is at home in his space during the weekend, when he is not able to do what he wants to do. He is yearning for a fantasy. He wants to benefit from both worlds but he is not prepared to change what he's got because it suits his routine perfectly.

But enough about them. I did find the whole holiday quite refreshing. I think I have mastered the theory now. I have a firm grounding and understanding of the concepts and methodologies. I have recognized all the concepts and put them into action. The next piece of the equation will be to find that zone, or space, or the void, or the zero point where I can master my thoughts and communicate or call upon consciousness or spirit or whatever we want to call it. How do you describe that point or that place?

ES: It is a different space. Initially, when you get introduced to it, it is scary, because you know something is quite different here and you don't quite know how to handle it. That is where it feels like things are really getting out of hand. You experienced things getting really tenser by the day in the two weeks or so before you went on holiday. That is when you start thinking "Do I really want this in my life?"

Then something literally snaps into place. Then you ask "How can it ever be anything other than this?" This happens in a split second but also over a long period of time, if that make sense. The way I have been given to visualize it is the spiral.

You start to the bottom of the spiral. As you work your way up, emotionally it gets more and more intense, until you reach the top. When you are in the exact right space at the top, it is as if you make a jump from the bottom of the spiral right to the top in a split second. You work your way up, but at the same time you are not getting anywhere, until you make that jump which is the quantum leap.

 Take a moment to reflect and make notes on what you have just read.
Have you noticed this spiral effect in your own life?

FH: You said you need to find the stillness to create the emptiness to allow the other things to fall into the emptiness.

ES: That's right. There has got to be a void first. You have been fast tracked on a path where you have been cleaning out a lot of things. You have been chucking away many things that you no longer need. You have now experienced that void. You also experienced the stuff that comes in to fill that void. It is not finished yet. The next two or three weeks will be really exciting for you in that sense. I don't know why I said that, but watch this space anyway. It is not something that you just get. It comes into your consciousness when it has already happened.

It grows over a period of time. When you initially become aware of it, it is a bit of hide and seek. You find that space, like you did when you were in the library while on holiday. You will have more of those experiences, and you will be aware of how it feels. You will get to a point where you realize that you think you go and look for it, but you don't go and look for it, because you are there all the time.

FH: I was trying to explain something to Wendy when we were on holiday, and I use the Kabala analogy. I said "imagine we are a cup or a vessel, and we can pour in the desire to activate the essence of what we want to achieve. We can replace the word desire with light. Quite often, we are too busy dealing with children, work, sales, money, and all sorts of stuff. We are not able to do the visualization and focus on the spirit. The human aspect of it which is the empty vessel, where we pour in the light or desire. Our problems tend to fill up the cup and we tend to get bogged down with that being the content of the vessel as opposed to emptying that out to allow the other positive things to come in.

I explained to Wendy that I was at a point, maybe 6 to 8 weeks ago, when I wanted to do something new. It was the fear of going to the next stage and slapping people over the head that was stalemating me. Terra incognita was the phrase that kept appearing from a number of different sources to tell me and wake me up. It was your explanation that got me to recognize that and to take things to the next level.

23 October: Always Dark Before the Dawn

FH: This has been a weird funny week. While I've achieved a lot, it feels real "down" and "empty" and I don't mean just as an anticlimax to being on holiday - maybe it's the weather, it is weird though.

ES: Interesting. Ever thought about the process of creation?
It takes a huge amount of energy which you are not even aware of, and then when stuff start to manifest it is a bit of a let-down because you are tired.

You have spent the past few months thinking and mulling over this business start-up product, and now it is happening and it feels like nothing.

FH: I took the afternoon off. The kids were away so Wendy and I had lunch out. I spoke about the kabala and the cup/vessel that needs to be empty for it to be filled up again. And I do believe that - but there is something else too. I am pondering it.

ES: It is like working for years to get a degree and you go through the ceremony and you wake up the next morning with a hangover and you still have to do the dishes - nothing changed but everything changed.

 Can you recall a massive change in your life that now, looking back, seems to be on a smaller scale that you experienced it?

When you are empty there is enough space for a tsunami to come in. Sometimes your attention is taken up by one thing while another thing is developing. And the awareness is still very much there. If you talk to like-minded people they will confirm that they have the same experience of "less aware".

It feels like being on a beach and the water pulls back and you think the wave disappeared. You are more in tune with the earth energy and waves coming and going.

 Take a moment to reflect and make notes on what you have just read.

As your awareness grows, you will go through these spells where you think you have done really well but suddenly things seem to be awfully quiet. That is when you should look out for the next wave of action and activity in your life.

That is also the time when you panic and think you have done something wrong – when that happens, remind yourself of the creation cycle. You create for six units of time and rest for one unit of time. A unit of time can be anything from a day to a year.

FH: I notice the SILENCE from the naughty ones.

If there's one thing I learned from you, I think it's not to rush things, and let them just unfold, but also not be surprised. The unfoldment has been leading up to that point (at any point) for months, even years - it's been able to know/become aware of the growing/spiraling that makes it all the more REAL/powerful - if that makes sense. The knowing means we are awake instead of being asleep and just reacting to situations and events. By being CONSCIOUSLY AWARE we can contribute more positively (or RESPOND) in ANY situation.

I've become a little better at being less hot tempered and tend to consider my responses better.

Damn, this whole thing is amazing/fun and what is really amazing is that there are SO MANY that have no clue about what "IT" is like.... they are all genuinely "half asleep" – I feel so much alive than ever before (albeit this week has been a tad draining).

ES: Carl Jung said "Who looks outside, dreams. Who looks inside, awakens"

209

26 October: A Lesson in Detachment

FH: Last week was strange. I think, in hindsight, I was experiencing a void. What I find of real value, is that - I do practice what I preach, don't get me wrong - but sometimes I can be my own worst enemy.

I can go 100 miles an hour like a Ferrari when I am creating and in my zone. But when it comes to the money aspect I fall back to below the speed limit. It was a beautiful metaphor that you mentioned a while back and I thought it was so true because I am not motivated by money.

In terms of my relationship with people and how they treat me regarding money that they owe me, I have let my own integrity down by not demonstrating that same level of energy towards that aspect of me. Does that make sense?

ES: It makes complete sense. It is fascinating how you have changed the emphasis. Initially the emphasis was "I've got work to do" in one box, "I've got money to receive" in a different box. "Work to do" is not a problem - you are very good at that. There is another box next to it, labelled "People owe me money, I have to receive money and that is a problem".

You are separating the two quite clearly. You have "no problem" and "problem". In this process, and with all the emotion that went with it, and with the learning that went with it, there are no longer two boxes.

There is only one box, which is "I am very good at what I'm doing, and therefore the money will come in. I need to go through particular motions but that is part of the job. I might not like it." Where you had any issue with money as being a separate part of yourself which you did not quite like, that issue with money is no longer an issue.

210

What area of your life do you see as separate when it is in fact part of the complete picture?

FH: I can relate to that.

What I find invaluable with the relationship that we have is that I can think something, and sometimes I think "Oh no, that's silly, that stupid" but I feel completely at ease with bouncing past you what my thoughts are. You have an independent, unbiased, detached perspective that more often than not confirms my understanding or perception that I have from a completely opposite end of the country.

I find it very useful. I get frustrated when I am not intellectually challenged. I love the content of our conversations and it is hard to find other people to engage in in-depth conversations on similar topics.

ES: You are no longer afraid to explore. There are still boundaries. You are no longer wondering whether you can get through the boundaries. You just jump over them.

FH: That was one of the things that you mentioned right at the beginning. You said I would be revisiting all my boundaries or words to that effect. That is so true. I have revisited boundaries in terms of judgment and awareness. The terra incognita has been a beautiful turning point in my life. It was all about fear of the unknown. I had a coaching programme up and running and I was asking what next. At the same time I said I did not want anything else. I did not want to incur more costs. I did not want to take my eye off the ball. With the business start-up program it has been so hard to put the content together.

ES: And you did not go out of your mind.

FH: We were going to go on holiday earlier on in the year. Then we went to Italy in October. And absolute turning point happened

211

in that holiday. It really allowed all to sink in to my being in preparation for the next stage.

I was able to recognize it. I don't know how you do it. With this level of awareness sometimes you forget and at other times you are almost on tenterhooks. You want to know what will happen next, you want to look out for it. I don't want to fall into that trap of a self-fulfilling prophecy. But at the same time I'm conscious that I create my own reality. I just want to make sure that it is not the opposite.

ES: You need to be aware of the balance all the time. It is exactly the same for me. On the one hand I know that every thought I think, everything that ever goes through my mind, is part of my process of creation. I am very aware of what I think.

I know I am creating my future and it is bloody brilliant to say the least. But is also part of me that says" Yes, but what if". I want to know what I can anticipate – to get the balance right, to have "Yes, but what if" not in a sense of fear but in a sense of confirmation - am I on the right track?

 Notice that spiral again – where you say "on the one hand" and "on the other hand". Only when you have accepted both sides fully do you realize that you do not need to choose, because both "hands" are part of you.

FH: That is what I think. I do not want approval of the path ahead. I want my awareness to confirm: am I on the right path, or am I making things fit to let me think I am on the right path?

Hans in South Africa has gone completely quiet on me. I have not had an e-mail or a phone call in more than two weeks. On the morning that I left on holiday I sent him a copy of our agreement by airmail. I thought that when I came back from holiday I would get something from him - a solicitor's letter or e-mail-but nothing at all. I don't know what the next stage is going to be on that one at all. So we can never tell in this game.

ES: Well, actually you can. It is a journey of both knowing and exploring.
Do you want to know about Hans in South Africa?

FH: Yes, go on.

ES: His whole empire is falling apart. It is very interesting that when you sent him that letter, it was the act that took out the linchpin for him. It is now all falling apart.

FH: How do you mean, linchpin?

ES: The linchpin is the one thing that holds everything together. If you remove that one thing, everything falls apart.

FH: Now you make me feel worse.

ES: No, no, no, no, no, you did what you needed to do. In that sense you are a teacher for him. Let me give you a different example. You are playing a particular role in his life by being a teacher for him. You have approached this, initially with kindness, by being helpful, with generosity. He did not get the message. Then you had to be firm and he did get the message. He might not thank you for it at the moment but he got the message. In that sense you are an incredibly strong teacher for him.

Everything is happening because of the whole process that was initiated with you sending that last letter to him and starting with legal action. All of that is steering his life in a different direction which he can only benefit from but he will not believe it at the moment. Right now he is blaming you for his world falling apart. If you did not do anything he would have continued to live a dream.

Yes, his world is falling apart, yes you were an integral part of getting the whole process moving, but eventually he will benefit massively from it, because he's going to learn a lot, and he will come back to you and thank you for this.

213

Also, while all of this is happening for him, to a huge amount is happening for you, which is opening up South Africa as a market. For you it was a big thing to send that letter, but in the greater scheme of things it was a small thing that started the whole process that both you and he are going to benefit from.

He will benefit from it in the sense that it will take his business in a different direction. He will grow up. You will benefit from it in the sense that you will be conquering a completely new market that you have never considered before. You are going to do that with the least amount of effort. It is one of those things that just happen and you look back at it and you say "now that was a miracle!"

 Whether we like it or not, our actions and decisions impact on the people around us, and also on the people that we have contact with. You do not need to be in the same room or even in the same country to make a difference in someone's life.

FH: As I dealt with each of these non-payerss - and it's an identical situation with Dieter in Germany, it is almost as if I become their body and their feelings. I almost adopt their persona and can feel their anger, frustration, and resentment towards me because of the situation.

I personally get torn, because I see it from their point of view, and I begin to question myself. Then I keep saying I've done nothing wrong, I have done what I said I would do. It is as if I am wearing their skin. I am experiencing their anger, frustration, and resentment towards me, more than I am able to justify my actions. I feel bad towards them. I know I did the right thing.

ES: You have to at some point make a conscious choice. Do you want to take on all their emotions? And if you want to continue that, what will you achieve with it?

FH: That is what happened to me before I went on holiday. It was not the financial aspect. It was the emotional attachment from their perspective which I was experiencing. It was very, very intense. I was questioning my ethics, my values, my principles, and I thought I had done everything right. I was really feeling it from their standpoint.

ES: Maybe the lesson in that for you is about detachment. Compare what you felt with them to what you felt when you also got a strong and negative emotion from your friend Colin.

FH: I felt as though he wanted to do one of two things. He was waiting for me to judge him or to be too understanding. I did not do either. I said "I am not here to judge you. It is up to you what you do, and I'm sure you will find the best way forward." It was a turning point in more ways than I could imagine but not for the reasons the average person would anticipate.

ES: That's right. If you still want to take on the emotions of the coaches, you have to ask yourself what is in it for you. Why is it so important for you to do that?

FH: I think you have taught me a valuable lesson with that. If I was to look back over the last three to five years, specifically on things to do with The Water Cooler, that has been one of my biggest failings. I become emotionally attached to people or situations or events. I think that has been a valuable lesson as well as I look back.

You have talked about reacting and responding. I suppose he is in exactly the same place that I have been previously. Will he react or respond to me? Initially it's going to be steaming and swearing and temper and anger. In due course he may see it and it will help him. That might come in six months or a year or two years' time - who knows?

 How often do you feel guilty or bad about the way you treat people? What if you treat them with integrity and they still play on your feelings? Remember, you choose how you feel. Ask yourself why you feel the way you do. If you need to, change your choice.

27 October: Feel the Force . . .

FH: I detect a period of hibernation from now until end of February. I suspect this is the time to perfect all the products ready for the coming out in bloom in early new-year/spring.

"Drains" and "Radiators"

Quite often, when we want more business or need more business, we can come across as needy, desperate or skint. It's often reflected in our handshake, the way we dress, the way we speak, even in the way we communicate in writing.

When we are in a state of need, we tend to focus all our attention on just one person - ourselves, often completely forgetting about the intended prospect and their needs. We can be so wrapped up in trying to get the appointment, or the sale, and wanting to focus all our attention on telling the prospect how wonderful we are why they should buy from us, we forget to focus our attention on the prospect.

Ever shaken hands with someone at a networking event, and it felt like a bit of lettuce? (And you had a funny feeling that the conversation wasn't going to lead anywhere.)

Ever shaken hands with someone at a networking event, who starts looking round the room, while you're talking to them? (And you had a funny feeling that the conversation wasn't going to lead anywhere.)

Ever shaken hands with someone at a networking event, and thought that they either need a good feed, a good wash or they simply didn't instil confidence in you? (And you had a funny feeling that the conversation wasn't going to lead anywhere.)

Ever shaken hands with someone at a networking event, and thought that the person was pushy asking for your card, as if they were on a mission or a sponsored business card collection campaign? (And you had a funny feeling that the conversation wasn't going to lead anywhere.)

Ever sat in a meeting with a prospective supplier, and instead of asking questions about you, they've talked and talked about

themselves without every wanting to know more about you - the intended client?

I bet at one point or another you have, and your prospects have as well, and remember the same too. Worse still, when we perceive ourselves as victims, it can be because of our choices and actions are sometimes selfish instead of selfless.

It's not what we GET that's important when working for yourself - it's what we GIVE that counts.
More importantly, what is it you GIVE to others that's unique and of VALUE?

Only when we're open to GIVE, are we truly open to RECEIVE.
Who do you know that "drains" your time and energy because they are always out to get something?
Detach yourself from the material gain of an end result you wish to achieve and allow the progress and results to begin immediately.

 Take a moment to reflect and make notes on what you have just read.

1 November: The Danger of Mobile Phones

FH: Margaret discovered Colin's affair.

ES: World war 3?

FH: Yes. She discovered messages on his phone

ES: There is another dimension to it. If we all create our own experiences, he created an affair to learn about himself. But at some level she knew - she also created the experience. And you also created the situation because it was your opportunity to detach and experience the situation above and beyond time and space - with no specific emotion and to become aware of how the whole puzzle fits together.

FH: I've made a commitment to myself today – 20 to 30 minutes commitment to try and meditate each day.

 Oh, the intrigue we live with. They say that when a husband has an affair, the wife is always the last to know. I disagree. She is the first to intuitively know, and then to choose to ignore every sign. Have you had an experience where you knew in your heart of hearts what was going on but chose to ignore the situation in the hope that it will change? Did it change?

219

2 November: Mirror, Mirror on the Wall . . .

FH: I have always viewed The Water Cooler as my playground and testing ground. In fact, one of the first things you said to me which was true is that I feel very, very safe in The Water Cooler because it is not costing me anything other than my time to play.

ES: And the interesting thing is that when I initially said to you that you will take on the world and move away from The Water Cooler, I thought that would mean offering your current product to the world. It turned out to be that will be only a small part of what you will be offering. That is very interesting.

FH: I wanted to come back to you on that today as well. I was curious to know if you could elaborate on that because I have felt a lot of change internally since we got together. I cannot remember the expression – it was like fish in a pond, and it is time to jump the pond and get into the sea . . .

ES: Yes. Get out of your hibernation and get into the world. I think is probably around the new product development, and – I wouldn't say giving a spiritual slant to stuff, but just allowing that creative energy to flow with no barriers, no obstacles, no inhibitions. That is what you have been doing.

FH: It is almost as if for a while I was creating products, but I was only creating some kinds of products as opposed to allowing the whole creative process to go with the flow and create what I was trying to create.

ES: Yes, and what held you back was "What will people say?"

FH: Do you know what? That is the first time you have actually said that as directly as that, and I can now see the logic and the rationale behind why things were the way they were.

ES: And what have people said?

FH: Well, I know that many people have commented. I have picked up a couple of clients who may not necessarily have become clients, because my approach has been different. Other people are beginning to think they thought they knew me. They have discovered another side of me. The perception of many of the forum members in The Water Cooler is that I am this brash, die-hard, insurance salesman type marketeer, which is not necessarily what I am.

That perception that they've got, I think has been altered considerably over the last few months.

I must admit, I have been reflecting on what we have been discussing, and it is really answering a lot of questions for me.

One of the challenges that I had, with everything you have shared with me, as I have tried to describe it to someone else, I had some real problems articulating it. I came up with this analogy: it is like a driving test. You know the theory, and you have the practical. Many people are not even aware of the test of what is available. They don't want to know the theory. They don't want to spend time reading or educating themselves as to the spiritual way of doing things. But even worse, they don't want to allocate the time to doing the practical.

 Fraser took a leap here and discovered his fear of "what people will say" was not only unfounded, but turned into unexpected encouragement. What fear is holding you back when it can in fact be an opportunity?

ES: That's right. They don't know what they are going to discover. They are just too scared to do it.

FH: All fascinating stuff. I think the energy in The Water Cooler is going down. Now is the time to not drop The Water Cooler, but to start pushing my new site out into the world. I am not restricted within the boundaries of The Water Cooler where I have had to wrestle with a lot of conflicting personalities. It is like breaking free from that to go and do what I really want to do.

It has been fun. Yes, but the energy feels different, I think it's dwindling, and it's failing. I think others will recognize this and leave it.

I must tell you what happened on Friday night.

I met Colin at the post office on Wednesday. He was in a hurry but asked if he and Margaret could pop over on Friday night. I did not have any time to think and said yes – I knew that Wendy and I did not have any plans.

Wendy decided to cook a nice meal with Colin and Margaret coming over, and spent most of Friday afternoon in the kitchen.

Come Friday evening, what really surprised me was that Colin and Margaret did come over, but they only stayed about 20 minutes, to then tell us they were going out for a meal.
Before Wendy and I had realized what had happened, they were gone – and we were left with their two teenage boys. It turned out that the boys also had no idea that their parents would leave them there, or where their parents had gone.

It was after 11 o'clock before Colin returned to fetch the boys. Of course I was furious, but Colin acted as if nothing was wrong and they left.

What stuck in my throat was that they hadn't told us that they were going out for a meal, and they had not actually asked us to look after their kids.

I realized that Colin and Margaret were still being selfish in trying to resolve their problems by not caring what was happening to the kids or their friends – they were so interested in themselves. And

222

part of me is angry about being angry about that. Part of me says "Don't worry about it, just let it go."

ES: What is it that disturbed or shocked or bothered you most about this whole thing?

FH: Good question. What is it that shocked me the most? There was no clear communication or understanding of what was actually happening on the Friday night. I assumed they were coming over to see us and they definitely did not communicate that they were either going out for a meal or asking us out for a meal, nor that they wanted us to look after their kids for the evening.

Even Wendy was fuming, having cooked a meal for 12 people, only to discover that once again she was looking after someone else's children.

I was thinking: talk about selfishness! I don't think – it was not my place to – do I labor the point and bring it to their attention as nicely as possible, saying "Look, I am glad you have things sorted out – that's brilliant. Can I just point out that you may want to see this from a different perspective as to how it affects the rest of us". Or do I not raise that? I don't think they recognize the impact this has had on other people.

I think it is significant because on Friday when they arrived I was convinced that they had got things patched up.

This incident had so many hidden messages and meanings for me. I understand that. The question was how I respond to the situation.

ES: OK. Various good things came out for you in terms of your own awareness and your own perceptions and how you have become aware of how you have changed as a person. The one thing that really still stuck there is: how can they be so selfish?

For me there are three sides to being selfish. The one side is that you completely ignore what other people want and need, and you

223

deliberately exclude people from your tiny little world, because the focus is on me, myself and I.

There is another side to being selfish, which is "I always just give. I always make life easy for other people. Why don't they do the same for me? It is time for me to receive as well and I feel I am not receiving. I am concerned about that."

Then there is a third side to it, which is "I am in a space where I have become important, where I have done a lot of introspection and the focus has been very much on me. Does that mean that I'm selfish to the exclusion of other people, or does it mean it is OK for me to focus entirely on myself and discover myself?"

We are not brought up in a culture where it is OK to focus on yourself. I don't know about you, but I was taught from an early age that whatever you do, you do for other people. If you do something for yourself, you are selfish.

 Who is looking out for you? Do you place yourself in the Number One position so that you can have something to give to the world? Or would you rather be "unselfish" and give until you have nothing left to give and then become a saint or a martyr?

FH: I was just gob-smacked at being able to recognize just how selfish the two of them were. It really stuck with me because it is not in my nature to be as selfish as that. But I don't want it to eat me. I know it has been getting the better of me.

ES: But the fact that it bothers you so much tells me there is something inside of you that you have not recognized yet, that you don't love yet, that you haven't integrated yet. And somehow, whenever you think about their behaviour it presses a button in terms of "Fraser, are you aware that in this particular aspect you are exactly the same as them, and therefore you have to love them for showing that to you?"

FH: Well, that was interesting and I recognize the way in which you were wording that with the three types. I was giving and not receiving. Was that subliminally or hidden? I don't know. I am honest with you. I recognize this really struck a chord with me and I am really trying to dig down through the layers of the onion to see what it is.

ES: Were you being taken for granted?

FH: Yes, yes. That is the expression.

ES: In slightly a different way than the various coaches have been doing by not paying you? They have also been taking you for granted.

FH: Ah. Now that's interesting. OK.

ES: You keep giving and they keep taking, and something in you is saying "Yes, that has been good for me, but is it still good for me?"

FH: You've hit the . . . damn, you're good! Damn, you're good! That's what it is. I've recognized it in me with the coaches and stuff with your help and guidance.

ES: And you've just fallen for a different version of it. This time it was not the coaches, but Colin and Margaret.

FH: That was something else I wanted to discuss with you. Thinking, doing and feeling. Many people know what they should be doing but are not doing it. Other people think about it, but they are not feeling what they should be. These are the three parts.

ES: The sequence is that you feel, then you think, then you do. There is a specific reason why I am saying that. Do you know the difference between a feeling and an emotion?

FH: No. I think I am a lot better at responding instead of reacting emotionally. But I don't understand the difference between feelings and emotions yet.

ES: I want you to think back to when you first realized that Wendy is the woman for you, and that you are going to marry her. How did you feel at the time?

FH: Gosh, she is a stunner. How did I feel at the time? I had a warm glow.

ES: Can you put that into one word? Did you feel happy? Did you feel glad? What?

FH: Excited.
ES: OK. If I tell you that you have just won a million pounds, would you have the same "excited"?

FH: No.

ES: You can get excited about many things. Was it the same at that moment?

FH: No, it was different. It was a calm, knowing excitement.

ES: Have you experienced it since?

FH: Pretty much, yes.

ES: Exactly the same?

FH: Yes.

ES: OK. And if I say to you "Fraser, think of something you can get excited about", would you feel the same?

FH: It's a completely different level.

ES: Would it make sense to say it took you to a place which is beyond time and space?

FH: I don't know.

ES: That's fine. There was at least one other moment where you had a feeling, and that is when at least one of your children were born. It was different from what you've ever experienced at any other time.

FH: Oh, when I had the twins. That was unbelievable. I was just crying. I was a wreck.

ES: So you were very sad about it.

FH: No, I was deliriously excited.

ES: Was it the same "excited" as when you decided to marry Wendy?

FH: Pretty much. No, I would say it was slightly different.
ES: So it was not quite "excitement", it was something different.

FH: No, it wasn't excitement. It was almost like "joy".

ES: OK. So, is there anything else that would give you joy, right now, at this moment? If I put a plate of strawberry cheesecake in front of you, would you feel joy?

FH: No. Joy would be the wrong word.

ES: A feeling is something very difficult to put into words, and it is just about impossible to experience it twice, even in a lifetime.

FH: Ah.

ES: If I say to you "How do you look when you get angry?", can you get a mental picture of yourself being angry? Is that easy?

227

FH: It was too easy. I got bright red and pink in the face

ES: Exactly. Get a mental picture of you feeling immensely sad about something.

FH: Yes.

ES: That is an emotion.

FH: That is fascinating.

ES: You can repeat an emotion as many times as you want to. You have control over that. An emotion is also triggered by situations and how you choose to interpret the situation.
You have no control over a feeling. It is there and you know what it is, and it is incredibly difficult to put it into words and that specific feeling never gets repeated in your lifetime.
You might have different situations where you have a feeling, but even then, the feeling you had when your twins were born was different from the feeling you had when you decided to marry Wendy. You cannot ever imagine or enact either of those two feelings again.

FH: So a feeling is difficult to articulate and it will never happen twice.

ES: And you know when you have experienced it, because it is different. For a split second you leave your body and you are somewhere where there is no time or space, just eternal bliss and gratitude.

 When in your life did you experience a feeling? Was it the culmination of an experience? Can you relive that moment in your imagination?

228

On the other hand, you can easily relive any emotion such as happiness, anger, sadness, because your body knows which muscles to use when expressing those emotions.

FH: That is an interesting choice of words. Eternal bliss and gratitude implies to me that it is the end of a cycle, the completion or fruition of a process, the manifestation of something.

ES: *Exactly – which is why, when you have completed a spiral, when you have that quantum leap which takes you literally from the bottom to the top of the spiral, you have that moment of insight where you feel that gratitude and you feel your heart opening up, that is when you experience a feeling. You even stop thinking.*

FH: Now coming back to Colin - the way he spoke about the other woman, using the analogy you have just given me, he spoke of his true feelings about the other woman as opposed to his emotions about his wife.

ES: *Both are emotions, because the one is the reality that he lives with, and the other one is the illusion of perfection that he is holding up to himself.*
I am sure you have also encountered instances where a person leaves a husband or a wife for somebody else and they live happily ever after, while in other instances the whole deck of cards just fall apart. When you have experienced a feeling with a person, nothing will stop you from being with that person.

When you have experienced an emotion with a person, you will continue to have that emotion until you get so sick and tired of being so blissfully happy with the person that you will find something to sabotage the relationship with.
Emotions require a hell of a lot of energy to keep up, whereas a feeling is like an infinite, eternal moment that determines the rest of your life.

FH: I am making notes as we speak because I am enjoying this.

ES: In terms of working for yourself, if you can come from a place of "feeling, thought, action", my God, nothing will stop you. But if you come from "emotion, thought, action", you will be exhausted.

I will tell you about a moment where I had a feeling that changed my life. Probably about 15 years ago I went to see an old clairvoyant woman in Pretoria. At the time I was living in Johannesburg. I had a job, and I was hoping to be made a director of the company. Everything was going very well for me. I went to see her and she said to me "you are going to live in England".

I thought yeah right, and the pope is going to get married. I didn't even think about it any further. I was not made a director for various political reasons. I was very unhappy. At that time I was transferred from Johannesburg to Cape Town. I implemented a project in Cape Town. It was highly successful.

My reward was to either be demoted two levels or accept redundancy. It was the most unfair redundancy. If I had taken them to court, I would have been financially settled for life. I just did not want to do that to myself.

The moment when I was told that I was going to be made redundant, the thought that went through my mind was "so this is where you move to England". At the time I felt the most incredible joy, gratitude, I don't know what. I actually got tears in my eyes and ran out of the room.

The person who was informing me of the options thought I was very upset about being made redundant. I didn't correct them at the time. I was just so . . . it was like seeing the rest of my life in Technicolor and falling in love with it. I didn't tell anybody about that moment.
Later I just went off like a banshee about how unfair they were, and the more I performed, the more money they threw at me so that I would keep quiet and not embarrass the company by going to an

employment tribunal. They more money they threw at me, the more I knew that moving to England was right.

I know now that if I did not follow my instincts at the time, I would probably by now have been dead from some cancer. I had a feeling. I recognized it and it shaped my life.

FH: Another thing which I realized over the weekend, and it is really reinforcing everything, is that life is all about trial. Life is all about lessons. The ability to recognize that you are busy with a lesson, or you have had a lesson, and you have grown as a result of that, is step one of the understanding, and you are beginning to awaken to the fact that there is more to life than meets the eye. That really reinforced everything that you have said to me today. I can understand it. I can relate to that. I know that it is right.

I am no longer in slumber. I have now become aware of so many things around me. I am more alert. I am noticing things. I am even beginning to know things because of the feelings that I have. I suppose it is leading up naturally to meditation. I don't even know if meditation is the right word. It is that physical act of connecting with a point of bliss, zero point, spirit world, whatever it comes to.

When I look back this year I laugh about how many trials and tribulations I have had and how I have been able to address them. Why would I want to meditate on the problems and resistance I have to meditation? I am asking for help to dispel that.

If I can find out what the blocks and challenges are and what my faults or the negative aspects of me are in leading up to the start of that process, and ask for guidance to address it, I will make a hell of a lot more progress much quicker, I would have thought.

ES: Yes, and you can pull all those blocks, challenges and everything else together in the question: what are you afraid of? What do you think is going to happen when you actually let go and do it?

FH: I think that is a good point as well. I don't think it is fear. I keep coming back to time. My brain says I can't find the time to do it. That is one of my greatest reservations. I am thinking if I spend the time – I don't know what the results will be – if I make the investment, the returns will come. It is almost a moot point.

ES: *If you really want to do something, the time is there.*

 What would you love to do with your life? What steps are you taking to spend some time every day getting closer to that goal?

Getting Emotional...

Are emotions and feelings the same when it comes to working for yourself? More importantly, how aware are you of the emotions of your target audience? How do your prospects use emotions and logic in their buying process? More importantly, how do you use emotions and logic as part of your working for yourself and selling process?

Emotions

Our emotions drive our behavior, and our role in working for ourselves is to find the emotions of the prospect that we can identify and activate. When it comes to understanding and manipulating people's emotions, it's all about being able to identify their "values".

Plutchik's Wheel of Emotions helps to identify the different emotions and their "opposites". Your prospects have different emotional triggers that you need to find in order to activate the relevant emotion, to get them to buy what you have.

When it comes to working for yourself, there are several key emotional triggers that you may wish to focus in on. Your mission is to identify which of the following is the driving emotion of your prospect, harness it in your copywriting and sales presentations, and lead them to the sale.

Fear (also Pain)

Prospects are inclined to make a decision quicker to get away from pain than moving towards a benefit. You need to identify their pain or fears and remind them of it - how much it hurts, how much it costs and how you can remove it for them. You may also wish to introduce a deadline, scarcity, exclusivity and other similar tactics. Fear of loss is an excellent motivator to action. You could also use negative case studies or examples of other people who chose not to take up your offer and "this is what happened to them", encouraging the reader or prospect to want to avoid a similar situation arising for them.

Greed

"Keeping up with the Joneses" is a common problem/opportunity that can be identified and harnessed to your advantage. Does your prospect want to remain the same as their neighbour living in a similar house, driving the same type of car, or do they want to live the celebrity lifestyle? After all they deserve better - don't they?

Exclusivity

Just like greed, some of your prospects like to belong to an exclusive group, they are not the same as the Joneses. They want to be better - in fact, some even think they already are - so play on it. Exclusivity can be leveraged especially well when selling cars, holidays, training events and seminars, property etc. You simply want the prospect to feel special and that they are one of a few who have been selected or are good enough for the offer.

Guilt

A good one for targeting female prospects. Why? Simply because when it's to do with family or friends, they are used to considering (and putting) everyone and everything before themselves. Many deprive themselves of the treats, that special pampering to ensure other people's needs are met, but then again, everyone loves a bargain - don't they?

Anger

Reminding prospects of their bad decisions and regrets of the past can help to activate anger in them, and you can remind them how to avoid this in the future if they choose your solution. Empathy is also a key word here; get your prospect on your side by illustrating that you understand their anger and frustration with being let down and how they can avoid it with you. If your prospects are having problems with one of your competitors, you might not want to name them, but you can certainly leverage the situation to your advantage.

Flattery

Everyone likes a compliment. Help the prospect to feel good about themselves and help them to understand how they can feel even better if they were to use your product or solution instead of what they already do.

Colours

Colours can also be excellent emotional triggers. Just ask any man what color of lingerie he prefers! What about jewelry? Which do you prefer - Gold or silver? The Bronze service or the Platinum Service? Colors can and do activate different emotional responses in your prospects too.

Remember, however, people may buy with their emotions but they use reason and logic to justify their buying decision. The bigger the item or the greater the price, the longer the decision, and the more weighing up, the more justification has to be done.

So after having activated the emotional triggers of your prospects, you may actually want to remind them WHY they want to purchase your solution, what they can avoid if they do buy from you, what they will get, and if appropriate, what they can SAVE.

You might want to win their heart, their mind and then their wallet.

 Take a moment to reflect and make notes on what you have just read.

3 November: It is my Understanding

FH: I was thinking of sending this to Hans in South Africa:

"It is My Understanding that it was lawful for me to send you the previous Notice.

It is My Understanding that I could and did provide, within that Notice, time for objections to be resolved honorably on both sides.

It is My Understanding that it is lawful for me to assume that, since you have not responded in substance (to the best of my knowledge) I have your tacit consent (by acquiescence) to … the statements I made/Proofs I requested … which now stand as My Truth, in Law.

It is My Understanding that it is now possible for me to assume that, since the proper time for your objections has expired, I have gained a lawful estoppel by your acquiescence.

It is My Understanding that I have acted in honor at all times, since you have not objected to what I said.

It is My Understanding that it is now possible for me to point out that you must henceforth cease and desist from all and any activity regarding this current matter, or that any further communications from you will be considered to be unlawful harassment, and can be disregarded by My Self without dishonor."

On another topic, refer the article "Getting emotional". I linked that into being able to identify the different emotional triggers that we use for sales presentations and copy writing. If you know what you have to offer it is fine, but identifying the emotional trigger is not the same as trying to blackmail people or manipulating them with what you have. If you are passionate about what you have and you believe you can help others, it is up to them to determine whether they fit your criteria and whether your solution can and will help them.

ES: It is a different reality. When you have this kind of freedom, it is wonderful. I recently dealt with a solicitor and had to demand my money back. He did not know what had hit him, because

236

nobody questions a solicitor. You just pay, and you pay more when he says so. And here I come and say "No, I am not paying for nonsense". Eventually he did not even want to speak to me. His partner spoke to me and I said "Look, I have learnt my lesson. Just give me back 60% of my money. I will make sure that I don't deal with you again." Next thing I get a cheque back in the mail for 100% back.

FH: You're right. If you start standing up for what you believe in, it's amazing how many different barriers you can break down. The deadline I gave was the 30ᵗʰ October to get themselves organized.

ES: And if you have any money issues, they have surfaced. What are you doing about them?

FH: You are right. I've got a big conversation with Dieter in Germany tomorrow. He has put his hand up and said "Yes, OK. I want to get things sorted out". But I notice the only one who has gone all quiet on me and who has not responded is Hans in South Africa. He's the only one who has gone to ground. I will have to sort them out.

ES: You are playing a part in his life. And yes, his whole empire is falling apart, but you are only playing a part in it. You are not responsible for it. He is 100% responsible for it.

FH: I was quite pleased over the way Dieter in Germany has responded and taken his responsibility seriously. Hans in South Africa is doing an ostrich – he is sticking his head in the ground and trying to deny it.

ES: It is not going to work. When you are supposed to learn something it keeps happening but in different ways until you've got it. For example, you have the problems with three individuals. Three of them, one after the other, did the same. They took you for granted. And so did Colin and Margaret. Different people, different situation, different agenda, the message was the same.

Where people take you for granted, it is not a "poor me" thing. It is more "Fraser, are you recognizing your own value, because other people aren't and they are just telling you what they see."

 This is really important. If you have the same experience with different people, it is because you need to have that experience repeated, until you learn what all the people involved are teaching you. For example, if you need to learn to stand up for yourself, you may be bullied at home, at school, at work etc. until you stand up for yourself. If you have one disastrous relationship after another, what is the common thread in that relationship – apart from you?

FH: I can see that now.

ES: And once you recognize what it is about, it stops.

FH: And the longer you put off making a decision, the more challenges you get to force you to make a decision one way or the other. It does not matter want your decision is. The mere fact that you made the decision will help you progress.

ES: That's right. It is not possible to make a "wrong" decision. Whatever decision you make will bring you to where you need to be.

FH: That's interesting. One the things that I have been reading over the last week or so is that I understand that as a soul coming to earth, before conception we have a blueprint and we forget that the moment we are born and put on our physical suit. I would like to believe that once you start getting into meditation, you can ask for guidance, protection, and to help recall what your blueprint is supposed to be.

ES: Yes. And if you ask to recall it, you speed up the process of recalling it. Once your head is turned and you see the reality you are living in, you are already recalling your blueprint. You have been recalling it for months. It just got into top gear over the last two, three months.

FH: I am now convinced that we manifest ourselves as humans in order to contribute to humanity, even the Universe, to leave our mark, to be unique for once in our lifetime. We are here with our unique offering to help others. That is why many are destined to work for themselves.

ES: That's right, yes.

FH: It's just been a bloody interesting summer in terms of waking up and understanding. I think coming out of my own slumber into this expansion and awareness phase has been an invaluable process and I think I have only just realized what's been happening. I think it is now about entering the understanding phase and learning what it is really all about.

ES: And giving you a basis for questioning more. If you stop questioning, you are in trouble.

 You cannot see the picture while you are in the frame. What picture are you still in with lots of emotional turmoil? What experience can you now see much more in perspective because you can think back to the time when it happened?

FH: That's very true. I think what I have been doing the most of over the summer is questioning, not so much do I want to, or curious about the future. It was a case of "Where am I in the process? What should I be experiencing? Am I consciously aware of where I am in the process?" I would say I have had a heightened level of awareness, to recognize things, not necessarily understand them, because I have often come back to you to say "This has happened, this is what I think, what do you think?" I think that understanding has been getting clearer and better. It is now about going to the next stage of learning and understanding about the resistance in my life and what has been holding me back.

It has been an action-packed year in that sense. I'm almost thinking yes, there is income and revenue coming into the business and I am getting new people, but I am looking at it from a selfish, happy point where I am able to do what I want to do without any undue pressure to go in any particular direction. Other people would view that as completely the opposite.

ES: That's right. You already have freedom. You just had to recognize it. And now you can have even more.

FH: I think freedom is very important. I shall reflect on that. I think that is the last phase in the process. Isn't that what working for yourself is all about – freedom!

Freedom: Fact or Fiction?

Are we fooled by statutes and legalese?
We Scots follow Scots law which relates back to Roman Law of years gone by, but your English law appears to be quite interesting, and I'm looking for clarification, not that it affects me, but crikey, a bit more research by some of yourselves could prove to provide startling information (one way or the other) I suspect.

Apparently....

All Councils in England are set up as COMPANIES/CORPORATIONS –

All COURTS in England are set up as COMPANIES/CORPORATIONS.

This is done apparently in order to set a Jurisdiction of an "unlawful" STATUTE.

(Note I say unlawful and not illegal - two completely different terms)

Would I be right in thinking then that if an individual living in England receives a summons from a court in England then...

A summons could be interpreted as an invitation to attend their place of business to discuss the matter in hand, thus is construed as an "offer" (under contract law)?

Did you know that all magistrates courts are deemed "branches" of the Ministry of Justice which itself is a registered Business/Corporation? Then I would hope you English chaps certainly do not agree to the jurisdiction of which it is governed.

Am I also led to believe that as "CORPORATIONS" they then create a legal fiction by addressing you as a "Person" (in UPPER

CASE) a separate legal entity to you, the named individual (under common law), to ensure that you comply with their requests and fall into their jurisdiction thus permitting them to deal with you in a matter as they deem fit.

If your COUNCILS are also registered Companies then are all these council tax bills that they want to take you for court are then unlawful too?

If they are setting the jurisdiction to that of a court de facto instead of a Court de Jeur, are they not denying you the added protection of the case being heard under COMMON LAW and a jury of your peers?

Is that not your right?

In fact, what are your rights?

Do you actually know?

In fact what are the implications (past, present and future) if any?

Perhaps it's time to paint your faces Blue and start standing up for what you could be losing....Your Freedom.

 Take a moment to reflect and make notes on what you have just read.

7 November: Actions Speak Louder than Words

FH: I got this response from Hans in South Africa:

"Hi Fraser,
Please find attached signed agreement.
I would like the opportunity to discuss things with you.
I still cannot understand or believe that you took such an
aggressive approach to this whole situation. You say that it was
purely a business decision. I could also no longer afford to
continue, even though I would love to. So my decision was also a
business decision - nothing more nothing less, yet I get the feeling
you have taken this personally.

Keen to discuss options.

Regards,
Hans"

 Emotional buttons are being pressed! How will Fraser respond to this? How would you respond if those were your emotional buttons?

9 November: It's Good to Talk

FH: Wendy was away with a friend yesterday. I did my domestic duties and then I sat down. I had maybe three hours of sitting down at the kitchen table where I wrote and wrote and wrote. So many things and thoughts were flashing through my head. I was consolidating my previous learning and it was able to flow from me in a coherent, logical manner.

Then Colin arrived. I was not expecting this at all and I thought "Oh my God".

Margaret has just had a small operation and has not been back to work. Colin told me that they had been away for a couple of days to talk things through. He said it made them look at why he had the affair in the first place. Something must have been lacking or missing in the marriage, and this enabled both of them to revisit who they are and the relationship they have. They both decided they wanted to make a go of it.

I said "Well, that's great, I'm happy for you".

Then I said "Can I share something with you that might upset you? I don't want to upset you unnecessarily but I think you should hear it. Do you mind if I say something?" I was in fact asking for his permission to be frank and honest.

I said "We had not seen each other in years. Then we met again just before your wife discovered you were having an affair. The two of you had to discuss it and you needed to fix it and deal with your marriage and kids. That's brilliant.

But you dragged me and my wife into this and made us your child minders. You never consulted us, and you never gave any thought to your own kids while doing this. Not only have you not been communicating with each other. You have also failed to communicate with those around you."

244

I could see he was getting a bit emotional but I thought I really had to share it with him. I was not trying to be awkward or a bad, nasty guy. I thought he had to hear it. He said the problem was that they just did not have the time together. I said "No. That might be, but do you want to hear my thoughts on it?" I kept asking for his permission so that I would not be seen to be ranting, pointing fingers, you know what I mean?

I said "I think it's been a lesson in being able to recognize how selfish you are – both of you. Margaret is very selfish with you because she obviously enjoys her work so much and spending so much time away from home. She is also selfish about wanting to be with you – understandable because of the bust-up you wanted to resolve but it goes much deeper than that.

You, Colin, just loved all the attention, all the focus on you because you have been so used to getting it. You have but you don't give. Neither of you give. You are so used to getting what you want. You will manipulate, you will lie - you will do things to get what you want. That is all wrong."

I then said to him "I could see all the signs of selfishness and I wondered what you give to other people? What do you share with other people?"

He could not answer the question.

I said "Here is one question you need to think about because you don't know the answer. It has nothing to do with sex or your relationship or your wife. Give a thought to that.

Another thing is that there is a very big change in your demeanor because you have been through this horrendous experience. You have now been taken down a peg or two. You now feel a little bit vulnerable and humility is beginning to shine through. We need that on occasion. I have seen it with me where in business I may become slightly overconfident or appear to be overconfident in the eyes of other people when my behavior amplifies things with them and they have reacted accordingly to that.

Wendy and I both think you have been really selfish in the way you acted towards us recently. Oh, my God, Elsabe, He got really upset. He said "I'm such a terrible person. I'm such a terrible person."

I thought, wait a minute, I'm not trying to get drawn into a poor me, victim scenario, to confirm his reality as he is trying to make it.

I said "Colin, you are who you are. You just don't recognize who you are. This has been really strange for me because I have become much sharper in my perception and understanding of how things are. Am I wrong in anything I have said so far, Colin? "

"No, you are 100% right".

I said "Well, I think what could work well in taking things forward is for Margaret to patch things up with Wendy. She went through all the bother of making a meal and you did not tell us you had decided to go out for a meal and leave your children with us. Wendy is a child minder - she is surrounded by kids five days a week. Over weekends she wants to take a break, not look after your kids."

That gave me absolute closure like you would not believe, Elsabe.

ES: I can understand that. How much of that did you prepare beforehand?

FH: Not a second of it.

ES: That's right. You just allowed it to flow in the moment and you did it with Love.

FH: As you rightly said, it is almost as if dormant thoughts and solutions are there, but you have given me a bloody good shake and awakening so that I can understand them in preparation for applying them in being able to review them and ensure they make sense.

I was thinking of Colin yesterday. Colin was coming across as broken, remorseful, I think, but he did not really understand why. He thought he had been caught out having an affair.

I was digging down a level and pointed out that he was selfish, and had always been selfish. That reminds me of the microwave oven analogy. Many people know how to use the microwave oven, either in business or in their personal life, but they don't understand how the microwave oven works.

You have been teaching me to recognize the difference between emotions and feelings. Most men are not in touch with their emotions. Colin was saying that he did not know how to discuss his emotions with Margaret.

The real test with Colin yesterday was that I did not want to come across as patronizing or a bully. I didn't want to come across as gloating or taking advantage of him. I didn't want to come across as someone scoring points and saying "look at me, I'm brilliant." I think the message did strike home.

ES: Yes. It was more like a heart to heart.

FH: Yes. I feel completely, totally happy with myself in the way that I managed it.

ES: The journey you are on is all about self-discovery.

 Often when we need to take action the decision to do so is like a mountain in front of us. Then, when we finally gain the courage to do so, and we do what we all along knew had to be done, the relief is incredible. Have you had such an experience? Then you will know what I am talking about.
Now what do you need to do that you have been putting off for far too long?

10 November: A Passage to India

FH: I appear to becoming more "philosophical" in my outlook. One thing is for sure - my faith is being tested by my delinquent coaches again this month.

ES: With the blueprint there are major things that happen which steer us in a direction (e.g. we met, your coaches and the way they behave) and nothing you do can prevent or change the outcome. Then there are smaller things that do not really matter, because there may be various routes but the outcome will be the same, e.g. what time do you have your meal? Time may vary, but you will have your meal.

I saw a movie the other day – "A Passage to India". An Indian doctor is in prison for false rape charge against a white English woman. Everyone talks about it, and then this Hindu professor comes to the main actor and wants to name a school after him. This is so mundane and out of place that the main actor says the professor is stupid because he does not try to defend the doctor in a major scandal. The professor says "it does not matter what I do, the outcome was predetermined and cannot change. What I can change is the name of the school."

ES: I have just had a number of thoughts about previous situations that I have been in, where I had a job, a really good job that went really well, and then things turned sour, and I had to move on, but I didn't. Eventually I was made to move on by being made redundant or by being bullied to the extent that I could no stay there any longer.

 Often we know well in advance that we need to move on, but somehow we cling to the known until the disgust with the known becomes bigger than the fear of the unknown. Have you ever been in a situation where the behavior of people turned so nasty towards you that you had no choice but to move on and leave those people behind?

FH: Now I can understand it. Now I think – oh golly, I think I am seeing this. Is this a recurring theme whereby I am being told why I have got all this knowledge, wisdom and gifts that can be given and shared, why do I continue to offer it in The Water Cooler where it is not appreciated for the value that it has? So perhaps it is time to stop doing what I am doing on The Water Cooler, cut my ties and just concentrate on what I want to do away from there.

ES: Find another forum which is bigger and wider and at a higher level. Yes.

FH: I wonder. That is very logical and seems a bit obvious in light of the journey that I have been on and the experiences I have had. One of the first things I said to you was everything in my life goes up and down all the time, but any pain I have had has been through The Water Cooler.

ES: Yes, but it was not like that initially. It was very good for everyone involved.

FH: Yes. So what has changed then? Because I have not changed in my outlook. I haven't changed in my attitude. I am still the giving person that I am. I have looked at myself periodically and I have made changes in that I have tried to improve in certain things. These were changes I knew I needed to make – not necessarily that somebody else would know about. To the outside world I continue to be positive, a free, independent, giving spirit. Is it because they are not doing the introspection and they are not changing, and they are building up resentment towards me, and that has been manifested in what they say or do in their interactions with me?

ES: Yes. And what would the reason for that be? Probably that that is the role they have to play in your life. And if you don't make that change, they will eventually get you to a point where you will make that change out of desperation if nothing else.

I've experienced this a number of times before where it doesn't matter what I do, it doesn't matter how well I do it, I get bullied

249

until I pack my bags and move on. And every time I've packed my bags and moved on, I've moved into something bigger and better and more satisfying. But I didn't want to make that move because I wasn't sure of where I was going. And better the devil you know than the devil you don't.

So people go out of their way to help you move. Your irritation with The Water Cooler has been growing for a long time, and they are not changing. So . . . they are not going to change. It is not up to them to change.

FH: OK. I think I am going to get a cup of tea and have a think.

ES: And don't stress about it. You will pass this "course" anyway. Think of it as "I have passed; I now want to see the proof".

16 November: The Force Grows Strong

ES: What is the one thing that is consuming all your energy at the moment?

FH: I am going to answer that. If I was to be truthful, I would say over the last 5 or 6 weeks I've been really contemplating my personal growth. I won't say I let my business slip – that is not true – but the emphasis has shifted completely from the business to my growth. I sometimes question whether there is too much contemplation or thinking about it. I try to get the balance right. Whether it is the right balance, I don't know. But there certainly seems to be a lot happening at the moment – that's for sure.

Things have changed with my business. I am waiting for something to happen. This is not a false hope. The skills in have been creating or developing on a personal basis – I go back to the Italy holiday, because I think that was a real turning point for a number of strange, weird reasons. It feels like I am developing certain skills personally in preparation for something happing or coming shortly.

Part of me is the curiosity element and the – not frustration – I still can't see the total picture. I am usually quite good in terms of my gut feel or intuition on where to go but in terms of – dare I say it – ourselves, I am genuinely at a loss as to what will happen next.

ES: I have thought about it since last week when you asked about some syllabus that you are working through and you wanted to know what is still waiting. I think I said something like what is still coming is stuff that you have never experienced. I sensed very much last week your – I don't want to say anxiety, but – "give me something concrete to hold onto". I have thought a lot about it over the past week especially. On the one hand, do I really have to sit down and say these are the topics that we haven't covered yet? On the other hand, do I say to you just go with that flow?

251

I actually realized from everything you have done in this working for yourself course and the conversations we have had, that you do want to see things quite concrete. It feels like you're looking for a checklist and you want to see how far you have progressed on the checklist. That, I realized, is part of the journey. It is not me copping out, it is me saying to you relax and just go with it. You are used to one extreme which is everything nicely packaged. You are not used to the other extreme which is nothing packaged at all. You have to experience that, so that you can come to the middle.

FH: I see it slightly different. Over the years I may have had a chaotic approach – a consistently inconsistent approach whereby the last couple of years, as I have been focusing on doing what I have been doing, I have taken a structured approach which has worked really well. Here I am, moving slightly away from that. It is not fear of the unknown – I have worked for myself for 20-odd years and that has always been there. I have an element of structure which I know is proven to work. Here I am in a new topic or subject area which I am trying to master. Not only do I not know the extent, height, width of it, there are no reference points to know whether it makes sense.

ES: Yes. I have also thought over the past week that the discussions we have had so far have touched on very specific topics, without us really having a plan behind it – or saying "today we are going to discuss this topic". There has been a natural flow in the topics we have discussed and the information we have exchanged. It is more about living it and then checking that we have got all of it.

FH: One thing you have helped me with is my perspective on The Water Cooler. Like you, I have given help to a number of people. The payback has not been there through The Water Cooler. I have questioned my integrity and authenticity, modus operandi, the way I conduct myself, the way I write, but I have also seen the way people interacted and behaved towards me, and I can laugh now.

I was getting quite upset because some people were behaving with malice and I really was struggling to understand why.

I needed to go through the process to learn and understand the benefit from it. Half of me wanted to break away from The Water Cooler earlier in the year – I chose not to, because I felt I still needed to go through the learning process, because it was all needed to build a better, solid foundation in going forward.

ES: Yes. It is not about you walking away from The Water Cooler in a huff – it is more about "OK, so you have proved that is not quite where I belong. Thank you for that, and I wish you well." Can you live without it?

FH: That was the conclusion I came to. With The Water Cooler several people have been really awkward towards me. I was really questioning myself. It has helped me to see that other people can become very threatened. Even when we are not playing the same games, the energy we give off – they don't know how to harness our energy or control it. A number of people want to keep us in a box and manipulate us, but because we like our freedom and we can behave in an unpredictable way, they feel threatened by that.
It just feels like a spiritual awareness of The Water Cooler. I can see myself returning occasionally, but – you used the expression "out of the pond, into the ocean".

ES: The Water Cooler has been your laboratory and you are coming out of it.

FH: I think that is very true. It feels like they are saying "Come on, Fraser, wake up, you have given" – what is missing? What is the nagging element that I have not mastered yet? And I think you said it last week – perhaps now is the time to move on, because the longer I stay there, the more awkward I am going to feel, but I have not accepted my decision to move on.

I think I'm quietly contemplating creating my own "Water Cooler".

Another way I could view this is that everything is still 100% appropriate and what they are saying is appropriate, but from the perspective of "you need to discover and acknowledge your consciousness so that in your awakening on experiencing awareness, you are going to help others become awake and aware of it as well. It has helped me contribute – the skills and talents and experiences we have, helps to create not so much the outcome, but it helps to contribute in our own unique way.

I can see the growth and the journey I've been on last couple of months, and I can also see how much people are running around trying to live a life that is so different from what they want to do - a bit like keeping up with the Jones' instead of living their life's purpose.

We are who we are. Everything IS as its needs to be. We are the sum total of experiences to date. We acknowledge it, are aware of it, understand it, and are thankful for it.
"Our life is about collecting experiences, not things!" (one of last week's lessons)

ES: Trust me on this one. There is no chaos - except the chaos we create with our lack of understanding.

 Many, many books have been written as "the definitive guide to awakening". You should have realized by now that there is no such thing. Each person's journey is different. You have had different experiences since you started reading this book. Which realization stands out for you?

19 November: Head in the Sand?

FH: What do you make of this . . . (Hans in South Africa is persistent, I'll give him that – I've not responded yet)

"Hi Fraser,
How are things going with you?
Sorry I have taken so long to get back to you, but I have really been working hard on trying to find a solution to our problem.
At no time did I want to cease working with your business as I believed when I started and I still believe now that the business and you could be the vehicle to my success.
However, for financial reasons, (which are not good at the moment) I had to make a business decision not to proceed.
It would be a lot easier to achieve results without the huge debt over my head which took all the passion out of my last efforts.
Could you please consider this proposal and get back to me.
Regards
Hans"

ES: *This does not feel good at all. He will continue to use your energy instead of generate his own energy for as long as you allow him to do so. He wants to scale down his problem, but he is the problem - that is my feeling.*

FH: I've done a draft for Hans, and am conscious I don't want to spend too long on it or allow it to drain me, but I would appreciate your thoughts on my possible reply to him:

"Hi Hans
Many thanks for your email.
Our agreement has been terminated by virtue of you not keeping to your side of the agreement.
You say that for financial reasons you could not continue. In not continuing you were in breach of our agreement which I had amended to suit your cash flow position, which you still did not honor.

255

As you say, a business decision has been taken. The line has been drawn.

We both live and learn.

While I wish you well in your chosen path as you go forward you still need to address the material breach in the agreement which triggered the termination clause and how you propose to repay the monies.

The debt which you incurred unfortunately is still there. It will not go away.

While I am prepared to evaluate your proposals for repayment, I must remind you that I am not, and will no longer be the solution to the problem you find yourself in.

I look forward to receiving and considering your proposals for settling the outstanding monies owed under the terms of our agreement, and when repayment will commence.

I want to settle this amicably without wanting to resort to legal collection and am open to considering your sensible proposals as to what is owed following your breach of contract.

Kind Regards
Fraser"

ES: *Perfect. You could expect some backlash, but that is the way he is - for him to deal with and not your problem. Now you could be drawn into his emotional turmoil, or just be your true self. The benefit for him is that your energy will tell him there is no way out, and he will find a way to comply - and that is how he will discover his own creative ways to generate the money. All part of the Great Puzzle. The major lesson for him is the universal law of "Say what you do and do what you say". I would not be surprised if he had never needed to take responsibility for his actions, and now is his time.*

FH: It's one of those rare moments, when I'm actually in the right, and yet still don't want to be seen as behaving like an ogre - if you know what I mean.

ES: I know - but the difference between a month ago and now is that you are calm about it, which means you respond and you do it with love. There is firmness in your response which he definitely will sense and react to.

FH: As you say…if people would just do what they say they will do, or at the very least communicate if there is a problem, instead of sticking their head in the sand hoping it will go away… (denial, blames, excuses).

Later:
FH: Hans in South Africa is not recognizing where he is in his own evolutionary growth, is he?

ES: It is his problem. First he said "I saw the problem first and I dropped you" and now he is turning around and saying "Actually, I don't want to go anywhere because I am comfortable where I am, latching on to you".
FH: If he cannot do one, he is not going to be able to do the other. The same concepts and principles apply regardless of what he does. It is as if he just wants to hang onto my coat tails. Yes, he is going to be getting an appropriate set of words from me.

What I was thinking yesterday was – as we were going through this process we became aware of it and we were documenting and re-affirming the process by which we were able to look back at each part of completing the steps in the process to validate and confirm and document. This was a real process – we were proving it as we were going along and it was work in progress as well – live R&D.

With this whole palaver with The Water Cooler, it really helped me to see and experience how some people think and behave, and how they go out of their way to try and knock you down because of their perceptions. You have been thinking about dignity. I also add integrity as well. If we can speak with integrity and authenticity and we are living what we are talking about, then we cannot be criticized. People will only judge us by what they want to perceive, and they will try and compare what we have achieved to what they have achieved and what they want to achieve. They will try and pigeon-hole us into their reality, not ours.

 Sometimes a relationship – business, personal or family – fails and we are ready to walk away, but we don't because we think that we can still salvage the situation. Often the weaker person in the relationship will become even more passive and wait for the stronger person to make the big move. If you are in such a relationship, are you the weaker or the stronger person?

21 November: Recognising the Signs

FH: I just got this testimonial from someone I been helping last couple of weeks.

"Fraser's knowledge is extensive, his energy infectious. Having just completed a series of marketing coaching sessions with Fraser I can highly recommend his advice and expertise. His coaching sessions are very well organized, structured and professional, tailored to your specific needs and area of business. Helpful, supportive and generous, his coaching is just what I needed. I can't thank him enough and would urge anyone wanting to develop their business to call Fraser - you won't be disappointed."

(She was often quiet, yet continually challenged my thinking, then went away.)

ES: This is wonderful - but you have an approach that makes you stand out from the rest.

FH: Again looking back today I think elements of doubt crept in this morning, yet I used the quiet time in the car park to reflect and give myself a mental reassuring boost, and this was confirmed by the testimonial in from this woman just about an hour ago - subtle but welcome!

ES: This was the Universe communicating with you - with the testimonial. Very interesting - I cannot see why you doubt.

FH: Again, I'm sending them not for looking for a pat on the head, more of confirmation to myself that I've awoken to them, recognized, assimilated and "hopefully) now truly whole heartedly applied/applying them (with my understanding) of them in context.

ES: I know. What I like is how you take the "irrational" stuff and turn them into bullet points that make sense.

FH: I can see how it all comes together. The Water Cooler provides the "teachers" on the various topics. and that why there's been an inner torment/tension with me and some of the people on there, because they think I'm trying to "sell" to them. Now that throws an entirely different dimension on things (and explains a lot too).

The internet has helped people working for themselves to reach a wider audience, but I also think the anonymity of the internet has created barriers with the relationship building of people.

It is almost as if I have been checking myself this year, and I had minor conflicts with a view to checking the foundations are firmly in place.

When someone asks me a question, I will be able to come back with a straight answer. If people have questioned my integrity, I have been able to stand firm and not get weak about a particular topic. I think this year has been a whole lot of testing in preparation for really ramping things up for next year.

ES: I got this in an email this morning from a friend:

"There are many who find a good alibi far more attractive than an achievement. For an achievement does not settle anything permanently. We still have to prove our worth anew each day: we have to prove that we are as good today as we were yesterday. But when we have a valid alibi for not achieving anything we are fixed, so to speak, for life. Moreover, when we have an alibi for not writing a book, painting a picture, and so on, we have an alibi for not writing the greatest book and not painting the greatest picture. Small wonder that the effort expended and the punishment endured in obtaining a good alibi often exceed the effort and grief requisite for the attainment of a most marked achievement." (Eric Hoffer)

FH: Yes, it comes back to excuses at the end of the day, doesn't it?

ES: Yes. The amount of energy that you can put into finding an excuse and in denying – if you can put that amount of energy into doing something that maybe you have never thought of before, but that you were even afraid of doing it – just do it and it may turn out to be something astonishing.

 What are you doing with total conviction, knowing it is destructive? For example, are you a committed smoker who has told yourself that you are unable to give up the habit?

FH: I think that was one of the first things you said to be when we started speaking – the energy I was putting into not actually progressing with the spiritual side of things, was more than doing it.

ES: We all have fear of what we might discover when we actually go this route. It is OK to have the fear, but it is not OK to hold on to it.

FH: I can see the logic in that. It is interesting how things keep adding on bit by bit.We were doing a lot of house cleaning today and I said to Wendy "Do you see what we are doing? We are doing some cleansing of our own".

ES: You have no idea how powerful that stuff is. I have a friend who was very unhappy. He got divorced and as part of the settlement got a dilapidated house. He has spent a lot of time fixing the house to make it habitable again. Do you know how that process has changed him as a person?

23 November: Dirty Harry

FH: I am not in a good place mentally this morning. A couple of things. I had about £6 000 due in this month and it is highly likely that it will not happen. Another client has paid most months but has now run into financial difficulties. She is based in Dublin and she is quite cantankerous. She is always very quick to blame others when things don't work for her.
S
he has admitted on several occasions that she has not done the work that she promised. However, she is also in arrears with what she owes me. She phoned up this morning, very quiet and subdued, and said that she can't carry on in any shape, manner or form, and she can't pay the wages for her staff in another business. She had to get financial help to pay that etc. She does not want to continue with me.

This is about £400 per month which is not a lot of money, but it all contributes to cash flow. Number one is: I don't think it probably would work out because she wasn't going to put in the effort. Number two –I don't know what to think in pursuing her for the balance and the breach of contract.

I really do think that I am doing what I was supposed to be doing. I am questioning my own ethics, morality and modus operandi, and I am really struggling to see one, what the lesson is, and two, what the solution is. Three, I am really concerned with this lady, as to how I deal with it. The one thing that I value in our relationship is not so much the solution from you, but another perspective on the situation. I had the wind kicked out of my sails and I can't understand the logic and the reason and where it is all heading at 10 o'clock this morning, if you know what I mean.

ES: Let's see what is going on here.

Don't worry; it is part of the plan. Imagine a web, like a spider's web, with long strands and the pearls connecting the strands. You are right in the middle of this spider's web. You are in charge here. The web is expanding, but you are in the middle of it. You are not caught up in it. You are right in the middle of it. You are actually more in control than you think you are.

Whatever is going on here will have an incredibly good outcome – the best you have ever had in your life. That is good news.

First of all, don't worry. Yes, you are concerned about the money. The money is going to come to you in a different format, in a different way, from a different source. It is like one door being closed and another door being pushed wide open. If you are thinking about financial difficulties and not being able to balance the books, the books will be balanced in a way that you least anticipate at the moment, so put that worry out of your mind.

About this particular woman, you have to be firm but gentle with her. You don't need to come down on her with a hammer, but you have to be firm with her. She is not telling you the full truth. She is playing on your feelings. She is trying to see how far she can go.

I can see you parting ways with The Water Cooler but that has been on the cards for a long time. The nice thing is that you will part ways much more amicably than you have anticipated.

Yes, there are a few interesting weeks ahead of you. What you have to do is keep your faith and keep your belief in yourself, and act with integrity. Act according to your true self. Put your fear aside. You are completely protected. The money is there, not from the source that you expect it to be, but from a different source. At this point, right now, the money that will be coming in will be exactly what you anticipated, up to the penny – very interesting – up to the penny, you will get what you anticipated, but not from where you expected to get the money.

That is going to change very soon in a completely different direction where you will never, ever, have any concern about money again.

Do what you feel you have to do. Do not be concerned about the consequences because the consequences will be the opposite of what you expect it to be at the moment.

I can see people queuing up to shake your hand and say "We will miss you" and they are honest and sincere in that. They really do feel it as a loss.

FH: Is that a reaction? I.e. am I saying goodbye as a reaction to something else? Or am I opting to go, as it were?

ES: It is something that you have no choice in. It is one thing leading to another, leading to another, leading to another and you saying "Oh! So this is how it works." It is not you walking away. It is not them saying "Now go away". It is something that happens as naturally as the flow of a river. It is actually going to be the best good bye that you have ever experienced, because everybody is smiling, including you. You will get support from the most unexpected sources.

FH: I had a phone call with the woman from Dublin and she said "OK, I have been busy and other things". She admitted on several occasions during the conversation that she had not put the time and effort in. So I followed up on our conversation with an email confirming that she admitted she had not put in the time and effort.

I have a really bad feeling about this in a number of different ways. I am concerned about my integrity more than anything else, and the amount of time and effort I have been able to put into this. I know she has the ear of some influential people.

ES: She also has no self-control and this is a turning point for her, much more than it is for you.

 We tend to only be aware of our own emotions and we do not stop for a moment to consider what is in fact happening to the other role players in our lives. When we do take a step back, we could learn so much from observing people. The secret lies in first gaining control of our own emotions.

FH: Interesting – she has no self-control over her behavior when she is cornered or when she finds herself in an awkward position. She comes out very aggressively. Being aggressive is her best form of defense by the looks of it.

ES: She is a bully. She has no self-control. She comes out with guns blazing. She has no experience of apologizing. She lives in her own world and she has been getting away with incredible things because "fools rush in where angels fear to tread".

She is not in a good space. Just by being firm and gentle with her you will expose her for what she is, without you doing much. All you need to do is act according to your true self. She will do the rest. She is standing there, ready to shoot herself in both feet at the same time, and there is nothing you can do to stop that. She is just so transparent. In fact, I have a feeling that she has been dealing with you with the intention of sabotaging you and she has not succeeded and she now knows that. Now she is like a lioness in a cage, which is why you need to be firm with her.

The one thing you do not need to worry about is the money. The money is in place, it is there, it is happening as we speak.

FH: From a cash flow standpoint, not one, not two, not five, but a multiplicity of events that should have happened in the last four to six weeks have not happened. From a cash flow standpoint I cannot understand it because all the normal stuff that I would normally do, I continue to do. This has really taken the wind out of my sails this morning. I must admit I have had many knock backs as you know.

ES: And you have always been flying.
FH: Today is different. I can't quite articulate it. It's as if – it's not the straw that broke the camel's back – it is slightly different from that. It's – I understand that we have to change and adapt, we have to face obstacles and challenges, and learn so that we don't repeat it. But in my dealings with this woman, I genuinely think I have been firm and fair all the way long but still they come back.

Part of me says OK, that is the Universe saying it is time to sever that relationship which I can almost understand – in preparation for getting new people to work with me.

But the amount of time, money and effort I have put into creating what I have created – half of me now thinks what I have been doing is not meant to be, and more so than ever before, and that concerns me, because I thought I have been doing the right thing.

ES: Yes. It was necessary, it did serve a purpose, and it was part of the plan – you had to do all of that. But that does not mean that you have to keep doing it.

FH: I don't want to spend time dwelling on things, but I woke up this morning to a phenomenal brick wall – mentally, spiritually, yes. I have been battered and bruised during the course of this year and that is what life is all about, but today I really don't know.

ES: It's a very definite transition where nothing is familiar any longer, and nothing is familiar yet. You have seen this coming for a long, long time. Now it is happening. All I can say to you is it is OK. Financially you will be OK initially, and incredibly rich eventually. Emotionally, you can get sucked up in it or you can become a spectator and have great fun. From my own experience it is interesting to be aware of what is happening and see people struggling like fish being caught on a hook. It is interesting to watch it.

 This is quite a challenging part of the change. When you feel like to only person on the planet and nothing is familiar any longer, it is scary. You look back and you no longer belong where you came from. You look forward and there is nothing familiar yet. The good news is that as you continue forward, new things become familiar. Have you ever been in such a lonely space?

FH: I understand that come the end of December things may take a turn around.

ES: Not may, will. There is something big happening. It is like – you just fastened your seatbelt on a rollercoaster, and so did I. And these people are extras in the background. They are not the main players.

FH: OK. I really am at a loss in terms – there must be close to £9 000 in revenue from these people that they haven't paid, and they make up all sorts of excuses.

My instincts tell me that they are not going to deliver as of today, and that I should draw a line with those people and say right, that's it. There are three parts to that. One is taking the decision, and as you rightly said it has been leading up to this. That's fine. The second one is – all choices, in my book, has consequences. In me making that choice, they have not done or delivered on their part of a bargain or expectation. Half of me thinks to spend money on legal stuff is negative, but by the same token I should not allow then to get away with it.

I spoke to Catherine this morning and said "You obviously phoned me to tell me this for a reason, Catherine. What do you propose as a way forward?" She said "I can't make that decision. It's you. You need to decide what you're going to do."

I thought she phoned me to say she can't pay me, yet she was in New Zealand two weeks ago, Elsabe. This is the thing that really annoys me. She knew she was going to New Zealand.

When she came back from New Zealand I said "Catherine, the money is still due".

She said "I can't pay you. I'm just back from New Zealand. You know that."

It is the same with Hans in South Africa – he went on holiday without paying me.

267

I am thinking "hmmm".

ES: Exactly.

FH: The way I am feeling today, I am a hair's breath from just quitting on The Water Cooler. And that is not a reaction. I think you are right – it is a considered response. I have considered it on a number of occasions before, but I think today I really just want to say "Oh, f*** it – excuse my French".

ES: Yes. It is inevitable. The only question is: how is it happening?

FH: How or why?

ES: The why is that you have outgrown them. This is your time to go from being the biggest fish in the fishpond to being one of the fish in the ocean. The fish bowl has become too small for you and you have known that for a very long time. That is the why. It is time for you to spread your wings, to take on the rest of the world. And that is happening.

FH: I think I can understand that, but all the stuff that I have been doing with the coaches almost tells me that it is wrong, or it is not right. In my heart of hearts I think I have got it right. But then this situation comes and I think "No, Fraser, you have got it wrong. And I am thinking "Heh?" This is where I also have the real problem.

ES: The contents are right. The people are not right. This is the time to leave the people behind. You know that. You believe in what you do. You know that what you have is top quality. Don't doubt yourself.

FH: Do you know what is ironic? The Water Cooler is about people who are trying to work for themselves. Many of those people are doing jobs that are not their true essence, so they are not getting the rewards that they want. They need help and guidance

268

to get their proposition right as to what it is that they offer. With everything that I have been doing in The Water Cooler it is as if many tried to copy me. All I want to do is help others.

ES: But some things you cannot stop. What would happen if you put a bath plug into the source of a fountain? Will you stop the fountain?

FH: It will overflow.

ES: Exactly. It is just not possible to stop that fountain. You are like that fountain. You will just keep flowing all the time. You have got these little bath plugs trying to stop you. It is just not happening, and it is causing a lot more frustration for them than for you, because they cannot stop you and they are not very good at imitating you either.

Let them do what they have to do. It is part of their life script. And you do what you have to do. That is part of your life script. Yes, they will do what you expect them to do, and they will be much worse off as a result of that. And you will be the one walking away, with people applauding you for the way you deal with it.

You know in your heart of hearts they cannot bring you down. That is simply not possible. So the best you can do is become a spectator, watch this whole thing unfold, and watch it go to its logical conclusion, and then that's it. You have made your transition.

FH: OK. I will try and go forward with that. I am not playing the victim here. I am trying to see a different perspective here, to question the challenge, the lesson, my intention, my attention to detail and the plan. I am questioning my authenticity, integrity, and I am even questioning how the other person will feel when I take action. I am thinking of the other people when making these decisions – I am not thinking about myself.

ES: That's right.   And yes, you have had a fair amount of stress. Do you think it is easy for a butterfly to get out of a cocoon? That's quite stressful.

And that is what stress is about – an inner tension because the world is not going to change.   You have to change.   And you have changed.   You are still changing rapidly.

What changes do you need to make now that you know the world is not going to change to accommodate you?

FH: I think I am changing.   As I look back at my notes, I keep finding stuff that I have produced and collected or assembled or done over the last few years.   A lot of what we have talked about has been inside of me.   I also see that I have recognized it as being inside of me as well.   So, one, it exists.   Two, I recognize it.   Are you thereby saying that the process that I am going through is applying what I have learned and identifying this within me? Because although I have been thinking it and I have been feeling it, I haven't done it and vice versa.

ES: Yes, and you are now applying it.   You are now living it.   It's like you have learnt over the years to speak a different language, which to them sounds so foreign, you might as well speak ancient Chinese.   And believe me; I am fluent in two languages.   I have encountered this attitude many times in England where people actually say to me "For a South African, your English is not that bad", but that always comes from a person who can only speak English, and sometimes their English is dreadful, and they in fact say "For someone who sounds like an idiot, you are not such an idiot."

That is what these people are saying to you as well.   "For somebody that sounds like an idiot, we have actually got a hell of a lot of respect for you, because we know that you are speaking a different language that we have yet to learn."

FH: I must admit – has my faith been tested? Yes, it has. What do I believe in? Where does my faith lie? Ultimately it is in myself – and that is not ego talking. That is a case of – you mentioned being true to myself. Everything I do, I think I am true to myself – much to the annoyance of my wife on occasion as well. I think I have been true and I am true.

ES: I am reading a fascinating book about synchronicity. There is a paragraph in there that says when you become aware of these flashes, these moments that have s significant impact on your life, you can do one of two things. You can either say "What a coincidence! Interesting" and put it aside, or you can start to take more and more note of it, but be warned. When you do take more note of it, you will exit the next junction on the motorway and follow your own path, which is far more interesting than staying on the motorway.

FH: I won't say I am feeling better, but I think I am in a state of knowing. I feel – it is almost like this feeling of emptiness has been growing. Certainly since I have come back from holiday – and I think today I have reached a turning point. A lot of coincidences happen, but the important thing is recognizing them as part of a process.

ES: Yes. And recognizing those coincidences as having a significant and profound and life-changing impact on you. That is the synchronicity.

FH: It is as if synchronicity happens as a result of recognizing the coincidences.

ES: Yes. Synchronicity and coincidences are individual experiences. What means a lot to me might sound meaningless to you. Coincidence does not lead to synchronicity. Synchronicity is a different type of coincidence. Synchronicity is the specific coincidence that has a profound, life-changing impact on you.

FH: I thought synchronicity was a linked sequence of coincidences that begin to have meaning.

ES: Synchronicity could be only one during your entire life, or it could be a series when you notice more than one of them.

FH: I think different coincidences can have different meanings which can lead to different realities. Time is not linear – there is only now. However, there are probable futures and depending on how we view our existing position, we can alter or change our actions and create - there are two analogies. One is where you go up the stairs in the dark. Another one that springs to mind is that you go through an art gallery with a torch. You don't know the rooms, and as you turn the torch on, you are looking at a picture in the art gallery, and that picture is you in the future. You have many different rooms with many different pictures that you can access in a moment of clairvoyance, but it is the conscious decision of combining feelings, thoughts and actions together that will determine the reality that you will experience.

ES: And how you interpret it.

FH: What is the final outcome of synchronicity? Is it reality? Or is there a different word?

ES: You create your own reality. You make of it what you want. There is a lovely example here. The Roman Emperor Augustus was involved in some outdoor religious ceremony and there was a bolt of lightning which hit a statue of him nearby. At the foot of the statue there were the words "Caesar Augustus" and the lightning hit the letter C which then fell off the statue.

His interpretation was that C is the Roman figure for 100, which meant that he only had 100 days left to live. Of course he got quite depressed about that. Then a friend of his said that is absolute nonsense, because it might as well mean that he has another 100 months to live, not 100 days. It could also mean that he had 100 seconds to live, and he had already passed 100 seconds, so it had nothing to do with time. Then somebody else observed that the

272

loss of the C changed Caesar into Aesar, which meant "of the gods". He gave one interpretation which was all doom and gloom, but there was another interpretation that he was going from a human to a god.

FH: We are talking about subtle indications that you are either on the right path, or you have to make adjustments to the path in order to get what you want.

ES: That's right. And all those coincidences reveal a pattern which you only become aware of when you start to look for the pattern.

 Have you had any experience of coincidence – things happening together? And have you had any experience of synchronicity – a moment that gave you a foresight of what was coming that you intuitively accepted?

FH: And that's why you need to go through the process, so that you can start to see the patterns and evaluate them. You need to do it regularly so that you can compare one point in time with another point in time.

ES: Yes. It is your own reality. It is your version of reality. I am sitting here on a Monday morning. It is 11.30. It is cold outside. It is raining and misty. That is my reality. If I was on the other side of the world, it would still have been Monday morning, but it would be 1.30 in the afternoon. It would be sunny, very hot and humid, and that is true as well.
So it is your own reality. It is how things add up for you and what you make of them.

FH: When I initially looked at your profile on The Water Cooler it did not register with me on that first day. When I looked at your website, I thought "Ah – I've got to share something with her." It was weird.

273

ES: Talking about synchronicity, I met a man earlier this year and we were talking about the stuff that I was doing. This man referred me to your three minute audit. There was no reason for me to remember that conversation or your name, but I did. I did nothing about it until August when I looked at The Water Cooler, saw your ad and made contact with you. That is where synchronicity comes in. Why on earth would I remember your name out of many names that I encountered?

FH: You talked about the chakra system. Last night I wondered if the opening of the chakras helps to create an energy which is then transmitted by us so they resonate with another frequency from another individual to help create the coincidences?

ES: Yes, that is how the energy flows. The higher up you go in terms of associating your actions with a particular chakra, the more you will become aware of these coincidences because the more the blueprint and the web gets exposed to you.

FH: Wendy and I went for a walk and I said to her Catherine has not done what she was supposed to do. She comes up with all sorts of excuses and I was laughing to myself, because blame, denial and excuses are all she has.

I also spoke to another chap today. I said "John, this will be a very hard conversation but you know why I am phoning you" and he said no.

I said "Since the 8th of October I am not aware that you have actually completed what I have asked you to do, so on the basis of that I am going to have to send you a termination notice. I don't want to fall out, I really value our friendship, but you know and I know you haven't pulled your weight. I just need to write to you and confirm that. We need to draw a line and close it."

He was actually OK with it. So I am getting a little bit more bolshie than I was a 8.30 this morning.

I sent this email –

"Hi Catherine
Further to your phone call of earlier today, I write to confirm that
as of today's date, (the 23rd November):
You have not complied with my three requests outlined in my email
of 8th October and thus our agreement is terminated.
You have confirmed today that you do not wish to remedy the
situation. You have entered into an arrangement with your
creditors and will need to advise them of your obligation of the
amounts owing under the terms of our agreement.

In an effort to resolve the situation without incurring any
unnecessary or additional legal expenditure for either party, I look
forward to receiving your proposals/offer of settlement as to how
we can conclude matters amicably no later than 30th November.
I have also enclosed an undertakings document to be signed and
returned to myself no later than 30th November.

Regards
Fraser"

(relatively short and sweet, and hopefully not too emotional)
Wendy knew I wasn't myself today, so we went for walk down the
back tracks with the dogs and I brought her up to speed with the
situation. I said I had no doubts in the medium and long term, but
next week or so I had no idea what was going on.

ES: Just have faith - you are protected.

FH: What did you think of that email - did you think it was too
heavy (in light of your comment "be firm and gentle")

ES: No, it was firm and gentle - you stated clearly what the
situation was and gave her a way out.

FH: I think so - time will tell. The one thing that confuses me
about all this though - over last 18-24 months, I've developed the

coaching programme, and it feels complete. I've really tweaked the coaching control panel to help coaches sell what is on offer and it feels complete too. Yet the recurring theme this year has been that I haven't been paid on time by people who continue to make excuses despite their written agreements with me.

ES: Maybe the real value is in what happened to you during the development of the programme? How did it change you? How did you grow from it?

FH: Putting the business start-up programme together enabled me to put it all into practice, and then produce documents and prove it. I walked the talk while expanding, learning, growing etc. at the same time (again walking the talk).

ES: So the person who finished it is not the person who started it.

FH: I think that is fair.

ES: And that is often far more important than the end result - and how they all fit together as part of the web - because it is all part of the plan.

FH: I think it definitely got me questioning the motives and actions of others and my own as well (which is where the real growth has been).

25 November: My Little Gepetto

FH: Wendy and I had a slight tiff yesterday to say the least. She said my head was in the clouds. The way I view it is that I am looking at this stuff as I am going forward, but I think I am a fairly grounded person. I think it is almost like a yin and yang.

ES: The moment you started talking about Wendy I thought "But that's her role". That's why she is married to you. The moment you go too high she has to bring you down. When you to go too low, she has to pull you up.

 We often experience "relationship problems" when our partner acts in a way which is the opposite of what we expect. The role of your partner is to provide an opposite so that you can both become whole. Imagine the relationship if you both are the same.

FH: I know the Irish woman who owes me money is definitely in slight panic mode. But I am staying true to myself. I gave her a process back in October. She has not followed that process. She has taken more chances than ever before. I have terminated the relationship and all choices have consequences. She doesn't want to renew the relationship. There are consequences for being in breach of contract. In that sense, my conscience is clear. My head is clear. As for other people owing me money, there is no point in getting bogged down. It will appear when it appears. I will just crack on and look to manifest what has been lost through other sources.

ES: That's right. It is a transition period. It is about shaking off certain things to make place for others.

FH: Wendy is very focused on the things which have not materialized. As you rightly said the other day I have been anchored in The Water Cooler and that has stunted my growth because the Universe has been the size of the Water Cooler membership list. I have not wanted to let go at the same time. 20% of my income has come from The Water Cooler.

ES: And it was necessary. It was good at the time, but like anything that goes up, it must come down at some point.

ES: If you look at each of those people who owe you money individually, not just the group that is successful and the group that is failing – if you look at each of them as individuals, I still have a feeling that there is something about every single person that you needed to experience – not something about the group, but something about each person. And I have a very strong feeling that all of this is not about the outcome, it is about the journey.

FH: Yes, we all have different personalities. We all have different circumstances. Some pay the money but don't put in the effort. Some put in the effort and don't pay the money. Some pay the money and put in the effort. So there is a real mixture. It is not them. It is me. It is what I am experiencing in my relationship with them. It is putting that into context in terms of a learning experience and what I want to repeat and what I don't want to repeat.

ES: Yes. But it is not about the outcome – about where you are with them now. It is about how you got to this point with them. I think if you look carefully at it you will see there were massive benefits for you, and now there is the downside.

You cannot see the picture when you are in the frame. We have to go through the entire process and document it and then say "Is that what it was about?" This is probably something you can say for every life experience.

27 November: Recognizing the Lessons

FH: An interesting week all in all. I also think I have come to recognize a key lesson. I think my sense of awareness is shifting from after the event and looking back to join the dots, to becoming aware during the situation as it is unfolding, enabling me (perhaps) to change the focus or emphasis of my attention and thus the outcome - heavy stuff.

And slightly different from wanting to hurry the situation as opposed to change the focus or emphasis of the situation (after all a coin has 2 sides, and a glass can be half full or half empty)

ES: There is another side to it which is now very clear - to do with the time lag and living the spiral. Your relationship with The Water Cooler went through specific phases:

- *This is hurting me - will I do fight or flight? (base chakra)*
- *This is not happening to me - my own tribe turning against me (sacral chakra)*
- *I will show them who is in control here (solar plexus chakra)*
- *If I stay with them, will they accept and love me again (heart chakra)*
- *This is not working and we have nothing more to say to each other (throat chakra)*
- *Time to move on and grow again (3rd eye chakra)*
- *Oh boy, watch this space for miracles (crown chakra).*

You lived this over months, and over the past week or so you lived all of it again (a much shorter and more intense version), which is where the time lag comes in - you finally severed the bond - probably last week already - and this week you did a "reality check" and whoops - no more blog on The Water Cooler.

And the difficult part is where you first have strong emotions, and then realize what it was in fact all about - the time lag.

We can live different spirals at the same time. You have been dealing with this Water Cooler one for a long time, but it became more intense over the last week. This is the end of it. When you told me this morning saying that you have moved your blog somewhere else, I thought "This is it. This is what it was about."

 Read through the explanation of the chakras again. There is a lot of sense and wisdom in the pattern that all our major life experiences follow. When you look back at some big experiences that have shaped you, what patterns do you see forming?

FH: I just thought it was so logical and so simple. What I was having difficulty with this morning- and what was interesting was the subsequent article that I wrote – was that I was talking about circumstances and how it is not the circumstances we want to change, because they are the last part of the creative process. We cannot change the circumstances. We have to change our thoughts, feelings and actions to create different circumstances. I have been focusing all my energy on The Water Cooler when I shouldn't be, so stop focusing in there. Instead of dwelling on it, there was a completely different sense of recognition or awareness within the situation.

ES: Exactly. I was referring to the process underneath that.

FH: Yes, and I thought the whole chakra thing I shied away from several times. I wanted to explore the greater, fuller meaning and understanding of it. I have got a basic understanding of them. I thought it was very interesting how you quickly summarised that the way you did.

This is so hard to explain. Instead of thinking I have all these challenges around me with people who have let me down and not done anything about it, I am thinking: stop. I am in a process.

Where am I in my own process? I am becoming aware of what is around me. What is the message to me? Am in reacting to the circumstances and the stimuli? I cannot change that. They are the result of what has already happened. So I need to start re-thinking and re-formulating positively in going forward and that will create the next natural part of the process. It just so happens that the next part of the process is re-writing and replacing the work I have already done, at a slightly deeper level.

ES: Exactly.

FH: Christ, that was hard to get to this, but now it is like – oh, man – it is like an Eureka moment. I've just had someone written to me in the last five minutes - after this realization, I hasten to add, to say "Hands up, apologies, you will be paid cash directly out of my bank account on Monday."

ES: Like he is rewarding you for "getting it"!

FH: That is beyond logic and consequence and coincidence by virtue of the nature and intensity of the situation this week. I have got one more thing where I am trying to work out what is going to happen, and that is Dieter in Germany. On five separate occasions he has promised and not followed through or delivered.
He has promised me faithfully that today was going to be the day that everything will be sorted. I am still not 100% sold, but in light of my own little breakthrough that I have had in the last 24 hours or so, I will see how the rest of the day pans out. There might be another reward at the end of the breakthrough I have had.

ES: You are creating frustration for yourself where you are expecting it all to happen at the same time. You expect to realize what is happening as you go through it, and that is not how it works. You first go through it and then you look back and you connect the dots and you realise "My God, that is what it was about."

Interesting how we go through a really painful moment, only to be rewarded by something that otherwise we would have seen as quite unrelated.

FH: The connecting of the dots is happening in a slightly different way than I expected. It is not a hindsight, looking back, aha moment. It is a real living the moment as I am re-experiencing it in a shorter and more intense, more – it is almost, dare I say it, in a separate reality.

I am re-living the experience from a different perspective and a different reality to say "I am looking back and joining the dots, but I am doing it now. Ah, that's why this is and how it is."

So as I look back over the last three, four months, as I have become aware of the process, we have been documenting things. I have been writing articles about the awareness. I have been learning things about myself, and at the same time I have been getting other people to question things about themselves by means of my articles.

I have done the awareness bit and the learning bit. It was this re-visiting why it is not working – all to do with resistance and beliefs and circumstance I have identified where I am in the process and what's the meaning behind the experiences that I have had.

ES: Yes, and looking for the signposts without getting emotional about it. Because when you get emotional about it, your emotions get in the way and you don't see the signposts.

FH: Yes, that is exactly where I am at, because it is not so much the answers you give, because I am in control. I am responsible. It's been the questioning the why, not the how. How things happen is going to manifest itself while I go through the process. I really have been struggling with why it is happening now, and it all comes back to "Look, Fraser, you have been in your own slumber, you have been in this area of comfort, all to do with The Water Cooler." You have said it, Wendy has said it, all the people have

282

said, aid it has not been that I have been fighting with it. I just got through the cycle of awareness, understanding and knowing. I just concluded the process that I wrote about.

ES: Yes, That is exactly what it is about. And that is why we are documenting this experience that people find very difficult to put into words, and therefore they feel really quite lonely on this earth.

FH: This is really why I need to move away from The Water Cooler. Although it has been good to me, it's actually inhibiting me instead of allowing me to grow. I am tempted to also write a goodbye blog to The Water Cooler to see the reaction to that. I might write it but not post it.

Mrs. Dublin is very conspicuous by her absence and silence. She is normally a noisy little critter. I think either she is away planning, stewing and thinking, or she has a few fires of her own she is trying to put out.

Hans in South Africa has just contacted me to get my bank details. He had to go through the same experience as Catherine. Hans has a few fires of his own he is trying to put out, I suspect.

One of the other guys phoned me last night and said *"Fraser, I signed an agreement with you. I have had an awful lot of shit that I have had to deal with this year. I'll be honest. My mind has been on so many different other things. I realize I have let you down and I have let myself down. I probably can't continue with you but I don't want to part on sour terms. Can we come to an arrangement that makes sense?"*

I said "if you are honest with me, I am happy to bend and twist. I really appreciate that."

ES: And you have been saying it to all of them all along.

FH: Yes. So the people who are taking me at face value and engaging with me are having a very simple, painless way of exiting the relationship with me, but the other ones who are huffing and puffing and creating a bit of a storm, are creating a rod for their own back.

I am getting slightly better at being able to distance myself and watch them implode as opposed to me getting involved in the implosion. It is not me that has not done what I said I would do. It is them, and I feel awkward trying to sympathize with them, because they are in that position which I technically created but all I have done is presented an opportunity which they have either not taken advantage of, or they have dug a bigger hole for themselves.

That has been my biggest challenge this year. I keep wanting to help them, when I shouldn't want to help them. One in particular is Hans in South Africa. He has again gone all quiet on me. I felt really bad because I thought I was creating a bad situation for them, but I wasn't. They just haven't done it and they have been taking the Mickey out of me for so many months.

ES: That's right – and waiting for you to do something about it. You did what you needed to so. You lived your script.

 Do you really think you are the only person being shaped by intense experiences? If you ask every person involved in this saga, they will probably give you their own version of the traumatic time they are experiencing. Think about people that you have been in conflict with. How did they show their stress and conflict?

FH: It started off as a very scary week. I am still not concerned about the financial aspect. It is more a case of where and why are these things happening at this point in time? What is the lesson? What am I to gain in preparing and going forward, so that I don't have to repeat this lesson again?

ES: *And I know from personal experience. Follow your heart, do what you need to do, and the money follows.*

FH: And that's been my philosophy in everything that I do. The one thing I have been struggling with a little is: why are the people around me not the right people? I know how long it took for them to get them to that stage where they made the commitment and signed the contract. Are you saying it was probably right at the time, but as things evolved they are no longer relevant or have that place?

ES: *Take a step back. You have an excellent process. You recruited people that you believed were able to do the job. Now let's assume that every single one of them did what is expected of them and are still doing what is expected of them. How would that change the situation? What I am saying is let's say you recruited these people a year ago. They know exactly what they need to do. They have every tool under the sun. They are doing the job. Great! How would that have changed you, and how would that have changed the situation you are in right now?*

FH: I wouldn't have had the challenges. I wouldn't have had to think. I wouldn't have had to grow. I wouldn't have experienced everything I had experienced.

ES: *And who would you have been?*

FH: I suppose I would still have been in my own relative state of slumber.

ES: *Yep. So did you recruit the wrong people?*

FH: Well, that was part of my rationalization to myself yesterday in that I may not have gained the financial rewards that I wanted or they wanted, but they have contributed to my cash flow. It was almost as if I can hear you speak to me, saying along the lines of "you have been protected. They have been provided to ensure that your needs are being met, but not necessarily to give you a level of abundance to make you lazy and sloppy.

ES: Exactly.

FH: I have been wrestling with my conscience in relation to the people who owe me money. Half of me says "Do I really go the whole hog and hold them responsible for every penny, or do I say pay me up what you owe me and we will call it quits?" I have been looking for the lesson – is this just the catalyst for me to say "right, everything stopped. Sign the undertaking that you will not have anything to do with the Results Academy in going forward, to give me the mental reassurance that I can go on with other things as well". That's what I have been wrestling with. Do I pursue it to the full extent of the law? Do I call it quits and just get rid of them? Do I hold them accountable for the back money that is owed? How far do I take it myself? Although I am in control of it and I can decide how far, I just don't know whether I spend time in dealing with this negative aspect of life, or do I just let it come to its own natural conclusion and crack on in other positive areas? And it's been a real juggling with it because Wendy says "get the money off them!"

ES: When you first asked yourself the question, what was your first response?

 Your first response is always the better one. It may not be the most logical one, and it may seem to you that you swim upstream, but invariably, if you follow that first response, the situation improves.

FH: My first response is still one of disappointment, where I question myself, wondering how I have let them down. And that implies an element of guilt, but it is not guilt, because I am trying to learn from what I have been through so that I don't repeat it again. One thing you have taught me is that I also have to respect my own boundaries because people have used my good nature against me and taken advantage of me because of it.

ES: You are your worst judge. You are very harsh on yourself. You are looking for a mistake, where you can do better, for how you can rectify where you went wrong. What if you did not do wrong? What if this is how it was supposed to happen? What if these people were used in their own way to actually bring you to where you are? Is that wrong?

FH: It might not be wrong. I might be able to recognize that as part of the lesson and the growing, but it is how that concludes and plays out in terms of the benefit gained in the next chapter.

OK, so they have been used to help play this part.
ES: Yes. And they achieved what they needed to achieve because you are different. You are a lot firmer in your approach because you know that what you do, you do with integrity. You know that you have given them the benefit of the doubt in every possible way. In that sense, they have achieved what they needed to achieve.

FH: OK, so a chapter in itself has come to an end because they will no longer be with me and those that are playing ball will be.

ES: Yes. And nothing you can do or you could have done will change the situation.

FH: I suppose there is still that element of fear, saying "God, maybe I haven't done something right, there is a loophole in that contract, it is going to come back; it is going to be 20 times worse on me . . ."

ES: Oh, no. You are so protected.

FH: I consider many of those I work with - my friends. I have also gone out of my way for them. I gave them many options to back out. They all wanted to do it. They chose and agreed to the terms. They signed the terms. The documents went back and forth two or three times until it was finally agreed and signed. I suspect I would prefer to walk away without really pursuing them for the total amount, knowing that I am able to hold my head high, and I know the true position. But half of me then says "They signed an agreement. You need to follow through, to remind them they signed that agreement." I really am walking the line as to whether I say "Bring it up to speed with the money you owe me, we'll call it quits, but you have to them stop using my business". I realize now I am in control. I just don't want to be the bad one.

I need to demonstrate that I have been firm, but I can take my foot off the gas at any time that I see fit. The more of a fight they put up, the more dogged I want to be, yet if they say "Hands up, how do I resolve it?" I am happy to work out an amicable solution with them.

 Remember what the professor said in "A passage to India"? There are things you can change, and there are things you can do nothing about.

ES: Sometimes you think people do one thing but they actually do something and you don't realize the context in which they do things until you look back. Yes, with the coaches, it is all about money and them being in breach of contract, but there will probably come a time soon when you will realize it is actually about more than that.

FH: I get it. We need the void, so that the vessel can be filled again. Even if it is half full, we can't recognize the experience of completeness and fullness. It is only topping it up.

ES: Exactly. You have to experience it being completely, totally empty.

 This is the whole purpose of change – to empty you out, so that you can be filled again. Have you experienced that?

FH: This is probably the hardest time I have had, and it is not a result of my own doing. I have been asking all the time "Why me?" but not as a victim. I really want to understand so that if I know the process, I can help endless other people in recognizing the process and what they can do to help themselves.

ES: Yes. But you have to live the process first so that you can look back at the process and think "So that is how that tiny little bit of the Universe actually works! Now I can see it. Now I can put the message into words. Now I can help other people.

FH: People go through an entire lifetime and they might increase one level of awareness or go down one aspect of a spiritual experience. The last three, four months have been so rapid, so intense, so fast – it is almost like double the intensity in half the time.

ES: Like a crash course – sink or swim. And you are swimming so far.

FH: And I will start thinking about my little good-bye epitome for The Water Cooler. I have made a conscious decision to stop doing things in The Water Cooler. I don't know whether I will delete my profile.

30 November: Guilty Conscience

FH: I just had a conversation with Catherine McQueen. She is prepared to pay me up until the end of the year, in total about £1 200.

I said she must send me the undertaking document today. This is a little agreement saying she will sever her ties with my business and no longer use any of the intellectual property.

She said "Fraser, if you want to take me to court, I would have to transfer it to Dublin and that would be more money, more expense, a lot more hassle, I don't have the money."

I told Wendy about her offer. Part of me said that I should take the money for the sake of the cash flow. Another part of me said "Don't say yes just yet. Let her squirm a little bit."

ES: If she offers you £1 200 she is probably prepared to pay three times that amount.

FH: I think so as well. For her to have a court action against her regarding a debt would have unbelievable repercussions for her reputation.

It is very seldom that I am in a position of strength with people who owe me money. I think this is a piddly little offer.

ES: She cannot be serious. She is in a situation that she brought herself into. She is still not realizing what is happening, and she is playing with you.

FH: If the boot was on the other foot, she would be getting very hard, very stroppy and very legal because of the nature of her personality.

ES: All this stuff we have been talking about is not just available to everybody. It happens every day to every person. But while you are living through it, you do not necessarily see what it is about. When you look back, you see what it is about. Now if you look back and see what it is about often enough, you start to realize what is happening while it is happening. You start to get the benefit a lot sooner, because if you look back and you see something that stands out for you, next time it happens you will not say "what have I done to deserve this, not me again, I am a victim". You will say "ah – I have been through this. Now I can recognize it while I am in it, which means I can get a shortcut out of it and get on with my life." You have been doing that. Initially you have been doing a lot of looking back, especially over the past year or year and a half. You had to look at all those situations and see them in a different light and understand why they happened. But then there was a fast forward – since you have started understanding that there is a lesson in every situation, things happen and you get the lesson much quicker.

You often get it while it is happening, not just afterwards.

1 December: It's in the Post

ES: Do you know that during our very first conversation on 25ᵗʰ August you told me that you are going to stop blogging on The Water Cooler and start blogging only on your website? It has taken you three months to actually take that step because that single statement required so much work under the surface before you could actually say "This is it, I am doing it".

FH: I am trying to work out what the core issue was – I suppose it was not being prepared to let go.
ES: Yes.
FH: Catherine McQueen phoned me back. I told you she made me an offer yesterday.
I got out the calculator and I just sent her this email:

"Hi Catherine
Further to our telephone conversation of yesterday morning, I write to thank you for returning the undertakings document, received by email earlier today.
With regards to your verbal "offer" of yesterday, I write to confirm the following:
The Balance outstanding on back payments as of today's date is £12 400.
If you were me, what would you think of your offer?
While you reconsider your offer, and in the spirit of wanting to resolve matters amicably, I may be prepared to discount what you owe me by £4 800. and once again is indicative of my willingness to resolve matters amicably, and to politely state that while I have to decline your offer, I am prepared to negotiate.
Can you also please furnish me a list of your other creditors, and the amounts owing.
If I have not heard from you by midday on Friday 4ᵗʰ December, I will assume that you do not wish to accept my discount, and I may have to pass the matter to my solicitor and her team to conclude matters by following the due legal process if we cannot reach a satisfactory, amicable and realistic conclusion.

I look forward to hearing from you
Kind Regards
Fraser"

ES: This is such a difference from how you have dealt with Hans in South Africa. You are obviously much more comfortable with what you are doing because it makes sense to you and it doesn't go against your grain, because your grain has changed,
FH: I think you are right for a number of different reasons. I have had confirmation that the agreement was water tight and she had better do something about it. That gave me an air of confidence.

2 December: Connecting the Dots

FH: I would like to point out that I am not a high maintenance individual, or an emotional wreck, but....

ES: You are human? And going through a massive transition?
FH: Read this –

"Hi Dieter
Further to my email of 8th October (see below), and all subsequent emails since, I write with disappointment that you have been unable to remedy the breach, and bring all outstanding monies up to date.
I write to advise you that as of today's date (2nd December), the amount owing is now £4 400, and I did not receive the phone call that you promised yesterday.
This, as I am sure you can appreciate, is unacceptable especially when you have made several promises to pay, and failed to make any payment on account during the last six months.
I have to say, I do feel very disappointed. I feel I have been very supportive and understanding regarding your situation.
I have offered financial holidays, discounts, and continued to make myself available to support you in the rollout of your business in Germany.
Our agreement is now terminated by virtue of you failing to continually to meet your contractual and financial obligations and comply with my subsequent requests.
I may be prepared to discount the above by £4 300 to encourage early settlement.
Once again this is indicative of my willingness to resolve matters amicably without having to formally engage my solicitor and her team to take matters to the next stage in the legal process.
If I have not heard from you by midday on Friday 4th December, I will assume that you do not wish to accept my discount, and I may have to pass the matter to my solicitor and her team to conclude matters by following the due legal process if we cannot reach a satisfactory, amicable and realistic conclusion.

I look forward to hearing from you.
Kind Regards
Fraser"

ES: The process is not finished yet. I was just going to ask you – apart form the money, what else ties you to these people? What have you invested in them apart from the money?

This is not about the money. It is about the severance of a relationship. Yes, it is a business relationship, but both parties fail to realize that the relationship is over and that it is time to let go. Remember when you held onto a disastrous relationship?

FH: My time and my effort – and I have helped every one of them on a personal basis as well. I spoke to Hans in South Africa this morning – I found his phone number by pure fluke – and his wife answered. I asked for him and gave my name.

I could tell by her attitude that he had not told his wife about the situation. I had a conversation with him and he was as nice as pie. He kept saying he was not trying to be difficult – it just did not happen for a reason. I said "I understand that, but what do we do to remedy the situation about the money you owe?"

He said "There's no way you will get the money in terms of the breach of contract. I just don't have it". I asked him about the money he already owed and he promised to send me an email with a payment schedule. Mentally I have drawn the line under this in terms of the people I want to work with. I am desperately trying to understand the meaning of it.

ES: With each of these people you had an initial contract and you had expectations and they had expectations.

FH: Yes, and on the phone call with Hans in South Africa, he said "I want you to know, Fraser, this is no reflection on you whatsoever. I want to make it perfectly clear that it is my problem and I just cannot do it. Going down the legal route is not going to be of much help either. It cannot and will not happen, because I don't have the money to give you."

I said "I appreciate that, you have just told me after 3 months that you want to deal with the back money that you owe me. This is the first time you actually said that. Can you please send me an email to that effect?"

I am still waiting – I will see in 24 hours. I have never been in a situation like this before.

ES: And there is a reason for it. There is more to come. When I read the first bit that you sent this morning, I was reminded of my own divorce and the process of divorce in general. People think that when you get divorced, you do the paperwork and go on to live separate lives. That is only the end of it on the surface. On a spiritual level it is always much more severe. Even with a friendly divorce, what happens on a spiritual level is much more serious and much more deeper felt, because when you enter into a contract with a person – either personal or business – when you enter into an emotional contract with a person, the silver cord that I was referring to between you and Wendy?

FH: Yes.
ES: A similar connection happens between you and any person that you enter into a contract with. It even happens between friends and between you and your children. When the physical contract comes to an end, it does not mean the entire situation comes to an end. There is still the cord that needs to be cut.

Cutting that cord is incredibly painful and difficult, and it does make you question everything that you believe in. it makes you question yourself, your own integrity. It does take a while to get back on your feet after that has happened.

What is happening here is that you have had that cord in place with all of these people. At least from your side it has never been just a business transaction. It has always been a business transaction with a friend, with some expectation – I suspect from your side – that it will make the friendship even stronger.

FH: I think that is a very fair assessment.

ES: That was your expectation, but it was not necessarily their expectation. This is why they can be quite blasé and abrupt about it. They experience different emotions than you. For you that also adds to the disillusionment, because you had particular expectations about this – not only about the contract, but about the relationship which is symbolized by the contract. They have not lived up to their part of the relationship. You have tried to overcompensate from your side for them.Also, what they are getting from you is by far more than what you are getting from them.

FH: That is stating the obvious. I am not being facetious; it is also a frustrated acknowledgement of what you just said.

ES: And because they are taking so much from you, that leaves you tired on different levels – physically, emotionally – sick and tired of trying to get to grips with this.

FH: That makes perfect sense. In terms of energy, they are draining my energy and not giving anything back.

ES: Yes. And you did get to a point where you realize that – where you started saying "Look, why is it that I have to give so much and get nothing in return?" And that happened over the last few months. For you, because you are far more sensitive – not fragile, I mean you understand your emotions and the bigger picture and the energy, you are experiencing it far more intensely than they are. You are actually cutting that tie, whereas they are trying their absolute best to keep the tie in place because they benefit from it.

That makes it so difficult. What do you do about this?

You want to cut those ties, because you realize you cannot continue to allow them to take their energy from you.

FH: Dieter in Germany is apparently a spiritual healer. I think he will recognize – as I said in the e-mail to him – I am very disappointed. I think that summarizes the whole experience. But I have drawn the line now. He had already terminated by virtue of not complying with about 12 or 15 different e-mails.

ES: And every one of them in their own way has been doing their utmost to keep that cord in place.

FH: I would agree with that.

ES: So what would you like to do? Would you like to keep the cords in place, or would you like to finally cut them?

FH: I think where I did cut the cord, it has been a hard, complicated process. I have let go by confirming that it is now terminated. Are you saying let go of the idea of suing them for the money?
ES: Let go of the emotional investment.

 A relationship breaks up on different levels. Everything you experience during that break-up is expressed in your physical body. You do tend to feel "sick and tired" and it does take a while to get your energy back. Have you experienced these symptoms?

FH: I think I did that with Catherine. The one with Dieter was quite hard because I have known him for five years.

ES: Probably also because you have invested a lot more emotionally in Dieter.

FH: Yes, I have. But when I look back to the past six months, he did not follow through on anything he said he would.

298

ES: And during that time, did you give him a lot?

FH: I have given him access to much material and helped him in his own business. The short answer is yes.

ES: Did he come to get a lot from you, or did he withdraw from you a while ago already?

FH: Well, he did come up with a number of excuses why he has not come to certain appointments by phone or Skype. He did say that Germany has had a real economic disaster. With him there is his own emotional attachment as well.

ES: And to you that is probably worth a lot more than money.

FH: It is, because I have never been motivated by money. I have only been motivated by two things – freedom to choose what I want to do, and the ability to help other people.

ES: And that is what you invested in all of these people. The money was just part of the physical contract. What you invested is much more emotional and that is what they did not deliver on. That is what makes it so difficult to let go.

FH: OK.

ES: To me this feels like a final clearing out. For example you go into the loft and clear out a lot of stuff. When you get towards the last bits, you start thinking "do I need to clear that out as well? Haven't I done enough yet? Maybe I can leave the last 20-odd bits and pieces for next year's clearing out? " But that is not how it works. You have to do all of it. And you have to do all of it now, because you cannot pour new wine in a jug that still contains old wine. For some reason that will become apparent, you chose to do this on a big scale.

Most other people do this on a small scale, but not you. But you only do it on this scale if you have the resources to deal with it.

FH: I really am questioning – not my mental stability – if this is a testing time, what is the test? Also, this test has been going on for ages.

ES: This is typical of any divorce situation – it feels like it never stops. Most people, when they go through a divorce – or the end of a friendship or a business relationship – have particular expectations. They get disappointed in those expectations, and they remain stuck there. That is why so many of these relationships end acrimoniously. They remain stuck there and they never try to see the other side.

All I can say to you now is: don't ever stop believing in yourself and your own integrity.

FH: In the normal course of business somebody might have a bad debt or be owed money. In the course of business somebody may have a bad month or even a couple of bad months. In the course of the past number of months I have been around people who do not do what they say they would do. As I observe that, I wonder how I contributed to their failure. I do so many things to support and help them. With the likes of Catherine for example, she would go away for up to six weeks and not communicate with me. I spoke to her about it and reminded her that I am a resource for her to use.I understand in a way that this perhaps is the Universe's way to say "You have learned what you needed to learn."

ES: The one thing you need to stop doing is to ask yourself where you passed or failed. There is no pass or fail. That is a judgment that you add to the situation. When things are really going well, you don't learn from it – you just cruise along because there is nothing to learn.

FH: Wendy said there are three coaches owing me money and the common theme is that it is not working. But when I do it, it works.

Part of me is thinking maybe they are trying to emulate me and they cannot do it, so it is not working. But that almost goes back to say the whole point of a franchise or a license agreement is that they take the system that works and they follow those. It works for me and it works for clients. So I think it is different when people roll up their sleeves.

ES: But that is the point. You have done everything you could. It did not work as expected. Does that mean you failed, or does it mean it is an experience you created so that you could learn from it?

You have not completely got 100% of what you needed to learn from it, and therefore it is continuing. That does not mean you failed. It would be the same as – let's say you have a person who is very happy with his life, everything is going according to plan and he is OK – there is no stress in his life.

But then he decides that he wants to run the 100 meters in 10 seconds. For starters he is overweight and smoking. He has to stop smoking and lose the weight, and then he can start practicing. He eventually stops smoking and loses some weight, and decides to start running so that he can lose more weight and get closer to his target. The first time he runs the 100 meters he does it in 25 seconds and he says "ah – I am not even going to try again because I failed." Did he fail?

FH: There is a learning experience that enables us to improve.

ES: Yes. And if you go through the same experience a number of times, every time you go through it, you learn something else about yourself through that. It is not possible to fail. That is a judgment we add because we love to punish ourselves. Especially when we are impatient and we like to do a perfect job and things are not going well, it is very easy to look in the mirror and say "you are a failure". We don't want to crawl, we don't want to walk - we want to run.

FH: I have been making notes about what I have learned while you were talking.

Written agreements are a necessity.
Less emotional attachment to the relationship and/or in dealing with issues People need to create, not emulate. Have clear boundaries. I have discovered that agreements can be interpreted in different ways, but I must have my own boundaries and decide what I want to allow in or not allow in.

ES: And also with every agreement there is an emotional investment that does not get acknowledged – even if it is with your bank manager.

Yesterday I used the example of a rubber band – the more it gets stretched, the more painful it gets. But it can only stretch up to a point, and then it snaps and the pain goes away and that is an amazing feeling.

FH: Andrew is due to have his first baby and things have been quite tight for them. He is generating monthly income by doing everything I cover. His cash flow is up and down. He was my first coach – therefore a strong emotional attachment. Also, if he goes, is that a failure on my part, and will people see it that way? I am trying to not acknowledge that or adopt the negative emotions associated with that.

ES: It is not that easy to see the picture when you are still in the frame. You can really punish yourself or you can go with the flow and see what happens. I feel you are really learning what you need to learn as you go along, and you need to give yourself credit for that. And with all of these coaches there is lot more behind it than just the money. Yes, the money is significant, but there is a lot more to it than just the money.

FH: I am not impulsive, but I can be quite decisive. I am close to going back to the last two and saying "Sorry guys, this is it".

ES: When you do get to that point, it will probably be a lot less painful. Until you get to that point, you will have other things to learn from them.

302

You have run your own business for many years and you have escaped many things that employed people have to live with, but you also have set up other challenges for yourself.

It is not easy to let go, especially when you know what you have and you don't know where you are heading. Then you are tempted to think "Better the devil you know than the devil you don't." But eventually you have to move on.

 This inner conflict continues until the entire process has been resolved. While you go through such a separation process, you don't even notice that you repeat the same pattern all the time.

The good news is that at some point you get sick and tired of the situation yourself, and that is when you are ready to move on to the next step. Have you experienced that?

FH: I shall go and have a think.

ES: And don't try and think where you "failed" – or do if you want to punish yourself.

FH: I am going to log this today. "I acknowledge that I have the courage to let go. In doing so I am asking the Universe for an acknowledgement of my understanding. I ask the Universe to confirm to me that I have understood the lesson."

ES: And when you get your confirmation, don't reject it. Say "Thank you, I accept it."
Don't say "Well, it is a bit small, I am not sure whether it is a confirmation", or "I am not sure I deserve because it is a bit big for me".

Later:

FH: Interesting wee development..... I spoke to Bob in Aberdeen and suggested that we draw a line etc.... He argued no, saying he was paying me on Friday, and that can we continue going until end of January, by which time it will give us both enough time to really appraise and know what we both want, but in meantime he will honor his obligations, and keep doing what he is doing (actually the first one to be honest enough about their own position).

Also, Dieter called me - quite emotional because I want to terminate our agreement, as he was trying "everything under the sun" to right the situation with him, and was also looking to bring all payments up to date by Friday and that I should trust him, and how he values our relationship etc..... He "warns me to do the right thing" etc. - (also a completely different tone to what I have been getting - might be because he saw how much he was in for, but I also think he really does want to work with me too.).

ES: Dieter cannot function without you, but you can function without him. He knows that. He will cling on but you will have much grief and no benefit. It does not feel good at all. Bob feels quite different – he is learning from you but using his own energy.

 This is again about the weaker clinging to the stronger and refusing to let go. Sometimes you have to be quite firm and end the relationship by breaking off all contact. What destructive pattern are you still holding on to?

FH: Yes, Bob appears to have woken up to his situation. He can see the writing on the wall, and has assigned himself an exit date. A pride thing I suspect - he thinks he is negotiating an exit on his terms and so perceives he is not a failure, but is being pushed.

ES: If he can succeed, nothing will prevent him from continuing? And as long as he performs and pays, he is OK.

FH: Bob has recently woken up to the fact that he has not put in effort all year. Now that he has done something, he is beginning to see some results. He doesn't want me to pull the rug just as he's getting going. I just think he had a bit of an "awakening" and realization of responsibility. He wants to take responsibility and on his own head be it – it is not down to me. He's evaluating the situation based on his own actions and results (or not by the end of January, as the case may be).

4 December: Recognising the Denial of Others

FH: Dieter in Germany promised faithfully he would call me by 12pm today.....he didn't.

Ah well.

ES: He is still dancing - has not realized yet that the music has stopped!

FH: He phoned me last week and said that if I push the legal side, he'll bust the company and I'll get nothing - he is telling me just to wait. Catherine in Dublin didn't comply with today being her final day, and Hans in South Africa didn't do the e-mail he promised - that just about sums up my week.

7 December: Stop Trying, Just Do it

FH: This weekend I was close to packing it in with my business. I thought about it and started flicking through the old testimonials and stuff and I thought "Hang on, I need to re-do some of these testimonials into the new look and feel." I think that was a good exercise. I was questioning whether everything around me was working. Perhaps this is a mid-life crisis – I don't know.

I have really been struggling with the reason why these things have been happening. Am I being tested to the limit to see what I do with it all?

ES: While you are in the process it is not that easy to see what it's about. You are always one step behind, because by the time you understand what it is about, it's already happened. There is a lot of stuff that is not in your awareness. By the time you become aware of it, it's already happened and a lot more is happening as well.

FH: Bob in Aberdeen just got a new client. He is ecstatic. He said "I can't believe how long it has taken me to actually read and apply what you offer. Now that I have done it, I have proven to myself that it works. All I need to do is repeat it on a more regular basis."
If one person can do it, the others can do it as well.

ES: One of the things that have come out of it is discipline. You no longer beg people to do it. Instead you say "You promised. Now you have to deliver or I draw the line."

FH: On Friday night I said to Wendy I have learnt an awful lot this year, including setting and respecting boundaries. Also, my opinion and beliefs about money has been different. While I respect money, I have not been respecting my own value in terms of getting people to honour why they said they would. In my book a deal is a deal. You made a comment about going as fast as a

Ferrari in creating things and moving them forward, but when I need to pull people up for not paying me, everything stops.

The agreements that I have are watertight. I needed to get people to follow their contractual obligations before I could move on to new things. I am now able to join the dots. It has been about money, boundaries and holding people to account – not just in the coaching program, but also in their financial dealings with me.

It has been hard.

In the last couple of weeks I have been thinking momentum is building.

I have become concerned about it. The number of people who stopped speaking to me over the past six to eight weeks has gone up by about 90%. I feel isolated in terms of sharing goals, aspirations and so on. I have often discussed things with a number of people. They are not calling me as much, and I am not calling them as much. It is not just one thing. Every part of my life is going through some level of transformation. It is very intense.

ES: Yes, it is intense. That rubber band is close to snapping and when it does, you will get back to being totally comfortable.

FH: Even with Dieter – he makes promises and commitments, and when I write back to confirm and enforce, it does not happen. Everyone around me seems to be not speaking with me. I seem to be the only common denominator. I know something will swing it around, but I am in the dark.

ES: There is something I have to tell you.
I feel a nervous twinge in my stomach – just a twinge, nothing serious or really significant, but it is there. It is there because you are new on this experience and you do not quite know what to expect yet.

FH: I know it – it feels like you're about to have a bout of morning sickness, but don't – it just keeps you in the state of excited stressful nervousness.

ES: You have had to live with much insecurity over the past few months. There was a purpose behind it all. Although you have had insecurity before, you have not had anything on this scale. You have always been in charge. You have always felt that you call the shots. You have always felt comfortable with that, because it kept your own fears at bay.

FH: It certainly hasn't felt like that since August. Has that then been your role, to open my mind up to the deeper side of life, to get me to log/record my experiences and so that we can share them with others, but also to help develop me and give me the grounding for next year, and beyond? The more searching I've done, the more I've been turning up pieces of the jigsaw not just for me, but even for you and a few people around me, even though they are oblivious to the path I appear to be on.

ES: This time round you have been forced to bring all your fears to the surface. You have been placed in various positions where you had to really dig deep. You will agree that more times than not you were pleasantly surprised. This process has made you stronger.
You have become a giant among men. You still do not think of yourself in this way, and that adds to who you are. That is the quality that will keep your feet on the ground in the coming months.

FH: Does this mean, therefore, that the whole sequence of recent experiences happened to get me to go within rather than look outside/externally for answers? I have contemplated more in the last four to six months than in the last ten to 15 years. While I don't feel stronger, I have continually tried to gain a wider/deeper perspective by using the vessel-void concept. It has helped strongly to have faith in what I am doing and also to recognize it in others and where they are in their own process. Often people choose not to explore/but rather to continuously deal with life at a superficial level, and not recognize the signs or where they are in the process.

I am now beginning to see through many people and things but feel that I can't say anything. It is not my place to interfere with other people's situations, but I just hate to see injustice.

ES: You have passed through a gate that you for many years have thought of as first not being there, and when you discovered the gate, you thought it was closed. Initially discovering the gate gave you great joy, but you were also quite relieved to discover that the gate was closed. Then you discovered that the gate was closed, but even the slightest push will open the gate. At the time you tried your very best to ensure the gate remain closed, while at the same time leaning against the gate to see how far it will open. Now, not only is the gate open, but you have walked through the gate and you are at a point of no return.

FH: OK, I see that as a metaphor of my personal growth – awakening in the sense I have a gained a much deeper insight and perspective on things, and a greater understanding of the ups and downs of working for yourself and how to respond to those challenges.

ES: Walking through that gate has made you a man among men. This is a new role for you and you are having some discomfort in this new role, but that discomfort will pass. Your footing is growing surer by the day. You are on the right track with everything you do. You are becoming more secure by the day, but this is different from the security that you have known before.

FH: I think the universe is beginning to show small confirmations (very small) and in weird random ways that I might be on the right path with the website/proposition etc.

ES: You have discovered that there are layers to your security, and you are far more comfortable with the layers that can be regarded as insecurity when you look at this through the world's eyes.

FH: I want to list those levels of insecurity and emotions:
- Mastery
- Certainty
- Faith
- Belief
- Confidence
- Uncertainty
- Doubt
- Fear

I love your take on "stop trying" - so different form the normal. Trying means you've already lost faith or certainty about the belief in the outcome. It just smacks you in the face, and tells you to wake up – I love it.

ES: Yes – it works against the Law of Attraction.

FH: But your explanation resonates with me (and how I think) and I suspect how 99% of the population interpret it.

ES: The process of creation is about searching waves for what you want to materialize, then finding the particles in the waves, then collecting the particles until they become what you searched for and the item/experience materializes. The particles have the potential to become anything you want, and they are anywhere, everywhere and nowhere until you go and look for them and attract them to you in the shape you decided on.

It is like ordering a beautiful car, to be delivered to your front door. Then you see some movement in the far distance, and it can be either a car or an animal or a whirlwind. You want it to be your car, but you cannot see clearly because it is too far away. If you are sure of the process, you see the outline of the car clearer and clearer as it approaches, and you feel your excitement growing. Then the car stops at your front door, and you say "Yes! I knew it, here is my proof. I am right."

311

If you are not sure whether what is approaching is the car you ordered, you say "If it is not my car, then I failed and I don't want to have my nose rubbed into it. So I am not even going to look any more, because it is probably an animal that is approaching." The car you are creating then changes into an animal because the Universe is so obliging. And what do you say? "I tried, but I knew it would not work, and see what happened. I am right."

 Be very careful with your thoughts – you are creating your future all the time. It would be a good idea to write down a few thoughts every day, just so that you can become more aware of what you think. Remember, every thought becomes either a word or an action at some point.

8 December: Quick – Beat the Germans!

FH: Let me tell you something that I'm VERY, VERY angry about today.... and don't know whether to REACT or not...

I read an article where Catherine from Dublin refers to her holiday in Majorca.

So much for Catherine lying about money problems etc.... She's currently on a beach in Majorca and hasn't replied to my e-mail about how she is going to solve the problem and how I was turning down her £1 000 offer v my £15 000 offer. She was pleading poverty etc., and the picture now appears quite different.

ES: This is where you DON'T react - you respond using that same strong emotion to come down on her, but you control the emotion like you control a wild horse - that is the test. You use your emotion, and don't let it use you.

It feels like a final test - do you react, or do you pull together all the strings from the past few months and respond and get noticed for all the right reasons?

It feels like she is teasing you in public - do you take the bait, or do you go step by step and remain authentic? Authenticity is powerful and I suspect the discount to her has just evaporated.

FH: I sent her an email and cc'd my solicitor:

11 December: More Blame, Excuses and Denial

FH: Darling Catherine has been getting somewhat braver in her interactions with me.

ES: Well, you did interfere with her time on the beach. What did you expect?

FH: She wrote back to me saying "My husband paid for the flights. We are staying in his parents' villa. He is very concerned about my health issues as a result of my negative dealings with you and your business. It is all your fault that my health is deteriorating".

 I can see you shaking your head here and laughing to yourself. When did you last hear the word "it is all your fault" when in fact it was not your fault at all and you knew it?

12 December: The Waiting Game

FH: I spoke to Dieter in Germany yesterday evening and reminded him that he was going to call me earlier the week. He said he would pay me very soon. I did not believe it. He is such a spiritual person but he makes promises and does not deliver. I do not understand it.

ES: Yes, he is, but he is also playing quite a specific role in your life which makes him put those things aside and act out of character or contrary to expectation.

FH: In every occurrence I have allowed him to set the expectation. He set the appointments and he said he would call me, and then he did nothing. So he set himself expectations and did not deliver. I told him that I did not want him to set unrealistic expectations. Each time he does it.

ES: How do you feel about it?

FH: Very drained and disappointed. He is now basically saying "Don't push me, because if you do I'll bust the company and you won't get anything. Allow me the time". I am not putting pressure on him. I am just asking when I would hear from him. I am concerned and empty.

ES: That makes sense. We had a conversation about him – when you called him on a Sunday afternoon. You were very emotional and intense about it. Now you are just reporting – the emotion is much less.

15 December: Hands Up

FH: Two interesting things happened this morning. The first thing was that I said "If somebody is listening to me, can you give me a sign, a real sign, that things have taken a turn because I have been learning the lessons and the application of that knowledge is now beginning to work. I would like a positive sign that I am going forward and things are improving with the application of this knowledge."

That was about 11:30 am. I stood up after I said it and walked from one room to the next, and then this e-mail arrived 40 seconds later.

"Hi Fraser,
My apologies in taking so long to get back to you.
I have taken careful consideration in submitting a proposal to alleviate the problem of the breach of agreement. I have even obtained legal advice in the matter.

Yes I believe that I may not have honored the agreement we made, but was this a deliberate breach of our agreement? No it was not.

Was it a failure on my part to succeed? Possibly.

But it certainly was not a deliberate attempt to rip you off or undermine your business in any way. I am willing to acknowledge the debt up to and including October of £12 720 and will contribute what I can afford on a monthly basis to pay this off.
At this stage I would aim for £1 060 a month starting on the 31st January. At this stage it is the very best I can do.
I have already agreed in writing to protect your intellectual property and the reputation of yourself and your business, and I am fully committed to this.
All I want to do now is to move on from a very unpleasant experience and get on with my difficult life.
The choice is yours.

316

I look forward to hearing from you soon.
Regards,
Hans"

FH: I think he has been to a lawyer and is trying to steer the letter to say it was not a deliberate breach of agreement.

ES: He is also saying when it went well, it was his decision, and when it went bad, it was your decision. It is about taking ownership of everything that happens to you – both the good things and the bad things.

 Now here is an interesting situation. When things go well, it is your doing. When things go bad, it is your enemy's doing. How do you explain that?

18 December: One Last Chance

FH: Let me tell you what happened yesterday. I walked up and down, I looked at it and I said "No, this is what I'm going to do".

I have delivered what I said I would do, and I understand that this was all about boundaries and me not holding people to account as I should. He also needed to be taught a lesson as well.

I sent a reply email to him:

I want to bring closure in order to open up the flow of the new things coming in. I don't want to spend too much time dealing with this negative energy when I can deal with it now in a way which is a fair compromise, to allow the clean flow of positive energy to come in.

I think I am dealing with this positively and it feels right to me. It brings closure so that I can focus on the positive stuff. Would I be deemed to be letting him off lightly?

Yes, I dare say I am, but I want to focus on bringing in new positive stuff not dwell on old negative "stuff". Afterall, the key lessons have been learned.

19 December: Feelings and Emotions Revisited

FH: The way I understand it is that emotions are triggered when we react to a situation that we create or are part of. Feelings are the start of a process and not the end of the process. So circumstances create emotions, feelings create circumstances.

ES: Feelings form both the start and the end of a process. It is the end of a process in the sense that when you are at the bottom of the spiral, it starts of with emotion, which is energy in motion. You want to get somewhere and you want to resolve something. When you get to the top of the spiral there is a quantum leap that takes you from the bottom to the top of the spiral and beyond space and time.

You are at the bottom of the spiral with your emotions and with all the circumstances around it that you react to. With everything that is happening and all the turmoil, you work your way up the spiral. You think well, I am climbing up the spiral, from the bottom coil to the top coil. In fact, you are climbing up the spiral, along the coils, but when you get to the top, you actually jump from the bottom to the top. That is when you experience a feeling.

On the one hand I am saying you are climbing up the spiral, and on the other hand I am saying you jump up the spiral from the bottom to the top, but you do both.

The emotions are what you experience as you go up the spiral. The feeling is what you experience when you reach the top of the spiral, which is also the bottom of the next spiral. That is the experience of becoming whole – the end of the experience, the moment of gratitude.

Emotions indicate division, duality and incompleteness. Feelings indicate completeness. Emotions are always disturbing, and feelings are always rewarding, comfortable – it is very difficult to put it into words.

The feelings that you pick up is the cosmic vibration. Once you have picked up the feeling, you add the thinking. You become consciously aware of the feeling and you attach your own emotions to the vibration. That vibration is always good, but we add emotions. This means we choose to make the vibration "good" or "not good".

You feel, then you think, then you experience, and at the end of the experience you feel again.

You have a "negative" experience while you are still in the process. The "negative" things are not the end of the process. The duality is still there you are still somewhere on that spiral. You have not reached the end yet. You will know when you have reached the end of the spiral because there will be resolution, peace of mind, complete clarity and gratitude.

And when I talk about feelings, I talk about qualia - what you cannot put into words. You can "do" an emotion on demand. Your body knows how to react when I say "do affluent, or absorbed etc." You experience a feeling only once, and it is very personal and unique, and you cannot repeat it - like when you first saw your newborn twins. Try and repeat that on demand. An emotion is energy in motion, and a feeling is a quantum fusion that takes your entire body permanently to a higher vibration.

FH: Now that I like...!

ES: You can "undo" an emotion, but you cannot "undo" a feeling, because once you experienced a feeling, there is no going back - your entire body changes permanently at microscopic level and you become "lighter". An emotion is nervous energy, but a feeling forms a bridge between your body and soul.

FH: I like that one too.

ES: You cannot choose a feeling - it happens to you when you have completed a spiral - it is the end result. When you win that jackpot you will know exactly what a feeling is - and by the time you try to define it, it will be gone.

 Read the explanation above again.   When you experience a feeling, that is the conclusion to the episode and you are finally able to move on.

21 December: Trying to achieve the Impossible

FH: I am making a list of feelings.

ES: I would love to see that list . . .   A feeling is neither positive nor negative – it is a state of being with no judgment. When you add judgment, you have emotions, not feelings.

You want to make a list of feelings? Describe the single drop of water in the middle of a stream, or the exact nature of a snowflake that has just melted, or the exact state of a bride who has just said "I do" or a mother looking for the first time at her first child. But you have to describe them in such a way that you can replicate them at will and there must be no doubt about their nature.
It is impossible to have a list of feelings. A list of emotions you want to experience is a good idea - because you can have positive as well as negative emotions.

All those lists are emotions. I am talking about creating a quantum of light at the conclusion of a spiral - it is impossible to put it into words - the closest you can get is qualia, but that still does not describe the uniqueness

22 December: Feelings and Emotions – the Penny Drops!

FH: Morning. The penny has dropped! Feelings are indescribable.

ES: Ha-le-lu-ja!

FH: Negative emotions are the resistance - blockages and disruptions to our "proactive creative thinking process" they block the energy flow. I am over the hurdle and my own resistance.

ES: And all those emotions come from one-sided interpretations and perceptions of situations that ALWAYS have two sides.

FH: Last night I was looking back to all the negative stuff and how this has all come together. I became aware of the little spiral and the cycle that I went through. I recognised it and the penny dropped.

ES: And when the penny dropped, how exactly did you feel?

FH: I can't describe it.

ES: Can you repeat that?

FH: I can't verbalize how I felt it.

ES: In that instant, a quantum of light was created.

 This is powerful stuff. When you have that indescribable moment, you actually create Light. You move to a different level of maturity that nobody can take back from you. Can you understand that looking back at your own conflict experience?

323

FH: Thinking about it, my mind was still. I wasn't focused on any form of external influence, and the realization just came into being.

ES: And what else happened?

FH: It was like missing a heartbeat, in fact. It was like that feeling in your stomach – not butterflies, but a physical reaction.

ES: If I say to you "Can you pretend to be angry?", can you do that?

FH: Easily.

ES: If I say "Can you pretend to be in that moment of realization again", can you do that?

FH: The short answer is no.

ES: Because the moment is gone forever.

FH: So feelings happen once only, while emotions can be replicated at will. So you still the mind and allow the feeling to come into being and it will manifest?

ES: You don't even need to do that. All you need to do is remove any emotion that you feel. When you have done that, the feeling will be there. You will not have that aha-moment until there is no obstacle in the way. A feeling is the creation of a quantum of light.

FH: Where does this quantum of light come from?

ES: The light is the result of a duality which is returned to unity. See duality as a proton on the one side of the world and an electron on the other side of the world. As you go up the spiral, the proton and the electron move closer and closer to each other all the time, but they fight each other all the time as well. It is as if they are being forced together and saying to each other "there is not a chance in hell that I will join you." The moment that proton and electron fuse together, it is like an atomic war ending. That is where the quantum of light is formed. The result is a quantum of light that makes your entire body feeling lighter and vibrating at a higher level.

 This is the whole purpose of life. We have these experiences and situations so that we can resolve inner conflict and become whole again.

FH: So the negative emotional energy prevents that from happening and keeps them apart. If you still the mind and remove negative energy and resistance, the fusion happens.

ES: That's right. It is inevitable that they will come together. It will happen, whether you want it or not. How painful the process is and how long it takes depends on how many obstacles you put in the way of the process.

FH: I have just had another ke-ching moment!

ES: And when you push over one domino with one aha moment, the other dominoes just fall.

FH: And now I can see I am at the bottom of another spiral. I understand why and how the process works.I can now see what happened yesterday. I was allowing all my external emotional issues to get in the way and that was stopping me.

ES: And while you go through this, you are not even aware of it. You have to have the experience and feel it in your own body before you can put it into words and describe it for someone else. When things really go bad and everything looks black, you don't understand that you are the light. You are looking for the solution outside of yourself and you cannot see it anywhere. There is nothing out there. It takes a while to realize that you are and have the solution.

4 January: A New Dawn

FH: I think that in the last few days I lost my sense of awareness. In fact, that realization in itself is awareness. I put it down to post Christmas blues. I have to get my batteries charged and get going again for my life's work is far from complete, and I have to apply all the learning of recent months.

ES: It is like being a boy and getting new long trousers - when you wear them the first time you are so aware of them and you feel them every time you move and you expect everyone to comment on how good you look and they do. But by the seventh time you no longer even notice the trousers, and then you have your eye on another new pair and you wonder what is wrong with the first pair - nothing wrong with it, you have just grown into it and got used to it.

And it gives new meaning to the story of creation - you work very hard for six "days", and you are totally exhausted on "day" seven, and you think "I have wasted all that time and energy for nothing, because you do not yet understand the entire process - the seventh "day" is the quiet before the materialization. And then the seventh "day" passes and everything gets going and you get too busy to notice the rhythm of the creative process - work very hard, rest, then see the results of your work.

Except that the "day" is not just a day - we have worked for months, but the concept is the same.

 Once you have had that moment of realization, it is quite natural to feel you have lost that sense of awareness. You don't lose it – it is put on the back-burner while you have the next significant life experience. All the time the awareness grows until you have it back again - but at a higher level. You never lose your awareness.

7 January: Three Blind Mice

FH: What an unbelievable 24 hours. Three of those owing me money, contacted me.

Catherine wants to settle out of court, so I agreed a sum with her just to close the books and stop draining me, and sucking my focus away - but she fully acknowledges she was in wrong etc.

Hans will start a monthly payment programme from next Monday - he contacted me last night at 10.30pm.

Andrew in Leicester acknowledges back money, but wants to pay at a silly £50 pm or he is threatening to go personally bankrupt.

All came "out of the blue" just when I thought that was it.

ES: This is a very new and different energy. It takes some getting used to. If you and I have to focus, imagine what it is doing to people who have no awareness. This year will go very well for you. It will be quite different, but will go well in every way.

FH: I now feel I understand what my resistance has been. I'm out of the dark period, and ramping up.   I now think I got my MENTAL closure on the coaches as they confirmed I was not in the wrong – I think that was my BLOCK - they were not acknowledging that it wasn't my fault. I also now realize that my EGO was dented and bruised and holding me back.

I have one serious question for you though. I have reviewed the past year, and I think it was all about overcoming self-limiting beliefs about ME - re Money (being too lenient), BOUNDARIES with others (not setting them), INTEGRITY (recognizing my own & POWER) - OTHERS BEING MIRRORS and using my power against me ... being TRUE to myself and not being molded into what others wanted me to do/be (namely being other people's scapegoat and chasing my coat tails), and almost like a final test of my own belief in what I was doing in preparation for the all the good stuff to come. However, one thing does puzzle me.

All these people failed in their contractual obligations with me. That does prove that my paperwork was good, but I think last year was almost like a live market test to get the wrinkles out, but I also don't think I want to be drained by similar people again.

Did they fail because the system didn't work? I don't think so. I think they expected me to do it for them, and they had no idea just how much work and effort I put in.

The criteria for any new people needs to be stronger - if I do it – I really am unsure about that one. I'm cracking on getting other new stuff finished. Do I continue with the licensing coaches, or after learning - not do it?

ES: As for those who owed you the money - it is all going according to plan. All you need to ensure is that you continue to act with integrity. You will get a very clear indication as to whether you should take on another coach or not. My feeling is that you will only get that clear indication once you do the spadework and see the results.

If you are concerned about taking on similar people, that will probably happen. If you are still looking over your shoulder, establish why you are doing that, and take what you need from it and move on. Do not build the future based on the past. Just build the future the way you want it and see it happen.

FH: The last 3 days have been unbelievably dark and yet, in the last 24 hours all three individually contacted me and wanted to resolve things.

I have just come off the phone with Catherine. She wanted to transfer money into my account and wanted final confirmation in writing that there would be nothing else afterwards.

Things have become a lot more intense – it is like wading through treacle. I appreciate that self-inspection was required, but the whole thing with the coaches is bizarre. I understand that they failed because I did not set and apply the criteria strong enough from the outset.

I have been really struggling to see what I did wrong, but I am now certain that I did my best, especially when I see how Catherine has been all over me to settle out of court.

All of these people were looking for a shortcut and instant fix. If they don't follow the process, it will not work. The process is simple and all they have to do is follow the process. Individually they applied the programme and it worked, but when they tried to sell it, they did not do what they were taught.

I have been doing so much soul searching – there is a whole different air of energy about me because I now have identified the source of my resistance and the cause of my negative emotions.

ES: This is about the interaction between you and those owing you money and the impact it has had on you.

 Everything in life is about the interaction between you and other people. Without people you will not be able to have any life experience, and you will never mature. Are there at this stage any people that you want to thank for giving you a life-changing experience?

FH: I agree. I may have had a contract with them, but my emotional boundaries have been ignored because I had an emotional attachment with the relationship instead of holding them accountable to their obligations.

ES: And if you want to continue as you are with everything as it is, you will know how to enforce those boundaries.

FH: So this was my own doing because I had to learn about managing my boundaries.

ES: Most people around you just do and don't think about anything. This scares people off "awareness". The moment you move away from the familiar and towards the unknown, you do enter a dark corridor. This is scary and different, but once you get out of it and you realise the extent of your own power, nothing can stop you.

FH: I have been in so many different situations in my life where I thought there was no way forward. I can safely say from the beginning of November I have been wondering about this, because it is dark!

Dieter in Germany contacted me to say he would have everything resolved by Monday. He apologized and so on and so on.

16 January: The Reality of the Situation

FH: Hans sent me this today –

"You need to be aware of certain points which I have listed below.

- *You are in a very long list of existing creditors*
- *All of these creditors have priority over your business as they relate directly to putting food on my family's table.*
- *I will more than likely enter bankruptcy the first quarter of this year.*
- *I have made a commitment to repay the money owed to you, but it will have to be under my terms and when possible by me.*
- *You can send your wolves and start legal action, but it will not change the situation. I am BROKE end of story. And whether you want £5 000 or £70 000, it doesn't really make any difference because I haven't got either.*
- *I haven't got any assets everything is mortgaged or money is owed against it. So there is nothing to claim against.*
- *I have already wasted over £10 000 of my money towards your business opportunity, and that has certainly contributed to the situation I now find myself in.*
- *You have trusted me before and had faith in my integrity. So now you must do the same and understand that I will repay the money owed to you as soon as possible.*
- *But it will not be paid under threats and intimidation.*
- *You will just have to wait until other creditors are settled and your turn in the line comes along.*

As always I will do my best towards you and my prior commitments, but you need to understand the situation."

This is pretty much as you predicted it.

Andrew in Leicester paid me my monies, but looks as though he going personally bankrupt too - and same with Dieter.   And Catherine has now settled with me "out of court".

ES: Hans is a nasty piece of work - and he is not telling you the full story. I feel someone told him to call your bluff. Be very careful of what you believe from him.

FH: I think that too, so my reply was very short and pointed to him –

"Hi Hans
In light of the seriousness of your situation, can you please send me –
- *The contact details of your solicitor and/or insolvency practitioner*
- *The full list of creditors and the amounts owing to each.*
Many thanks
Fraser"

ES: You cannot pour new wine in a container that still has vinegar in it - once all the vinegar is out, the new wine will pour in. You can punish yourself about it all or you can look forward and wait for the miracle, because there is a miracle coming as sure as I am sitting here.

25 January: Looking Back

FH: This has been a hard, long journey, I have to say.

ES: Yes. But it would not have happened to you if you were not ready and able to do it.

2 February: Time and Timing

FH: The one thing I don't think we have mastered yet is this whole thing of time and timescale – not just on putting the project together and getting launched, but also on information that we receive from the other side and how it chronologically fits in with our own circumstances.

I am still a little unsure as to when the launch date is, and I also think the information we get form the other side – dates and times can be out.

You have told me a number of times of things that were going to happen and I am still waiting. That is not a criticism - it is rather me wanting to understand how the process works.

ES: Time is quite fluid. It does not matter exactly when something is going to happen.

We know it will happen and the journey to get there is a lot more important than the end result. That sounds like a cliché, but it does become meaningful as your awareness grows.

3 February: Half Empty, Half Full or Broke?

ES: Hey, it is darkest just before the sun rises.

We will get there. What to do next? First, follow your own advice.

Listen to the quantum vibration. Then take away the barriers you have put in place.

You have now reached the bottom of the vessel. From here onwards the vessel will fill up.

5 February: Remaining True to Yourself

FH: I have been doing a lot of reflection since yesterday. I have been putting everything that we have been talking about in writing and practicing. It is reaffirming my belief, not just in what we are doing, but also in myself. I am reaffirming my own position and where I am on my journey.

ES: The way you are and with the approach you have towards people – you are a good person. You are open and giving. You don't have a hidden agenda. You share what you have. You look out for other people. All of that is good. But with everything in this world there is a dark side as well.

Maybe your experiences have taught you that you should continue the way you are, but be aware that there is another side of you that people will reflect to you. You can reject that other side of you, or you can accept and integrate it and have balance. You can have two-sided coin rather than a one-sided coin.

FH: I thought I was becoming better at responding and having clearer boundaries.

ES: No doubt about it. but without all these experiences you would have remained stuck in reacting emotionally – feeling hurt, angry, and repeating them like a tape that is stuck in one space.

 Some people never grow up – they get stuck in those emotions and they find someone to blame until the day they die. Who do you blame for your life?

FH: I totally agree. You came up with a wonderful quote the other day. You said we talk from the heart, not from the head, so we don't have to think about a response. That is so true. All the things we talk about in the course are appearing, re-appearing and reminding me that what we offer is very special.

8 February: The Plot Thickens

FH: Andrew in Leicester owes me a reasonable amount of money. Over the weekend he sent me a sarcastic email. He alluded that he already had a list of creditors. I asked him for a copy of this list of creditors and his income and expenditure. Then we can come to some arrangement on what he owes me.

He sent me a sarcastic message saying I don't need to know the information.

He is £50 000+ overall in the red. Alarm bells rang when I saw that. If he owes that amount of money to 10 people and he has had an arrangement with them for 12 months, whereby he has been paying them every month without telling them that he owes me money.

He had also entered into an arrangement where he was paying all of them less than he owes me. For the last year he had been paying me more in monthly payments than the total amount his creditors were receiving, and they did not know I existed. I think he should have declared it, but I really don't know whether he has or not.

Because of his breach of contract with me, I suspect I am now his largest creditor.

18 February: Yet Another Line is Drawn

FH: I'm getting faffed about by one of those coaches who owes me money, and he sent me a stroppy email this morning - (he is posturing, but I don't like way he is doing it):

"Dear Fraser,

Before we proceed any further, there is something I would like to clear up, for the record.
The tone of your recent emails and phone calls has been as if I had 'borrowed' money from you, and you were now entitled to demand repayment. That is not the case.
We are now in the position of trying to bring things to a fair, equitable and tidy conclusion, so that we may continue with our respective lives.
I'll be in touch again shortly to continue working things out with you.
Also, please can we continue all correspondence regarding this matter in writing (or email)?
Thanks,
Andrew"

ES: *Excellent idea to do it all in writing - he does not think about what he writes and is already tying himself into knots.*

FH: He is saying I have been leaving messages, when he disabled the feature from his phone (after agreeing to speak to me on a particular date).

ES: *I am always amazed at how some people can twist facts to reflect a version of reality that only they believe - and when you talk to them, they seriously only believe their version.*
I really believe that it is a form of art.

FH: But it really gets me questioning myself, my ethics, sanity etc

ES: And you get consistent answers whereas he changes with every communication, so why are you questioning yourself?

FH: Oh I don't know, I'm just getting battle weary I suppose.

ES: You have a conscious choice - react with emotion, or respond from that quiet place inside yourself where you always find your choice. One way is to write him a letter and get all the emotion out of the way, and then go to that quiet place where you always find your truth.

 Here is a powerful way to get anger or resentment towards a person out of your system.

Write that person a letter, explaining in detail what they did and how you were affected by their actions. Be totally honest. When you have written the letter, cut it up or tear it into pieces. Burn or shred it – whatever you want to do while symbolically getting rid of the emotions that are not doing you any good.

24 February: It's a Fair Cop, Gov . . .

FH: Aye, aye, finally another one...

"Dear Fraser,
WITHOUT PREJUDICE
Further to my earlier email, I'd like to add that I am willing to negotiate, in the interests of bringing this matter to a conclusion so that we can get on with our businesses. And also because it would be a shame to fall out over this.
However, before we continue, there's something I need to make clear. Due my financial position, I am only currently in a position to make very small payments towards any agreed amount.
Obviously, I am working to improve things, so it should get settled more quickly in future, but I can't promise what I don't have, and I can't do anything that could be seen as making preferential payments.
(Otherwise, in the event of my declaring bankruptcy, you could be faced with a demand from the Official Receiver for reversal of the transaction. And yes, I have kept the debt management agency in the loop, and am acting on their advice. Thank you for your concern.)
The reason I raise this is because in our previous conversations, you seem to have been under the impression that I might have access to some sort of external funds. I don't.
I'm as keen to be in a position where I can pay things off in one go as I'm sure you'd like to see me in, but unfortunately that's not the case right now.
Oh, and in answer to your question from your earlier email – the £125 per month left over is what is paid to the debt management agency and distributed amongst creditors.
On that basis, I am prepared to offer a settlement of £2 500 + VAT, payable in instalments, to bring this matter to an expedient close.
I await your reply.
Please note I'll be away from my PC for a few days, so will get to read it next week when I return.
Kind regards,
Andrew"

25 February: Viva le Force

FH: I've had 2 hours sleep. Snow and ice on the roofs and gutters caused a drip, drip, drip in the bedroom ceiling due to a leaky loft. Three roofs tilt into one flat roof! I took off a chunk of ice 4ft x 1.5ft ice, three inches thick.

ES: Holy Moses!

FH: The gutters were frozen. The water backed up behind it on a flat roof and froze. The snow then slid off the three roofs onto another roof and froze. This all happened because of a change in the weather over the last two days. There is more snow but it is slightly warmer. As a result the ice started melting but couldn't flow into the drainpipes, and stayed on the flat roof. I look like the back end of a bus after impact.

Hopefully this does happen only every 58 years - like they say in the weather report.

There I was, up on the roof with a torch, snow blowing in my face and I get this thought... All this manual labour is to unblock the ice and water that is causing resistance to the flow of melting snow from the roof, and I'm personally putting in the effort to fix it. This was somewhat symbolic, I think.

The drainpipes and roofs are now clear of mud, leaves, snow and ice etc., and have been rinsed out with boiling water to ensure water from the roof can flow off and all the way down. The garden is covered in huge lumps of ice that we shoveled off.

I really hope it is a turning point as I have genuinely had only two hours sleep. We had buckets, basins, towels and jugs on the bedroom floor. The washing machine is packed with towels, and there is a big pile still to go. My fingers are all shrunk and shriveled white despite wearing gloves.

There's always something for us to fix, address, learn from and grow…

ES: Oh yes. You do get to a point where you just take it in your stride and you have virtually no emotions - like Ghandi or Mandela.

And it will increase over the next few years because of the planetary energies - it is happening and people are unaware and feel like victims all the time - which is why we need to get this up and running - but not today. Part of the change is listening to your body and sleeping when you need sleep.

FH: I was truly gob-smacked about my realization about my own resistance. That wasn't a reflection while speaking to you on Skype. It was while I was up a bloody ladder in the dark and snow.

ES: You had a feeling!

In Conclusion

ES: At this point the delta (referred to in our first conversation) had merged and Fraser was ready for the next challenge in his business. This journey has taught him to identify the spirals in his life and understand the meaning of challenges. We are not victims on this journey – we are just ignorant until we recognise the patterns that we consciously create every day.

Fraser has also discovered that everything in this Universe is balanced. Book 2 will contain information on other events that are not covered in this book, which clearly illustrate that the ups and downs in life result in a balanced view.

The journey towards Fraser's first conscious feeling was both frustrating and amusing. The end result is a much improved control over his emotions, to the extent where he uses his emotions to get a better outcome, rather than him being used by his emotions to complicate matters.

Fraser and I have taught each other more about patience – a real virtue which only comes to its full right when you understand the difference between time and timing. Everything happens at the right time and for the right reasons. Where we disagree with this, it is based on incomplete growth, because we still do not understand that time is not relevant at all.

What is relevant is that we detach ourselves from our experiences, so that we can see the patterns and lessons. That is what we are here for.

Being self-employed is not just a different work status. It is also a life experience where you have to have peace with yourself, because often there is no-one else that you can rely on. This journey was all about becoming aware of who you really are, so that you can get rid of all the extra baggage and use the greatest resource available for any self-employed person, namely your own intuition, to manifest the riches you already have within.

FH: I am reminded of the soliloquy by Sylvester Stallone in *Rocky VI: Rocky Balboa* that I would like to close with. I feel it helps to typify what working for yourself is all about. It also helps to illustrate the journey I have been on. Whenever we face resistance in our life, the secret is not to fight it, but to let it unfold to see where it takes us next on our path –

"Let me tell you something you already know. The world ain't all sunshine and rainbows, it's a very mean and nasty place and I don't care how tough you are it will beat you to your knees and keep you there permanently if you let it. You, me, nobody is gonna hit as hard as life! But it ain't about how hard you can hit, it's about how hard you can get hit and keep movin' forward, how much you can take...and keep movin' forward. That's how winning is done! Now, if you know what you're worth then go out and get what you're worth! But you gotta be willing to take the hits and not pointin' fingers sayin' you ain't where you wanna be because of him or her or anybody! Cowards do that and that ain't you! You're better than that! –

Don't fight the thought of following your dream regardless of the challenges that lie ahead, they are there to keep you on your path to wherever it may lead you. Don't be scared to face your fears or to venture into Terra Incognita. It doesn't matter whether you have faith in others or not, or whether they have faith in you or not. It's all about having faith in yourself, being true to yourself and following your heart. To those who have now settled with me out of court, thank you for teaching me some of the best lessons I needed to learn.

And whilst we all recognize that things don't always go according to plan, instead of lashing out, accusing or blaming others, sometimes it pays to stop and reflect and think how we can change *ourselves* for the better.

344

To my past, present and future clients, thank you for allowing me to dance my magic and share what I have to offer.

To Elsabe, thank you for becoming a wonderful coach, teacher, mentor and friend.

And Wendy, thank you for your patience, tolerance, unconditional love, support and understanding for allowing me to follow my heart - I love you forever.

A summary of The Journey to date

As we both reflect on our journey to date and each of the issues, challenges and obstacles we have had to address or overcome as detailed in the previous pages, we can recognize four distinct stages to our personal journey and evolutionary growth:

- Slumber
- Expansion
- Learning & Understanding
- Freedom

Slumber

We start our evolutionary process of personal growth and awakening by reacting to situations and events, based on our conditioning and belief systems to date.
Our understanding of how life works is based on generalizations and social conditioning. We tend to do what we think we should be doing, and what is deemed acceptable and "the right thing to do" by others.

Many people don't stop to question where they are in their life. They need to experience some real challenging times and events in

346

their life before they wake up and start to search for answers, and how they can change themselves and/or their situation. The awakening from slumber often occurs when we don't want to face some particular home truths or deep routed fears, or want to venture into terra incognita.

One thing is for sure; instead of living life on automatic pilot we need to awaken to our true purpose, what our heart-felt goals, ambitions and dreams really are, and what it is we need to do to overcome our self-limiting beliefs and self-imposed fears. This can only come from self-inspection and reflection – some people also call it meditation or contemplation.

On a practical level we evaluate WHERE we are in our life today and identify how we are spending our time and energy.

The more self-inspection and reflection you do, the more you will begin to question whether your own thoughts and actions have been taking you closer to your goals or further away from what you want to achieve. More important, this awakening from your slumber a heightened level of awareness and purposefulness nearly always comes about as a direct result of

- Recognizing your unwillingness to accept responsibility or
- Taking ownership of the situations and circumstances we find ourselves in or
- The negative challenges we face.

Quite often, when things don't go according to plan, many people blame others, come up with excuses, or worse, enter into the denial of the real cause of the situation they find themselves. The do not search within to see what or how they can improve from within, so that they can create the external environment they crave.

We do, however, create our own reality, and the process which we have discovered, experienced (and documented) has enabled us and many others to recognize where they are in this 4 step process. By performing the exercises and activities in this book (and the

347

advanced exercises we refer to in our coaching programme) you will develop a much deeper understanding of yourself, your nature, your purpose and how you can apply simple, practical and powerful techniques and tactics for identifying, addressing and overcoming many if not all of life's challenges.

An aversion to risk, fear of being unpopular, avoiding criticism, or refusing to stick your head above the parapets, can all ensure that you don't wake up from your slumber of non-performance and lack of results in many areas of our lives.

Quite often people in this phase of the S.E.L.F. evolutionary process don't understand why they think the way they do, or why they hold the opinions or views they do about the world and their lives. Many are too busy reacting to the symptoms of their unbalanced thoughts, to recognize why they're not generating the results they want. In hindsight I can see that now, as I reflect and look back on the various challenges I've had to face over months.

Quite often, at this stage in the process, people simply aren't doing any introspection, meditation or contemplation to identify and address the inner imbalances. As we have come to learn, our outside reality is a reflection of our internal reality and we become what we think about and dwell upon.

Feelings create circumstances. Circumstances do not create feelings. In our Coaching Programme, we expand on this, enabling you to identify the powerful difference between feelings and emotions. You learn how to manage your emotions to create the circumstances you want, rather than just perpetuate your current circumstances.

Feedback of people who have read our book indicate that if you're at this stage of your personal evolutionary process, then perhaps its time, to wake up, take control, and stop following the herd. Just because everyone else is asleep and following the herd, doesn't make it right for you to do the same.

In short, many people experience life on auto-pilot. They live by habit, unconsciously reacting to circumstances and people. They don't take control of their life, and thus they prevent themselves from achieving the results or success they want. You need to know **WHERE** you are.

Expansion & Awareness

Explanations, realizations, and the ability to look for and interpret the signs are all parts of recognizing where you are in this stage of your personal evolutionary process.
You become aware of the small, insignificant indicators that help you accept your position, and you recognize the current trends and what your corrective actions need to be. Corrective actions mean becoming aware of your own actions, your own behaviors, and the patterns in your life. As you connect the dots, and recognize recurring themes in your life and business.

As part of taking stock and identifying WHERE you are in your life, where you've been and where you are heading, you become aware of the things you need to change in order to achieve the things you want. A desire to achieve a particular goal or objective is good to encourage and motivate us to action. However, many people reach stage 2 of their evolutionary process and they discover that they don't know WHAT it is they want.

Sometimes you want to fix or address a particular issue, challenge or problem. The question is: What do you want to achieve? If your circumstances only create emotions, but feelings create circumstances, then we need to focus our attention on mastering those emotions that run our lives, so we can create the experiences we desire.

Many people delay the achievement of their goals and objectives because they have not become aware of the true obstacles in their path – their own thoughts, fears, behaviors, actions and self-imposed limitations. In other words, become aware of your own thoughts first, instead of identifying where others have gone wrong. Rid yourself of your greatest fears, and watch how quickly you grow, develop and achieve real breakthroughs.

When you learn to read the coincidences, recurring patterns and themes in your life, you become more aware. You recognize it is time to come out of your slumber and stop following the crowd. Many people can take a lifetime to recognize that they need to change, and become aware of their true situation. That is where our Personal Success Quiz can help initiate your awakening or increased awareness.

In summary, before you grow you must first recognise what you want to change and be prepared to give consistent attention to what you want to change. But **WHAT** is it you want to achieve, change or experience?

Learning and Understanding

Learning occurs when you become aware of the signs. You can identify the reasons WHY you have been in your auto-pilot slumber, and WHY you've been experiencing the lack of progress and results you so desperately want.

You very quickly discover the real reasons for your lack of progress and what you need to do to address them.

Taking stock, and asking yourself some good soul searching questions can really help you in your evolutionary process, as can discussing your situation with a personal coach, confidante or someone who understands and has experienced the four-step process we are summarizing here.

You learn WHY you need to change, why you're not making the progress you want, what it is you OFFER, and to whom.

You get to understand the myths that all your false assumptions have created and why you've placed limitations on yourself. You understand WHY you have certain experiences, and attract certain people, circumstances or events into your life.

When you reach an appropriate level of understanding, you will recognize that the results you are experiencing now are the cumulative total of your prior thinking, conditioning and actions. Once you complete this step in the process, some areas of your life will still require attention, but you understand what these areas are, and more importantly what needs to be done about them. The more you become aware and understand your current situation and how you've arrived at it, the less likely it is that you will return to your old, destructive behaviors. Once you have completed a personal success quiz, it will all seem obvious what needs to be done, and you will kick yourself because you hadn't realized this before.

In summary, for the 3rd part of the process, the more you learn about your true self, the more you will understand **WHY** you have not reached your objectives and **WHY** your progress has been so slow.

Freedom

Freedom comes from knowing what's holding you back and what you need to do to remedy the situation. You are much closer to living the life or lifestyle you want.

When you KNOW something, it is more than just a basic understanding of the mere mechanics of cause and effect. Knowing does not come from reading a book or e-book or from attending a workshop, seminar or teleconference.

Knowing means having experienced (or endured) and applied what you've learned, having consciously completed the previous 3 stages of the process.

You look at your life, thoughts and actions in a different way. When you know what you need to do as part of the next stage of your personal growth, you feel alive. You have a sense of purpose and a plan of action. You recognize your outdated reactions, and are changing them. You know what needs to be done, and you know how it needs to be done and why.

You begin to know things in small chunks, but by stepping back you begin to see patterns emerging. You begin to see all the parts of the problem as well as the solution and what to do next. Knowing also means knowing the truth about who you are, what you want, and whom you can really help. It means becoming better centered, better grounded, and having a better feeling of what's right for you. Many people have a fear of failure, fear of success, or a fear of a whole wide range of issues. The fear paralyzes them and they don't want to become aware of what they could do, or understand how they can achieve their dreams. They stay the same, they don't grow, and they don't achieve their full potential.

The secret is in knowing WHEN to do something. It's all about timing. Many of the negative experiences you've had to endure have in fact been important lessons in preparing you for the freedom and positive experiences you crave.

In summary, **WHEN** you change your limiting beliefs and apply what you've learned, you will experience freedom, results, and abundance unlike anything before.

Once you have completed all four stages of your personal evolutionary process, be mentally prepared for an almost overnight transformation in who you are, what you offer, and what you really want to (and will) achieve.

As a result of the personal journey we have both been on, we have each created our coaching programs which go much deeper.

We share very practical exercises and activities to enable you to live your life purpose and achieve your entrepreneurial goals and objectives.

This is not the end. This is just the beginning for those who want to embrace it.

Fraser & Elsabe

Engage With the Authors

Fraser and Elsabe are available for public speaking, engagements and private consultation.
What is your next goal or objective? What would you like to resolve?

Unlike many business coaches, Fraser has helped entrepreneurs from 44 countries to identify & address over 2000 common small business issues, challenges & obstacles that have been holding them back & preventing them from achieving their entrepreneurial goals & objectives.

Each of these issues have been documented and shared in his other 12 books on Amazon, his webinars, keynotes, workshops and coaching programs.

He offers no prescriptive advice, but best of all - Progress is measured, documented & guaranteed.

Can he help you?

Elsabe Smit is an international coach, facilitator, public speaker and author.
She works with individuals and business owners/managers around the world who lack confidence, clarity and purpose and who are seeking help to overcome their fears, doubts and reservations about the future.

She also works with business managers and entrepreneurs to help them overcome their obstacles – to spark creativity, increase personal development and motivation, identify opportunities, improve efficiency and contribute to business growth.

Yes, if you want to:

• Acquire entrepreneurial skills
• Document your model, vision or new marketing strategy
• Get engagement online or position yourself as an expert
• Generate more leads, enquiries, sales or referrals
• Add new revenue streams or create new passive income
• Grow Your Business®

www.fraserhay.co.uk
fraser@fraserhay.co.uk

Elsabe has an MBA (Master Business Administration), a MA in Industrial Psychology and extensive experience in the business world.

She is the author of 10 published books, covering human resources, strategic management and practical spirituality.

www.elsabesmit.com
AskElsabe@elsabesmit.com

One Last Thing...

If you enjoyed the book, would you have any objection in leaving a positive review on Amazon?

If you believe the book is worth sharing, please would you take a few seconds to let your friends know about it on Linkedin, Facebook or Twitter? And if you know someone who is thinking of starting a business or currently owns one and is facing a few challenges at the moment, simply send them the link to the book on Amazon accompanied by a short positive comment. If it turns out to make a difference in their lives, they'll be forever grateful to you, as will we.

Thank you for investing your time in us. Now it's time to apply what you've learned from the book in preparation for bigger and greater things.

Fraser and Elsabe

Printed in Great Britain
by Amazon